# The Use of Land

# The Use of Land: A Citizens' Policy Guide to Urban Growth

*A Task Force Report Sponsored by
The Rockefeller Brothers Fund*

Edited by
William K. Reilly

Thomas Y. Crowell Company
New York
*Established 1834*

Published simultaneously in Canada by
Fitzhenry & Whiteside Limited, Toronto.

Design by Marilyn Housell
Manufactured in the United States of America
Printed on 100% recycled paper

Library of Congress Cataloging in Publication Data
Task Force on Land Use and Urban Growth.
  The use of land.
   Includes bibliographical references.
  1. Land—United States. 2. Cities and Towns—
  Planning—United States. I. Reilly, William Kane,
  1940-   , ed. II. Title.

HD257.T37 1973     333.7'7'0973     73-8215
ISBN 0-690-00267-x

## Members of the Task Force on Land Use and Urban Growth

*Chairman*
Laurance S. Rockefeller
New York, New York

*Deputy Chairman*
Paul N. Ylvisaker
Dean, Graduate School of
    Education
Harvard University
Cambridge, Massachusetts

John F. Collins
Consulting Professor of
    Urban Affairs
Massachusetts Institute of
    Technology
Cambridge, Massachusetts

John R. Crowley
Chairman
Colorado Land Use
    Commission
Denver, Colorado

Henry L. Diamond
Commissioner
New York State Department of
    Environmental Conservation
Albany, New York

Walter E. Hoadley
Executive Vice President and
    Chief Economist
Bank of America National Trust
    and Savings Association
San Francisco, California

A. Wesley Hodge
Lawyer
Hodge, Dahlgren & Hillis
Seattle, Washington

Vernon E. Jordan, Jr.
Executive Director
National Urban League
New York, New York

Virginia Nugent
Chairman
National Land Use Committee
League of Women Voters
Washington, D.C.

John R. Price, Jr.
Vice President
Manufacturers Hanover Trust
New York, New York

James W. Rouse
Chairman of the Board and
    Chief Executive Officer
The Rouse Company
Columbia, Maryland

Pete Wilson
Mayor of San Diego
San Diego, California

**Task Force Staff**

*Executive Director*
William K. Reilly

*Senior Staff*
John H. Noble
Thomas A. Barrington
Gordon Binder
Phyllis Myers
Michael Rawson
Sara M. Mazie

*Report Staff*
Jo Tunstall
Elizabeth Arensberg

*Support Staff*
Barbara N. Gray
Josephine Haley

# Contents

PREFACE                                           page 1

THE REPORT IN BRIEF                               page 13

I    CHALLENGING THE IDEAL OF GROWTH:
     A NEW MOOD IN AMERICA                        page 33

II   BUT GROW WE WILL                             page 75

III  PROTECTING WHAT WE VALUE                     page 103

IV   ADAPTING OLD LAWS TO NEW VALUES              page 145

V    CREATING WHAT WE WANT:
     REGULATING DEVELOPMENT                       page 177

VI   CREATING WHAT WE WANT:
     INCENTIVES AND OPPORTUNITIES                 page 219

VII  SUBDIVIDING THE GREAT OUTDOORS               page 263

VIII CONSERVATION AND DEVELOPMENT:
     THE ROLE OF THE CITIZEN                       page 295

NOTES                                             page 305

PHOTO AND CARTOON CREDITS                         page 309

INDEX                                             page 311

# Figures and Tables

Figure 1    POPULATION PROJECTIONS    *page 78*

Figure 2    HOUSEHOLD FORMATION TO 1990    *page 80*

Figure 3    POWER PLANT NEEDS THROUGH 1985
            IN THE WESTERN STATES    *page 81*

Figure 4    URBAN REGIONS: YEAR 2000    *page 83*

Figure 5    VISITORS AND ACREAGE OF STATE
            AND NATIONAL PARKS    *page 108*

Figure 6    STATE PARK EXPENDITURES    *page 109*

Figure 7    GREENBELTS AND PARKS IN
            ENGLAND AND WALES    *page 134*

Figure 8    ANNUAL HOUSING STARTS    *page 244*

Figure 9    RATIO OF LOTS SUBDIVIDED TO
            HOMES CONSTRUCTED IN
            SELECTED SUBDIVISIONS    *page 265*

Figure 10   INDICATION OF INTERSTATE
            LAND SALES    *page 271*

Figure 11   IMPACT OF RECREATIONAL LOT
            DEVELOPMENT ON POPULATION    *page 280*

Table 1    POPULATION AND LAND AREA OF
           URBAN REGIONS: 1920-2000    *page 84*

Table 2    POPULATION BY PLACE OF
           RESIDENCE: 1950-70    *page 85*

Table 3    PREFERENCES FOR RESIDENTIAL
           LOCATION    *page 86*

# Preface

The Task Force on Land Use and Urban Growth was created in the summer of 1972 by the Citizens' Advisory Committee on Environmental Quality (a body established by presidential executive order in May 1969). It seemed then to the committee that the institutional apparatus and laws for dealing with such environmental problems as air and water pollution were in being. The problems were not by any means solved, but governments at all levels were organizing to deal with them. The problems of land use and urban growth, however, had received far less attention even though they are equally, if not more, serious. Laurance S. Rockefeller, then chairman of the committee, saw the environmental movement as a force of great vigor and excitement which, if it were to broaden its vision and direct its energies to urban growth problems with equal commitment, could achieve impressive results.

Granted, land use is a far more complicated issue than pollution. There is no physical ideal of "pure land" to guide us or even to indicate when we are making progress. But land use is a fundamental environmental issue—one that vitally affects transportation, housing, recreation, and even job opportunities. It is an issue that needs subtle accommodations and balances because it is basically concerned with seeing that conservation and development occur in the right places.

The citizens' committee set up the task force in August 1972 and named to it three committee members—Laurance S. Rockefeller as chairman, Commissioner Henry Diamond (the present citizens' committee chairman), and Mayor Pete

*The meeting of the task force in November 1972 in Washington, D.C.
Clockwise, from left, Laurance S. Rockefeller, William K. Reilly, John F.
Collins, Walter E. Hoadley, James W. Rouse (back to camera), John R.
Crowley, and Pete Wilson (back to camera).*

Wilson—and nine other individuals whose backgrounds are broad and whose interests and associations include banking, law, planning, government, universities, civil rights, and citizen action. A full-time executive director was borrowed from the Council on Environmental Quality. His staff came from the disciplines of planning, law, architecture, journalism, economics, and biology. The task force is bipartisan and private, with all funding provided by the Rockefeller Brothers Fund. Although the citizens' committee advises the President and the Council on Environmental Quality, the task force is making this report to the committee.

We convened on four occasions beginning in September, meeting twice in Washington, once in New York, and once in San Diego. In the course of our work, we surveyed virtually all of the major reports on land use and urban growth from the previous five years. We examined significant national and state legislation, pending and enacted. We attempted to identify opportunities for immediate improvements in the way our cities grow and we also sought to determine desirable long-term trends in values and at-

2

titudes. As a citizen group we inquired closely into the attitudes of citizens in four parts of the country. Our recommendations are intended to be responsive to the concerns and anxieties about urban development that people expressed to our staff.

As a group, we proceeded by general consensus and did not vote on each recommendation submitted to us. Rather, it was understood that, if a member was strongly opposed to a recommendation, he or she would indicate that. If no satisfactory accommodation could be worked out, the member could write a statement of dissent for the report. Although the report contains no such dissents, it is conceivable that individual task force members may differ with particular points, although all members share the strong conviction that the basic direction of the report is sound.

Commissions and task forces have been convening for more than a decade to study land use and urban growth in the United States. Although many of their recommendations have been ignored, and some of those implemented have had disappointing results, the nation owes these groups a debt. They have raised the national consciousness about urban problems. They have suggested why many Americans feel dissatisfied with what is happening to their communities and the land surrounding them. And they have kept before the public the notion that urban deterioration, environmental degradation, suburban sprawl, racial and economic segregation, and lack of community—the all-too-familiar problems of metropolitan areas and even of many smaller urbanized areas—are not inevitable. But from our vantage point in the 1970s, many of these problems seem even more intractable than they appeared a decade or so ago.

No longer do experts think governmental programs can remedy most of the defects in the way urban growth occurs. No longer do many authorities claim to know what to do, for example, about the drabness and lack of variety of much new residential and commercial development, the unwillingness of many suburban communities to provide housing (and, thus, access to jobs) for people of modest means, the dehumanization of even our prosperous downtown areas, which are increasingly given over at street level to bland, nine-to-five enterprises that contribute neither delight nor charm to our community life. It is as though the drive has gone out of our search for solutions, and a great weariness has set in. Proposals for more research, for experimentation, for demonstrations are more common now in professional journals and reports than are recommendations for new programs and specific laws.

We appreciate and share the frustration felt by many who have striven for so long to find answers to these pressing problems. We are aware of the danger of appearing to suggest that government can solve society's ills when, in fact, many of the most severe problems—too few jobs to go around; people without the skills, energies, or confidence to get available jobs; hostilities among groups and classes; dishonesty among officials and others responsible for the physical development of our cities—have to do with human conditions that change slowly, if at all, and rarely in response to legislation. And we are aware of the great difficulty of making original or, at the very least, useful proposals. No government can save our souls. That we must do for ourselves, and it can be a cruel distraction to direct the energies of people to political solutions when government cannot help.

Nevertheless, we believe that America can do better than it has been doing in planning and controlling urban development and in protecting our natural, cultural, and aesthetic resources. Although many urban and social problems are far from being solved, we see a few decidedly promising trends and we believe we can identify some fruitful courses for the future.

We are encouraged by the speed at which far-reaching change can occur in the United States. Consider the following: the new willingness by several states to assume responsibility for major land-use decisions; the three-year-old requirement of detailed environmental assessments of federal actions; the unprecedented technological improvements demanded in automobile design to improve safety and lessen air pollution; the emerging consensus in favor of universal health insurance; the increasing assumption by states of financial responsibility for primary and secondary education; the growing respectability of federally supported income maintenance. A decade ago, many of these propositions were unknown or unacceptable to all but a very few. Now, many have become policy and the others are not even considered avant-garde.

Most of these changes have been preceded by widespread public awareness and concern. Citizen interest and action by non-governmental organizations has kept issues before the people and pressure on public officials. In each field, the ideas involved

4

gained currency even when their implementation was momentarily blocked.

The most progress has occurred in environmental improvement. In just a few years, public concern has led to the enactment of comprehensive pollution-control legislation and the establishment of an institutional apparatus sufficient to suggest that, if pollution levels themselves have not yet begun to come down (and in some areas they have), then at least the laws and agencies are now in being that can bring them down.

The energies of the environmental movement are fresh and powerful and their victories, impressive. If those energies could be focused on the problems of land use and urban growth with the same persistence and sophistication that have characterized pollution battles, who knows what might be achieved.

We are therefore hopeful, and we present a hopeful report. Many of the "first generation" urban reports issued in the 1960s had enthusiasm, excitement, and moralizing, to be succeeded by sober, cautious, reflective resignation in some "second generation" reports of the early 1970s. We have attempted to write a "third generation" report, one that acknowledges the political constraints in our cities, states, and federal government, one that realistically assesses what we can and cannot influence, one that

*Laurance S. Rockefeller and William K. Reilly confer before the San Diego meeting of the task force.*

5

sets out a selective strategy for improving the way in which our cities, suburbs, and even some remote areas are physically developed and redeveloped.

We have written a "bottom up" report that looks first to the concerns of citizens about urban development; then to the opportunities and incentives of the private sector, of landowners and developers; then to the ways in which local government can create an environment that frees the private sector to use its opportunities well; then to the states to correct the limited view and property tax preoccupations of local governments; and, finally, to the federal government to provide national recognition of the need for institutional reform of state and local land-use laws and programs and to adapt key federal programs to the new policies of lower level governments.

In most instances we have favored the rearrangement of processes and the redesign of incentives to get the system working for, not against, quality urban development. We have consciously focused less on negative compulsion than on creating positive inducements, less on increasing public expenditures than on making sure that the governmental entity with the proper perspective is the one responsible for dealing with a particular issue, less with tilting the balance toward environmental groups or to development interests than in trying to make certain that a newly emerging balance between these forces is maintained.

By and large, our proposals are for immediate implementation. Many of the measures we recommend could alter the tone of American life as early as the 1976 bicentennial year if the country were clearly committed to their objectives.

And it may be. There is a new mood in America that questions traditional assumptions about urban growth and has higher expectations of both government and new urban development. We view this new mood as offering an extraordinary opportunity, for out of the willingness of citizens in many parts of the country to say "stop" or "wait" to development can come greater assurance that the development we get will be of higher quality than much of the development since World War II. We will continue to accommodate new development, of course; rates of anticipated household formation through the end of the century leave us no choice. It is essential therefore that we give constructive focus to the new mood, that it come in most places to mean not no growth but quality growth.

6

Although most of our recommendations are for immediate action, we also foresee a need for long-term changes in basic attitudes and values toward land. It is time to change the view that land is little more than a commodity to be exploited and traded. We need a land ethic that regards land as a resource which, improperly used, can have the same ill effects as the pollution of air and water, and which therefore warrants similar protection.

The message of this report is intended for many ears. We address several recommendations to the President and Congress, most notably a suggestion that they enact and implement national land-use policy legislation providing federal recognition, guidance, and financial assistance to states that undertake the reform of their land-use laws and institutions. We have a considerable amount to say to states, for the largest opportunities in directing land use and urban growth lie with that level of government constitutionally empowered to tax, regulate, and condemn land. We address one chapter to the courts and the legal profession. We have things to say to the cities, particularly to those cities trying to manage growth. And we have much to say to professionals and citizens concerned about the quality of American life.

We will be very pleased if our report is found useful by the many audiences to which it is directed—not as the last word on the problems but as a constructive advance in our thinking about land use and urban growth. We have tried to rethink a number of propositions long accepted in this country, particularly the rights and responsibilities that accompany property ownership. We have made far-reaching recommendations affecting historic preservation and open space protection, zoning, new communities and other large-scale development, and lot sales in rural areas for vacation homes.

In a word, the report is a call for more responsibility in the way land is used. Responsibility in respecting natural systems and cultural values; in recognizing the legitimate rights of others to move to the places they value just as our parents or we have done; and in leaving to those who will come after us an environment that will endure and enrich. The sense of responsibility we wish to encourage transcends our obligations to be good businessmen, lawyers, accountants, or public officials. It emphasizes obligations to the wider society. People should not have to be paid to refrain from victimizing their neighbors with excessive, inappropriate, or destructive development, and our laws should reflect this.

*The task force meeting in December 1972. From left, John R. Price, Jr., Virginia Nugent, Henry L. Diamond, Paul N. Ylvisaker, and Laurance S. Rockefeller.*

We would hope, too, that humanistic values would guide development, and we have sought to determine where such values lead. They have led us to favor protection of vibrant neighborhoods and historic areas; to appreciate the need for more flexible criteria that go beyond minimum development standards for evaluating new proposals; to value broad environmental and social impact assessment procedures for new development; to propose that governments play a more active role in making land available for development on a scale large enough to include generous amounts of open space and a wide variety of housing types; and to propose that governments assure that land is not developed inappropriately.

We have confronted the bleakness of many center city areas by pointing out how conditions can be changed in the next phase of growth. The land-use policies of local (particularly suburban) governments have exacerbated the concentration of lower income people in cities by rendering land outside the cities unavailable for inexpensive homes or moderately priced rental apartments. We suggest ways to alter the economic incentives that have been partially responsible for local exclusion of low-income people, and we propose state-supervised limitations on the powers of local governments to take arbitrary actions that have the effect of saying to any segment of the population "go elsewhere."

In the eight months available to us, we have not attempted to be comprehensive or exhaustive. We set to one side many more areas related to the quality of life—education, jobs, income, public safety, health—than we considered. Why, it may be asked, have we not dealt with matters of such fundamental importance? Surely, if we have learned nothing else about urban problems, it is that they do not lend themselves to a piecemeal approach. But in the areas in which the problems are most severe, so much appears to be wrong—and most of what is wrong appears to be related. The awareness of such interrelationships can lead to a numbness, a paralysis in the face of complexity that we hoped to avoid.

For the most part, we have addressed the issues we have because they all relate to aspects of the physical environment, the natural and man-made environment that is the arena for all human endeavor. As a task force of the Citizens' Advisory Committee on Environmental Quality, we have addressed the problems most appropriate to our consideration.

We have tried to deal in detail with those subjects we have addressed, looking always for the point of leverage at which public policy might improve circumstances and free private energies to contribute to, not work against, the broader public interests. Our central concern has been with the use of land as it affects other conditions of life: what happens to the environment we rely on and enjoy, where we live and shop and work, who our neighbors and our children's classmates are. We have attempted to identify ways in which our policies toward physical development and conservation might be improved so as to encourage a strong sense of community among our people.

We would like to signal a new priority to the American people and their leaders in and out of government. The massive urban growth foreseeable by the end of the century must be managed without destroying what we most value in the distinctiveness of our neighborhoods and communities; the beauty of our countryside, coastal lands, and mountains; and the delicate rhythms of nature. And it must be managed so that opportunities are not shut off to any segment of the population.

When we describe our report as hopeful, we do not wish to appear overly optimistic. Essentially, the task before us consists of learning to do what we have not yet successfully accomplished on any scale: creating communities that are socially open and environmentally sound. In learning to do so, it will be necessary to consciously maintain a balance, a creative tension, between the forces of development and the forces of conservation. Only now are the conservation forces—those who would apply high humanistic standards and criteria to new development—acquiring sufficient strength to be taken seriously by traditional spokesmen for development. Thus now some reconciliation between growth and environmental objectives may be realistic.

This reconciliation can take many forms. The pending national land-use policy bills, on which President Richard Nixon and Senator Henry Jackson have both provided leadership, are examples of a constructive response to developmental needs—including social needs—and environmental protection. New state laws also offer positive examples of this balance.

Both groups—developers and conservationists—have a stake in achieving an accommodation. For, on the one hand, increasing citizen disenchantment with development could conceivably stop growth in some areas, with immediate economic harm to developers. On the other hand, courts will never sustain environmental land-use restrictions that exclude development from one area unless there is a process for accommodating needed development somewhere else. The price for upholding strong environmental regulations must be a fair accommodation of essential needs. And the price for allowing major development to go forward must be a careful regard for environmental protection and for orderly growth.

The vastness of the work ahead does not argue for leaving it all to the experts. There are probably few other fields in which citizens, adequately informed about problems and alternative solutions, can be so helpful to public decision-makers as in the field of urban growth. A generation of urban experts has produced fewer important changes in the growth process than five or so years of sustained citizen action. The need now is to assure that citizens are informed in their efforts to affect urbanization. We hope that our report will help fill that need.

The December 1972 task force meeting. From left, Laurance S.
Rockefeller, William K. Reilly, Pete Wilson, Walter E. Hoadley,
James W. Rouse, and John R. Crowley.

Many individuals have helped us with advice, analysis, and encouragement. We wish to thank particularly those who made oral presentations or wrote papers for task force meetings, including: Fred P. Bosselman, David Callies, and John Banta of the Chicago, Illinois, law firm of Ross, Hardies, O'Keefe, Babcock and Parsons; Lois Craig of the Federal Architecture Project; Herbert M. Franklin of the Washington, D.C., law firm of Frosh, Lane and Edson; Robert H. McNulty of the National Endowment for the Arts; C. Willis Ritter of the Washington, D.C., law firm of Haynes and Miller; and Don Detisch and James Goff of the San Diego city government.

We are also grateful for the papers prepared by Stan Ross and Michael Feinstein of Kenneth Leventhal and Company, Los Angeles, California; Roy Mann Associates, Cambridge, Massachusetts; and Ecology and Environment, Inc., of Buffalo, New York, and for the interviews conducted and photographs provided by Janet Mendelsohn of Cambridge, Massachusetts.

Helpful advice, information, verification, and critiques of drafts were provided by many agencies and individuals. We wish to acknowledge particularly the comments and advice of Stanley D.

11

Heckman of New York City; Frank Beal of the American Society of Planning Officials; Lawrence N. Stevens, executive director of the Citizens' Advisory Committee on Environmental Quality and G. Merrill Ware of the committee staff; Boyd Gibbons, Timothy Atkeson, and Philip Soper of the Council on Environmental Quality; Randall Scott of the National Association of Home Builders; Robert Cahn of the *Christian Science Monitor;* Ralph Field of Westport, Connecticut; Art Davis and William Duddleson of the Conservation Foundation; Huey Johnson and Greg Archbald of the Trust for Public Land; Robert Stipe of the Institute of Government and Jonathan Howes of the Center for Urban and Regional Studies, University of North Carolina; Steven Weitz of the Department of Housing and Urban Development; William H. Whyte, New York, New York; Fred Anderson of the Environmental Law Institute; Edward J. Logue, Steven Lefkowitz, and D. David Brandon of the Urban Development Corporation of New York State; Richard Wiebe of the New York State Office of Planning Services; and Calvin Kytle and Don Lief of Washington, D.C. William Dietel and Marilyn Levy of the Rockefeller Brothers Fund provided encouragement and assistance that went beyond the financial.

We would also like to acknowledge the helpful comments and data provided by the following agencies: the U.S. Bureau of the Census; the Tri-State Regional Planning Commission and the Regional Plan Association, New York; the Southeastern Wisconsin Regional Planning Commission, Wisconsin; the Metropolitan Washington Council of Governments, Washington, D.C.; the Division of State Planning, Florida; the Metropolitan Areas Planning Council, Massachusetts; and the Division of Planning Coordination, Office of the Governor, Texas. And we would like to thank the firm of Parsons, Brinckerhoff, Quade and Douglas, who loaned us Thomas Barrington.

Finally, we are grateful to the hundreds of citizens in New York, Florida, California, and Colorado who freely shared their views on urban growth. Our assessment of their attitudes leads us to believe that many of the far-reaching proposals we have made are realistic, timely, and, most important of all, responsive to the emerging concerns and values of Americans.

*Washington, D.C.*
*May 24, 1973*

# The Report in Brief

This is a hopeful report, one that acknowledges the political constraints in our cities, states, and federal government, one that tries to assess realistically what we can and cannot influence, one that sets out a selective strategy for improving the way in which our cities, suburbs, and even some remote areas are physically developed and redeveloped.

\* \* \*

Our central concern has been with the use of land as it affects other conditions of life: what happens to the environment we rely on and enjoy, where we live and shop and work, who our neighbors and our children's classmates are.

\* \* \*

We have looked for the point of leverage at which public policy might improve circumstances and free private energies to contribute to, not work against, the broader public interests.

## The Situation

On the one hand, unrestrained, piecemeal urbanization—supported by a value system that has traditionally equated growth with the good life—has produced too many dreary, environmentally destructive suburbs of a single lifestyle; too many bland, indistinct city centers; extensive mismanagement of the earth's resources; and rising popular discontent. (In many areas experiencing especially rapid growth, citizens are questioning the desirability of more growth. People concerned about urbanization tend to be against high-density development and to sanctify the

13

single-family home. They challenge rezonings that would accommodate more growth, propose studies of optimum population, and approve height limitations on buildings. Often, they seem to be viewing development itself as the enemy, as a kind of pollution that causes congestion and destroys views.)

*On the other hand,* the needs of the American population, existing and projected, can be met only through continuing development. (The fertility rate would have to stay at the low replacement level for about seventy-five years before population growth would stop. The number of U.S. households is increasing even more sharply than the number of people: from now until 1985 more than 27,000 new households are anticipated every week, equal to a city the size of Kalamazoo, Michigan. This increased household formation rate is one-third greater than the rate from 1960 to 1970. With high incomes have come high levels of consumption—automobile ownership, recreation, travel, the purchase of bigger homes and even second homes, with the result that people are spreading out farther over the land. As a consequence, urban land area is increasing far faster than the size of the urban population or the number of urban households.)

## The Problem

How shall we organize, control, and coordinate the process of urban development so as to protect what we most value in the environmental, cultural, and aesthetic characteristics of the land while meeting the essential needs of the changing U.S. population for new housing, roads, power plants, shopping centers, parks, businesses, and industrial facilities?

## Main Obstacles to a Solution

Historically, public opinion has favored development almost irrespective of the cost to the environment. Our laws and institutions, many of which evolved during a time when growth was a national ideal, reflect a pro-development bias.

Although public opinion is now changing and agencies that play by the old rules are increasingly coming under attack, new rules have yet to be formulated and accepted.

Processes that allow for sensitive accommodations and balances—that assure protection of critical open spaces and historic buildings, but also assure that essential development needs are met—are not yet in effect in most areas.

Many citizens lack confidence in official land-use plans. They distrust the way zoning decisions are made.

Landowners expect to be able to develop their property as they choose, even at the expense of scenic, ecological, and cultural assets treasured by the public.

Most developers lack the opportunity to significantly improve the quality of projects. The small scale of their operations, or the restrictive policies of local government, work against variety, protection of important open spaces and other environmental lands, and the accommodation of low-income people and mixed lifestyles in many areas.

Developers are increasingly having difficulty getting land in sufficiently large parcels and with zoning and sewerage adequate to permit large-scale development. The land market is a large part of the problem; so, in some areas, are anti-growth attitudes.

Incentives created by the local property tax and the small size of many local governments lead them in some growing suburban areas to resist essential urban development, to exclude the poor, and to make decisions that will not raise property taxes or visit change on established residents. The same incentives can sometimes lead them to permit development in the wrong places.

## Our Working Assumptions

The United States has institutions and policies for solving the problems of air and water pollution. We have neither adequate institutional processes nor the necessary legal doctrine to solve the problems of urban growth.

We have not yet learned to build communities that are environmentally sound and socially open.

We are in a period of great ferment when citizens' groups, the courts, a number of state governments, the national administration, and congressional committees have begun to consider fundamental reforms in the way state and local responsibilities for land-use control are distributed. At the heart of this ferment is recognition that states must have the responsibility to control land-use decisions that affect the interests of people beyond local boundaries if critical environmental lands are to be protected and if development needed by a regional population is not to be blocked by local governments.

Public land acquisition cannot, need not, be the whole answer to the problem of open space protection or historic preservation.

15

With private property rights go obligations that society can define and property owners should respect.

It is not enough to think only of conserving what we have. Conservation must be part of a larger effort to create what we want. In a time of massive change, the task must be to maintain a creative balance between the forces of conservation and the forces of development. Only recently and in selected areas where people are applying new high standards to development is this balance becoming possible.

### Our Conviction

There is no need for people or their governments to accept a future of blanketing urbanization in which individuals and communities lose their identities.

Nor is there need to put up with some of the suburban barriers that limit the mobility of people with low and moderate incomes.

Nor is there need to accept development stretching endlessly along the edges of roads and sprawling across scenic hills and valleys, forests and farms.

There is opportunity, in short, to have urban regions that contain natural beauty, to have new and renewed urbanized areas more varied and satisfying than those we are familiar with.

### Our Approach

Before we came to our conclusions:

—we surveyed the major reports on land use and urban growth of the past five years;

—we examined significant state and national legislation, pending and enacted; and

—we conducted field studies in:

*Florida* ("Paradise in Peril"), which attracts 4,300 new residents each week, 550 to Dade County (Miami) alone; which includes three of the fastest growing metropolitan regions in the nation (South Florida, Tampa-St. Petersburg, and Orlando); which from 1950 to 1969 lost 169,000 acres of estuarine habitat to dredging and filling; which in April 1972 passed one of the strongest set of state land and water management laws.

*Long Island, New York,* where 2.6 million people are concentrated in two counties fragmented into 110 taxing jurisdictions; which in ten years (1954-64) lost 29 percent of its coastal wetlands; where the NAACP is suing Oyster Bay on charges that zoning has been used to keep out poor and black people; where environmentalists now form more than a hundred diverse groups.

*Colorado,* where in November 1972 voters barred the use of city and state funds to support the 1976 Winter Olympic Games, pulling in a welcome mat that had been out for twenty years; where, in Boulder, citizens considered (but defeated) the first referendum in the nation to limit population size but approved a city study of ways to reduce population growth to a level "substantially below" that of the 1960s; where longtime U.S. Representative Wayne Aspinall was defeated in the 1972 primary by a law professor running as an environmentalist; where a statewide land-use plan is due to be completed by December 1972.

*California,* probably the only state where concerned private citizens have produced a comprehensive plan to provide alternatives to the development proposals of federal, state, and local agencies; where environmental impact statements are required for significant private as well as public developments; where a powerful independent regulatory agency has been authorized to control all development along the shores of San Francisco Bay; where voters have now empowered the state to take a similar approach to regulating all development along the California coastline and, in most instances, 1,000 yards inland.

## Conclusions

A new mood in America has emerged that questions traditional assumptions about the desirability of urban development. The motivation is not exclusively economic. It appears to be a part of a rising emphasis on human values, on the preservation of natural and cultural characteristics that make for a humanly satisfying living environment.

This new mood represents a force of great energy. On the one hand it presents opportunity; finally, a broad, popular concern for planning and regulating land use has emerged that can be offset against the one-sided, purely economic values that have characterized much development pressure. On the other hand, it presents a challenge, for it encompasses a range of negative attitudes that are sometimes confused and even hostile to the needs of our society for new development.

Nevertheless, this new mood is the most hopeful portent we see. Although it expresses a range of anxieties and discontents, it can be used as a lever to achieve the changes in land-use planning and control that will make possible a qualitatively different future for us and for American generations to follow.

The most serious charge against the new attitudes is that public policies developed in response to them would necessarily impose their heaviest burdens on the least advantaged members of society. It must be recognized that the disadvantaged have legitimate needs that only development can meet—and that a measure of urban growth is inevitable in our lifetimes, for the poor and for nearly everyone else.

No growth is simply not a viable option for the country in the remainder of this century. The case for more development is not based simply on demography—on the fact that we must house the people who are already around or whose birth is foreseeable—nor even on projections of economic growth. There is also an ideal involved, that of respecting the free choices of Americans to move in search of a better job or a better life. Mobility has been a traditional road to opportunity in America. Wholesale growth restrictions, imposed by many communities, could block that road for the many who still want to travel it.

Efforts to divert growth away from metropolitan areas and into "lagging" areas or to small towns have had little success. The likelihood, in the absence of major changes in attitudes, is for continuation of metropolitan concentration.

The urban region is a fact of life. The vast majority of Americans will live, not predominantly in cities as we have known them, but in suburbs and exurbs that will be contiguous in many areas. The issue is not whether there will be urban regions—that is, regional constellations of urban centers and their hinterlands as opposed to single super cities—but what form these urban areas will take.

High-density or highrise living are not the only alternatives to sprawl. Even with low densities, utilities and services can be provided economically and substantial open spaces conserved.

***

*In most instances, we have favored the rearrangement of processes and the redesign of incentives to get the system working for, not against, quality urban development. We have consciously focused less on negative compulsion than on creating positive inducements, less on increasing public expenditures than on making sure that the governmental entity with the proper perspective is the one responsible for dealing with a* particular issue, less with tilting the balance toward environmental groups or development interests than in trying to see that a newly emerging balance between these forces is maintained.

*** 

Although we recommend a number of measures to inject higher levels of government into the development guidance process, we think that the broad base of regulations should be established by local decisions.

## Findings and Recommendations

### Open Space

We believe there is an enormous opportunity for the federal government to encourage open space protection by formulating, mapping, and publicizing a set of advisory national open space classifications for consultation by federal agencies in the planning of development projects, for use in support of state and local plans and regulations, and for consultation by private land buyers and sellers.

Especially in newly urbanizing areas, we see both recreation and social needs best served by establishing as public policy that the limited natural supply of prime recreational open spaces, particularly beaches and other waterfront areas, should, to the maximum feasible extent, be acquired by government, preserved, and made publicly accessible.

Federal spending for open space acquisition should be maintained at levels commensurate with needs. We see particular merit in continuing to extend the network of parks, seashores, and lakeshores that are owned and managed by the federal government itself. States, many of which are currently enjoying budgetary surpluses, should also adjust open space acquisition plans to rising needs, particularly with respect to areas where urban growth is anticipated and where waterfront land is beginning to appreciate as a result of pollution-control activities.

Since no combination of federal, state, and local land purchases is likely to acquire enough open spaces to satisfy demand, other techniques must be used as well.

State and local governments should assert and protect often neglected public rights in beaches and other recreation land. Similarly, the federal government should exploit its full range of powers, including its permit authority and public works activities, so as to promote protection, public access, and use.

Federal estate tax laws and regulations should be amended to permit the transfer to the federal government of land determined by the Secretary of the Interior to be of national significance, with the fair market value of the land offset against federal estate tax liabilities.

Governments at all levels should actively solicit open space donations and should facilitate the work of responsible private organizations, such as the Nature Conservancy, by granting them charitable status for real estate tax purposes.

Mandatory dedication requirements (imposed on developers) can be an equitable and inexpensive way to provide essential urban open space. We believe the requirements should be used even more widely than they already are.

In newly developing areas, developers should contribute open space or cash for the purchase of open space, sufficient at least to satisfy the reasonable needs of the residents of their developments. Local governments should adopt regulations requiring such contributions, preferably in connection with "cluster" provisions. States should authorize and encourage the adoption of these local regulations or should adopt similar state regulations.

State legislation and local regulations should assure that adequate public accessways exist before allowing the subdivision or development of private property adjacent to public beaches and waterfronts.

To protect public open space against diversion to other public use, states should, at a minimum, provide that (1) alternatives to the diversion of parkland be formulated with full opportunity for public comment; (2) any open space taken be replaced by other open space that will, wherever possible, meet similar public needs; (3) additional procedural protections be established to ensure careful evaluation of proposals by one agency to condemn open space under the jurisdiction of another agency; and (4) methods for determining the value of open space be improved so that any open space may be replaced by land of at least comparable monetary value.

Since it is neither feasible nor acceptable for governments to acquire the vast agricultural and natural areas that ought to be conserved within future urban regions, mechanisms to protect privately held open space are essential. Without such mechanisms, even moderate objectives of protection programs are

20

unlikely to be achieved.

The land market, as it operates today, is the principal obstacle to effective protection of private open space.

To achieve permanent protection, open spaces should be insulated as completely as possible from the market forces that now inexorably press them into development. One way to accomplish this objective is for owners of open spaces to give up or sell part of their property rights. Another is for local or state governments to regulate development of open spaces, requiring owners to maintain them as they are.

State as well as local governments should establish protective regulations to prevent development that would be incompatible with open space needs in critical agricultural and environmental areas. Where protected areas are carefully selected through comprehensive planning, states should authorize and encourage, in appropriate cases, very low density zoning, including, for example, requirements for 50 or more acres per dwelling unit. Enactment of pending national land-use policy legislation is urgently recommended as a means to encourage state and local regulation in a balanced framework that is respectful both of conservation and development priorities.

Decisions to construct sewers and to provide other public services should be taken only after careful consideration of whether these decisions will stimulate or discourage the development of designated open spaces. Plans for the location of federally assisted sewers should be consistent with state, regional, and local plans.

Governments and charitable organizations have a significant opportunity to preserve open space by providing owners with a just and convenient method of donating urbanization rights and then persuading owners to use it. In time, we believe, ownership of open spaces without urbanization rights should become as commonplace as ownership of land without mineral rights.

Incentives are often needed to encourage protection and to back up regulations. Because incentives involve a trade-off—offering the landowner something in return for a desired response—care must be taken to assure that public benefits are commensurate with public costs.

Measures that grant partial relief from real estate taxes on farms in urbanizing areas, in force in about half the states, should be re-examined to assure that the public benefit in open space protection warrants the substantial expense reduced taxes entail.

Provisions that grant reductions in the absence of permanent restrictions should be regarded as half-way measures, justified only when permanent restrictions are politically unacceptable.

We are persuaded that a mix of techniques, including public acquisition of land and of development rights in strategic land parcels (those located along highways, directly adjoining urbanized areas, and along waterfronts) but with primary reliance on federally supported, state-administered, non-compensatory regulations appears to present the only realistic hope of achieving the permanent protection of critical open spaces, including buffer zones between urbanized areas.

We see the need for a National Lands Trust to be established either within the Interior Department or by federal charter to assist public bodies, particularly state land-use agencies, in the designation, planning, and conservation of extensive greenspaces in and around major urbanizing areas. The National Lands Trust would advise on regulatory and acquisition measures and make funds available for acquisition of full or partial interests in strategically located lands within greenspaces. For this purpose, federal funding of $200 million should be made available annually on a matching basis with a 75 percent federal share.

A changed attitude toward land—a separation of ownership of the land itself from ownership of urbanization rights—is essential.

Historically, Americans have thought of urbanization rights as coming from the land itself, "up from the bottom" like minerals or crops. It is equally possible to view them as coming "down from the top," as being created by society and allocated by it to each land parcel. We think it highly likely that in forthcoming decades Americans will gradually abandon the traditional assumption that urbanization rights arise from the land itself. Development potential, on any land and in any community, results largely from the actions of society (especially the construction of public facilities). Other free societies, notably Great Britain, have abandoned the old assumption in their legal systems and now treat development rights as created and allocated to the land by society.

*Historic Preservation*

Historic areas need protection, too. Many communities have important or unusual historic buildings or whole streets and neighborhoods with historic integrity, where the buildings, by their age, design, and scale, form a unit of visual continuity and character. Such areas may already be registered historic districts, as in Charleston, Boston, and Santa Fe, or they may be stylistically varied areas lacking any significant single buildings but forming units of pleasing proportion and providing a sense of the past. Such historic properties are vulnerable to the same threats as open space, and their preservation often poses the same buy-it-or-lose-it dilemma to local authorities. We see historic districts and buildings benefiting from the approach and many of the techniques we recommend for protecting privately owned open space, an approach based primarily on regulation, not purchase.

We need broadened classifications for historic areas. Present criteria for listing in *The National Register of Historic Places* are that the area possess integrity of location, design, setting, materials, workmanship, feeling, and associations and represent a significant and distinguishable entity. These criteria discriminate against areas with a stylistic mixture, areas that can often support a varied rent structure and provide a refreshing diversity of uses and people. We urge that urban neighborhoods characterized by a mix of uses, a vitality of street life, and a physical integrity be recognized on the *National Register* as "conservation areas."

For historic preservation, as for open space protection, the first requisite is a framework for regulation, preferably a statewide system for registration of historic districts and properties and a clear policy favoring preservation. States should enact appropriate legislation to implement the Model State Guidelines for Historic Preservation recommended by the Council of State Governments among its 1972 suggested legislative proposals. Such legislation would establish a state institutional structure for review and regulation of historic sites, structures, and districts and would enable local governments to protect the integrity of historic areas.

## Adapting Old Laws to New Values

To protect critical environmental and cultural areas, tough restrictions will have to be placed on the use of privately owned land. These restrictions will be little more than delaying actions if the courts do not uphold them as reasonable measures to protect the public interest, in short, as restrictions that landowners may fairly be required to bear without payment by the government. The interpretation of the "takings clause" (which has sometimes been construed to prohibit governmental restrictions on the use of

23

privately owned land as, in effect, "takings" of the land itself for which landowners must be compensated) is therefore a crucial matter for future land-use planning and regulatory programs.*

Many judicial precedents (including some from the U.S. Supreme Court) date from a time when attitudes toward land, natural processes, and planning were different than they are today. Many precedents are anachronistic now that land is coming to be regarded as a basic natural resource to be protected and conserved and urban development is seen as a process needing careful public guidance and control.

Ignorance of what regulations higher courts have been willing to sustain against landowner claims that a restriction amounted to a "taking" has created an exaggerated fear that restrictive actions will be declared unconstitutional. Such uncertainty has forestalled countless regulatory actions and induced numerous bad compromises. The popular impression of the takings clause may be even more out of date than some court opinions.

Extensive case preparation is necessary to demonstrate the constitutional validity and public benefit of land-use regulations. To facilitate that preparation, the trend toward "environmental divisions" within the offices of state attorneys general and county and municipal attorneys should continue, and attorneys in these divisions are urged to devote a substantial share of their efforts to land-use regulation.

Existing nonprofit organizations should be supported and appropriate additional organizations established that will provide governmental attorneys with the expert testimony, research assistance, and skilled tactical advice needed to prepare for important land-use cases.

State and local legislative bodies should continue to adopt stringent planning and regulatory measures whenever they believe them fair and necessary to protect natural, cultural, and aesthetic values. This legislation, in addition to its direct benefits, can help create a climate of opinion in which lawmakers and judges will regard strong, needed restrictions as a proper exercise of governmental power.

The courts should "presume" that any change in existing natural ecosystems is likely to have adverse consequences difficult to foresee. The proponent of the change should therefore be

---

*The so-called takings clause in the Fifth Amendment to the U.S. Constitution: ". . . nor shall private property be taken for public use, without just compensation."

required to demonstrate, as well as possible, the nature and extent of any changes that will result. Such a presumption would build into common law a requirement that a prospective developer who wishes to challenge a governmental regulation prepare a statement similar to the environmental impact statements now required of public agencies under federal programs.

It is time that the U.S. Supreme Court re-examine its precedents that seem to require a balancing of public benefit against land value loss in every case and declare that, when the protection of natural, cultural, or aesthetic resources or the assurance of orderly development are involved, a mere loss in land value is no justification for invalidating the regulation of land use.

### Development: Regulations

The mechanisms used to regulate development need improvement. Under present laws, localities can take many—probably most—of the regulatory steps needed to control development. To do so, however, localities must often distort their regulatory process to fit a mold established by half-century-old state legislation. The distortion—particularly the overemphasis on detailed preregulation and underemphasis on flexible response to what is actually taking place—often obscures how development is guided (even to decision-makers), seriously misleads the public, and deprives landowners of essential procedural safeguards. We look forward to completion and release (scheduled for the spring of 1974) of the American Law Institute's model land development code, which promises to furnish invaluable aid in the modernization of out-of-date state enabling acts.

Except for small projects with limited impact, discretionary review should be at the heart of development guidance.

The best regulatory mechanism so far for development review is environmental impact analysis. The great benefits of the process are its focus on proposed development, its consideration of feasible alternatives, and its replacement of the "minimum standards" concept with a concept of seeking among feasible alternatives what is best for the public interest. In the long run, the greatest importance of the environmental impact analysis process may lie in its establishment of a higher standard of conduct for development agencies, requiring them to publicly evaluate opportunities within a broad spectrum of public objectives. States should enact legislation, modeled on federal environmental law, requiring environmental impact statements in connection with major state, local, and private actions that significantly affect the environment.

For the convenience of all concerned—builders, neighbors, administrators, the general public—a convenient, nondiscretionary mechanism must be provided so that the mass of small projects can proceed without elaborate review—a mechanism resembling today's nondiscretionary building permit.

As agencies gain experience with environmental impact statement requirements, they should seek increasingly refined ways to identify the actions and issues important enough to warrant such review. Plans, minimum standards, or other criteria that assure some alternative form of control over the less important actions may prove most acceptable.

For power plants and other critical development, project review procedures should be modified so that disapproval of one development proposal must be accompanied, in the same proceeding, by approval of an alternative (or abandonment of the project if need cannot be satisfactorily demonstrated). A much more thorough planning process is needed for this purpose as well as review agencies with larger geographical jurisdictions. Passage of the proposed power plant siting legislation would be an important step toward fulfilling this need.

Every element of the regulatory process, including deliberations, advisory recommendations, and final decisions, should take place at advertised meetings open to the public. Local and state laws should establish open meeting requirements for all governmental agencies responsible for land-use regulations.

To reduce the reality or appearance of conflicts of interest, state and local laws should disqualify local and state officials from voting or otherwise participating in any regulatory decision whose outcome could confer financial benefit, or could appear to the public to confer financial benefit, to themselves, their families, or their business or professional associates. All persons having any responsibility for land-use regulation, including elected and appointed officials and employees, should also be required by law to make periodic public disclosure of their financial interests and real estate holdings within the jurisdiction over which they exercise responsibility.

Citizen suits appealing from local regulatory decisions should be permitted by any local resident or civic organization in the public interest, without regard to property ownership or other financial interest. Citizen suits to enforce ordinance requirements should also be permitted. Safeguards against premature or frivolous litigation may be necessary to guard against abuse.

Local officials and citizens should periodically try to identify aspects of local procedures that may give rise to citizen mistrust. Insofar as practical, measures that cause mistrust, whether or not the resulting suspicions are in fact warranted, should be changed.

Fairness alone is not enough. The regulatory process will not merit public trust and respect unless decisions are based on consistent policies and plans. A process of planning and policy-making far superior to the one now found in most localities is essential. Such a process will include clear protection policies and plans for existing neighborhoods and critical land areas as well as frank acknowledgment of uncertainty about the nature of unforeseeable new development.

## Development: Incentives and Opportunities

Even though communities must be more effectively protected against inappropriate development, additional protection is not the most pressing need at the community level. The greater need is to remold the development process—not only the regulatory process but also the methods by which land and utilities are made available—in order to foster quality development

Important development should be regulated by governments that represent all the people whose lives are likely to be affected by it, including those who could benefit from it as well as those who could be harmed by it. Where a regulatory decision significantly affects people in more than one locality, state, regional, or even federal action is necessary.

Congress should enact a national land-use policy act authorizing federal funding for states to assert control over land use of state or regional impact and concern. Such legislation should include incentives in the form of federal financial aid and sanctions in the form of reduced highway, airport, and open space funds.

Just as state governments are intervening to provide more protection in some areas, so must they intervene for more development, particularly the sort that local governments often exclude.

State legislation should deprive local governments of the power to establish minimum-floor-area requirements for dwellings in excess of a statewide minimum established by statute.

The continuing efforts of civil rights groups and other litigants to obtain court decrees invalidating exclusionary regulations are encouraged as essential steps toward achieving the state legislation and administrative action that are ultimately necessary to safeguard fundamental rights and assure needed development.

Economic self-interest often leads local governments to concentrate less on achieving quality than on prohibiting development altogether. To discourage excessive reliance on local cost-revenue criteria as the basis for evaluating the acceptability of new development, and to increase public acceptance of state responsibility for guiding locally excluded development, we encourage the states to enact measures that would reduce the impact of new development on local tax rates.

Revisions to existing federal housing assistance programs, particularly those introduced by the Housing Act of 1968, should concentrate on a restructuring of incentives to encourage private investors to take a long-term interest in their investments. Expanding the options of assisted persons through housing allowances should be considered in designing new housing programs.

The small scale of most development remains a major obstacle to quality development. Although an increase in scale does not guarantee higher quality, it significantly increases the developer's opportunity to achieve quality. To promote large-scale development, communities should adopt planned unit development (PUD) regulations that permit flexibility in project design, subject to overall design review. The community, as well as the developer, should have the power to require that significant projects be reviewed under PUD procedures. A part of the review should be patterned after environmental impact statements.

Governments should use all acceptable means to channel development into new communities or, to the extent that these are unachievable, into "growth units" of 500 or more dwellings with related services, as recommended by the American Institute of Architects. The success of this policy will rest on overcoming the obstacles that now keep developers from operating at larger scales.

Density bonuses are one way to encourage larger scale development. Even though few localities have yet been willing to grant sizable bonuses, and despite the risks in awarding vastly increased density (and thus vastly increased land value, which raises the risk of corruption), we believe that large density bonuses should be authorized, in appropriate cases and after careful design review, to new communities and other sizable projects.

The federal government now guarantees bonds issued by developers to finance new communities that meet the social, environmental, and other criteria set out in Title VII of the Urban Growth and New Community Development Act of 1970. The aggregate of loan guarantees now available under the act should be increased and the guarantees made available for developments as small as 500 housing units together with related facilities.

The states should establish governmental entities, comparable to New York's Urban Development Corporation, responsible for assisting and when necessary directly undertaking large-scale projects. These entities should have the full range of powers, including the power of eminent domain, the power to override local land-use regulations, and the power to control the provision of public utilities, when necessary, to overcome the barriers that now prevent most developers from operating at the larger scales that the public interest requires.

The development process should, insofar as possible, be shaped by planning and regulatory bodies, lenders, accountants, appraisers, and other participants so that developers, home-buyers, and other consumers come to perceive the maintenance and enhancement of quality as the key to profitability. Divergence between quality and profitability should be minimized.

## Lot Sales in Rural Areas

An estimated 95,000 second homes were started in 1971—up from an estimated average of 20,000 per year in the 1940s, 40,000 per year in the 1950s, and 75,000 per year in the 1960s. Second home starts are expected to reach 150,000 annually during the 1970s.

Nevertheless, rural lots are being created far faster than second homes. For the nation as a whole, at least six recreational lots were sold in 1971 for each second home started. Much of the excess of lots sales over second-home starts is the result of demand artificially inflated by high-pressure sales practices. Many buyers are encouraged to think of the lots as speculative investments rather than as building sites to someday use and enjoy.

There should be no effort to discourage the creation of bonafide recreation communities. In the absence of specific problems, such as consumer victimization or environmental damage, there is nothing wrong with second homes. The over-all goal should be to encourage the creation of livable, enjoyable, and ecologically sound recreation communities and to prevent lot sales where such communities seem unlikely to come into being.

Recreational home developments should be required to satisfy the same environmental and land-use policy standards that ought to apply to first-home developments. This does not mean that such communities need have curbings or sidewalks any more than communities for first homes in every case require such facilities. It does mean that local governments should establish subdivision requirements sufficient to assure that all subdivisions, whether for first or second homes, will attain acceptable development standards. Adequate public facilities, including water supply and sewage disposal facilities (installed or bonded) should be required as a condition of subdivision approval.

Although strong local controls are essential, states should establish their own regulations to assure that planning expertise is applied, that adequate facilities are required, and that inappropriate subdivision is prohibited, even in remote areas.

Every effort should be made to bar lot sales projects in which management and sales practices encourage sellers to disregard the suitability of projects as places to live and to enjoy. Particular attention should be given to projects in which the manner of the seller's operation enables him to make substantial profit—or to show a substantial profit on his corporate books—before he installs water supply and sewage disposal facilities and the other rudimentary essentials of community existence.

To reduce opportunities for high-pressure salesmanship, the federal and state laws requiring full disclosure of lot sales information to protect lot buyers should be amended to give buyers of lots (in projects governed by the acts) a nonwaivable cooling-off period of 30 days instead of the present 48 hours. The cooling-off period should be granted to all buyers including those who have seen the land before they buy. The acts should also be amended so that projects containing more than 50 lots are covered, irrespective of the acreage contained in each lot.

Congress should amend federal securities legislation so that the sale of lots in any project containing more than 50 lots will, unless all obligations of the seller are performed before any payments by the buyer, be regarded as a securities transaction subject to the prospectus and other requirements of the Securities and Exchange Commission.

The Securities and Exchange Commission should require that descriptions of development programs be made available in conjunction with financial statements of land sales corporations, including pertinent information concerning the types and scheduling of promised community facilities.

For the inexperienced buyers likely to be purchasing unimproved lots, the protection afforded by disclosure requirements is insufficient. We believe that a warranty is needed as well. Federal and state legislation should obligate the sellers of lots (in projects containing 50 or more lots) to guarantee to each buyer that his lot will, for one year after the date on which he is scheduled to obtain title, and again for one year after the date on which the contract obligates the seller to complete all improvements, be fit for construction of a dwelling (or for any commercial or industrial use specified in the sales contract). Fitness for use should be defined, by statute or regulation, to include suitable water supply, the availability of lawful sewage disposal facilities, and safety elements (such as that the land is not subject to flooding). The warranty should be unwaivable and breach of warranty should entitle the buyer to return of all his payments, with interest and damages, up to the date of breach.

We recommend that careful consideration be given to requiring that a portion of the lot buyers' payments be deposited in escrow until the seller has fulfilled his obligations to the buyers. Escrow accounts could be held by banks and released to the sellers as facilities are completed. If promised improvements are not made, escrow money could be applied to construction costs.

## The Role of the Citizen

The vastness of the work ahead does not mean we should leave it to the experts. We believe that civic organizations can make an important contribution to the quality of life in their areas by helping to decide what should be protected and preserved in their localities and how and where essential development needs are to be met and by helping to assess systematically the adequacy of local plans, laws, regulations, and procedures affecting urban growth. The 1976 bicentennial year would be an appropriate time to complete of the first phase of such an assessment. We urge that federal assistance be made available for these citizen efforts as part of the bicentennial program.

# Chapter I
# Challenging the Ideal of Growth:
# A New Mood in America

There is a new mood in America. Increasingly, citizens are asking what urban growth will add to the quality of their lives. They are questioning the way relatively unconstrained, piecemeal urbanization is changing their communities and are rebelling against the traditional processes of government and the marketplace which, they believe, have inadequately guided development in the past. They are measuring new development proposals by the extent to which environmental criteria are satisfied—by what new housing or business will generate in terms of additional traffic, pollution of air and water, erosion, and scenic disturbance.

This mood defies easy generalization because it springs from a melange of concerns—many that are unselfish and legitimate, some that are selfish and not so legitimate. The mood is both optimistic and expansive in its expectations of the future, and pessimistic and untrusting about inevitable change, even (perhaps especially), in places where change is the only constant. Its demands range from managed growth to no growth, from "stop-til-we-plan" to "stop," period.

There have been isolated instances of such reactions before, of course. But today, the repeated questioning of what was once generally unquestioned—that growth is good, that growth is inevitable—is so widespread that it seems to us to signal a remarkable change in attitudes in this nation.

Once, citizens automatically accepted the idea that growth—in numbers of people, in jobs, in industries—would ease the public burden by increasing the tax rolls and spreading per capita costs. Now they have doubts. They seem to be expressing the belief that larger size means not only lesser quality but also higher costs. Pressed by inflation, they listen carefully to arguments about the hidden costs of growth.

The new mood reflects a burgeoning sophistication on the part of citizens about the overall, long-term economic impact of development. Immediate economic gains from job creation, land purchases, and the construction of new facilities are being set against the public costs of schools, roads, water-treatment plants, sewers, and the services new residents require.

But the new attitude toward growth is not exclusively motivated by economics. It appears to be part of a rising emphasis on humanism, on the preservation of natural and cultural characteristics that make for a humanly satisfying living environment. There may not be a willingness to sacrifice achieved economic status by throwing out industry already there, but many areas are ready to forego a measure of future economic advantage by keeping out new business and industry, maintaining a stable population, and preserving existing low density and scale. A letter to the editor of the *Miami Herald,* which appeared in October 1972, expresses the new mood well:

> In the past few years we Dade County residents have watched roads, sewers, water mains and telephone ducts being torn up and replaced to accommodate sudden increases in residential and commercial density. We have seen the shadow of rising skylines creeping toward the places where we live; the walling off of Biscayne Bay; vehicular traffic thickening at our doorsteps and the cost of it all swelling our tax bills or rent. In the rush of alleged progress, authorities have had little difficulty in clobbering the outcriers. ... But now it is different. A better informed public knows that a concentration of population means a concentration of pollution, snarled transportation, greater physical danger ... and a higher cost of living.

Four successful candidates for local office in Dade County, Florida, who banded together as the Committee for Sane Growth, put it more succinctly. According to their platform, they "joined solely to ... seek to solve the paradox of 'the more people who come to share our good life, the less good it becomes.'"

This mood is apparent in many parts of the United States, particularly in those areas which residents regard as environmentally superior. Vermont, Maine, Massachusetts, Delaware, Colorado, Florida, California, Oregon, and Hawaii—in all there are statewide movements concerned with protecting scenic areas, preventing "over-growth," and halting developmental processes

34

that threaten to degrade the environment. In Colorado, Florida, Hawaii, and Oregon, state officials are even considering optimum population levels and reflecting on how to assure that population does not increase beyond levels that can be adequately supported by existing land and water resources.

The new mood has political viability as well as grassroots energy, as confirmed by even a partial rundown of 1972 election results:

—Coloradoans, in a heavy vote in two separate ballots, barred the use of state and Denver city funds for the 1976 Olympic Winter Games, bringing to an abrupt end a twenty-year effort to attract the games in the name of progress and civic pride.

—In New York State, 70 percent of the voters approved a $1.15 billion bond issue to finance facilities for cleaner air and water, solid waste treatment, and the purchase of environmentally sensitive areas.

—In Florida, voters approved, again in a heavy vote and by a large majority, a $240 million bond issue to purchase environmentally endangered lands, thus enabling the state to acquire lands under the authority of a vital section of their new land-use act.

—California voters approved Proposition 20, which authorizes the creation of state and regional commissions to control development along the coast. The opposition waged a bitterly fought, heavily financed campaign. Although an earlier campaign against a similar initiative to regulate coastal development had been successful, this time the big spenders were the losers.

—The citizens of Boulder, Colorado, and Santa Barbara, California, voted height limitations for new buildings. Voters in San Diego passed a similar measure for coastal structures.

—Voters of Boca Raton, Florida, set a maximum to the number of housing units that could be built in their city, the first successful effort to curtail growth by a citizen-approved limit.

—Suffolk County, New York, voters approved a zoning change that will give the county more say over local zoning decisions affecting wetlands.

—Environmental bills of rights were ratified in Massachusetts and Washington to facilitate public complaints against polluters.

—Santa Barbara voters placed on their city council two advocates of slowed growth.

—Three major open space purchases were approved in California, in San Mateo, Santa Clara, and Marin counties.

—Oakland, California, voters advised the city government to double the money spent for parks and open space.

—And of fifty-seven candidates for Senate, House, and gubernatorial posts endorsed by the League of Conservation Voters, forty-three, representing twenty-five states, were successful.

## The New Mood in Four States: A Reaction to Rapid, Unmanaged Growth

Task Force representatives went to four states where the new attitudes toward growth were strong: Florida, Colorado, California, and New York. In each state, the communities visited were ones in which embattled citizens and public officials were in the midst of heated controversies: Dade County, Florida; Boulder and Denver, Colorado; San Diego and San Francisco, California; and Long Island, New York. In all these areas, population has doubled, trebled, and even quadrupled since the 1950s, with the pace of growth considerably more rapid than the nationwide average in metropolitan areas alone (where most of the nation's population growth in the past twenty years has occurred).

In the areas visited, the rapid pace of development, the despoliation of sensitive environmental areas by piecemeal, unplanned, and often rapacious development, and the unwillingness or inability of local governments to help had so aroused citizens that they were demanding change. In one area, a water crisis spurred action; in another, it was smoggy mountain air; in another, the repeated filling-in of a valued bay. In all but one area, the threatened despoliation of overwhelming scenic beauty was the energizer of citizen concern. The presence of such physical factors helps explain why these communities are in the forefront of the new mood, but the waves being generated in these areas, far from being isolated, are part of a rising tide of citizen sentiment against rapid, unplanned development.

### Florida

"Paradise in Peril," the *Miami Herald* called it in December 1971. "Not that all is lost but that all still might be preserved," the paper explained. And paradise it is, with woodlands, wandering streams, glades, quiet bays, hidden estuaries, miles of beaches, green savannahs, golden sunshine. The beauty and peace that delighted Ponce de Leon continue to delight, attracting 4,300 new residents each week, 550 to Dade County alone.

But many Floridians are skeptical about the desirability of such growth. In the fall of 1971, the *Miami Herald* visited the smog, the concrete, the sprawl and jumble of Southern California for a vision of what the Florida paradise could become. A university expert there told its editors, "If you had as many people in Florida as we have in California, you would have all the same problems."[1]

The skepticism about growth began in South Florida and since has spread to the newer boom areas in the state and beyond. Such a concern may seem surprising in a state whose population is only 6.8 million and whose area is largely rural by the standards of the more populated parts of the country. But Florida includes three of the fastest growing metropolitan regions in the nation—South Florida, Tampa-St. Petersburg, and Orlando, home of the Disney World complex.

The eye of the anti-growth storm is Dade County, the most densely populated area in the state and one of ten counties in the ecologically sensitive peninsular region south of Lake Okeechobee. Home of Miami and Miami Beach, Dade has 1.3 million people. Its growth rate has slowed from the hectic pace of the 1960s, when the population jumped from 500,000 to almost 1 million in a decade. Other counties in Florida are faster growing, but Dade is where, in accommodating new residents and tourists, the most environmental damage has been done and the most environmental battles have been fought.

The land in Dade County is flat and green, much of it reclaimed from swamp by dredging and filling. Water is everywhere, not just along the coastline, where the people cluster, but by the many roadways and in fields, bays, and artificial canals. Ironically, the ubiquitous presence of water is not evidence of a plentiful, clean supply but, rather, of a vulnerable, sensitive ecosystem that has been violated by development. Satisfaction of the insistent hunger for a home, a seawall, and a place to tie one's boat resulted in routine destruction of ecological values. Beaches were lost; major waterways polluted; plants, fish, and wildlife killed. As people continued to pour in, hotels appropriated the beaches; condominiums and office buildings, the land nearby. Sewage treatment was often primitive, with sewage dumped into inland canals or overloaded ocean outfalls. (Two of three ocean outfalls, including that of Miami Beach, release totally untreated wastes.)

Now, building and zoning moratoriums hang over portions of

Dade, initiated by a countywide referendum. The referendum sponsor, attorney Harvey Ruvin, says that parts of Dade County should not be built on any more—and he was elected county commissioner in 1972. Ruvin, along with Dade's new mayor and two other county commissioners elected at the same time, ran on a platform that called for no rezoning if one or more of the following is lacking: adequate sewage treatment, sufficient road capacity, required dredge-and-fill permits, and a guarantee of fresh, potable water. These limits on development would reverse the time-honored process familiar in Dade and elsewhere, where builders build first and then demand services that are provided by acquiescent local officials.

The new mood in Florida means a kind of "guerrilla warfare" against countless rezoning attempts. It means elections in which,

*"Unlike other movements, the environmental one is here to stay. The beauty of it is, it's the first issue that cuts across all lines—race, religion, class. Land is a very basic thing."*

increasingly, the candidate's stand on building moratoriums and single-family homes is *the* issue. It means a shift for old-line conservationists from polite living-room meetings to aggressive political action. It means increasing numbers of people taking up the arguments of the conservationists. It means widespread acceptance of a governor's claim that "there are necessary and reasonable limits on the use of property." And it can entail an across-the-board thinning of planned density, as in Boca Raton, which recently voted a ceiling on the number of building units the city could accommodate.

What is most distinctive about Florida today is the response of government to citizen pressures. All over, in cities and towns, in counties, at budding regional agencies, there are new regulations and new procedures; people who have in the past stayed out of local government are now attracted to elected and appointed posts, and the old-liners are being challenged.

The most remarkable transformation is at the state level. From a state whose previous role in land use had frequently been that of ratifier of private development decisions, in April 1972, Florida passed one of the strongest sets of land and water management laws yet to clear a state legislature.

*Long Island*

The ecology of Long Island is in some ways similar to that of Florida. The Island population—2.6 million people in two counties, Nassau and Suffolk, which are fragmented into 110 political jurisdictions with taxing powers—is solely dependent on fresh water recharge for its water supply. Its shores are lined with wetlands and beaches and its waters stocked with valuable fishlife, although not so much as in past years. The Island, however, was subject to even greater population pressure than South Florida, as tens of thousands of young families poured out of New York City after World War II in one of the nation's earliest, most powerful surges to suburbia.

Now, a new drama is taking place on Long Island, revolving around its latest and perhaps last great push for growth. At issue are the pace and shape of new development on now-vacant land (most of it in the eastern end of Suffolk County) and of redevelopment in Nassau County, where towns born in the 1950s are coming of age.

Long Island remembers the damage and discomforts from

previous waves of growth, when population in Nassau County jumped from 672,000 to 1.3 million between 1950 and 1960. Today, Nassau County, to its critics, stands for untrammeled growth, an unrelieved pattern of low-density single-family homes, shopping center sprawl, and haphazardly sited business, industry, and entertainment. Once-blue bays are polluted; once-common shellfish have disappeared; wetlands are bulkheaded and beaches are eroded; in many areas open space is virtually gone. As traffic jams, multi-laned highways, and smog close in on the suburbanites in Nassau, many are questioning the quality of the growth they have witnessed. Some are eying the green land of Suffolk County to the east, where dunes, empty beaches, rolling farmland, streams, and hills still beckon.

However, it all seems about to happen again, in Suffolk. The old lures of "more house for your money" and "plenty of green space" are reappearing. Acreage-for-sale signs and the onset of strip development already mar some of Suffolk's highways. Although farmlands still yield a high economic return, acreage in active agricultural use is declining, down to less than 50,000 acres from 60,000 in 1966. (One town reported that, as of January 1973, 60 percent of its farmland was owned by speculators.)

Though not so forceful as in Florida, the questioning of growth is quickening on Long Island. "The old direction was build and grow, laissez faire zoning, the Robert Moses philosophy, when roads were decided first and land use after," said Carlie Larson, staff director of Suffolk County's year-old Department of Environmental Quality. "Now, progress means we can accommodate a normal rate of growth. You can't plan when the population increases 10 percent a year."

Environmentalists alone now form over a hundred diverse groups, most loosely confederated since 1969 in the Long Island Environmental Council. The council's director, Claire Stern, says the difference even in a few years, is "close to phenomenal in terms of the awareness and concern."

A good fight is guaranteed against any request for zoning variances. Requests for multi-family zoning or higher density are bitterly protested, whether for apartments for the well-to-do or for low-income Long Islanders. Shopping centers are questioned, and a town's courting of industry is hotly criticized.

Despite the potent pressures of the Long Island Builders Institute, the protection of agricultural lands in eastern Suffolk has recently been attempted through more restrictive zoning and tax abatements. The Suffolk County executive has proposed that the county buy 3,000 acres of farmlands and lease them to farmers.

Supported by citizens aware now of the value of wetlands, the town of Islip has proposed spending $1 million to purchase threatened wetlands over the next four years; several other towns are considering similar actions. (Between 1954 and 1964, Long Island lost a full 29 percent of its coastal wetlands.) These local purchases are being coordinated with state purchases of environmentally sensitive lands, made possible by passage of the 1972 bond issue. Strongly supported by Governor Nelson Rockefeller and the State Department of Environmental Conservation, the issue provides for $18 million to acquire tidal wetlands, which are located primarily in Suffolk County. Some money will also be available in Suffolk and Nassau for wetlands restoration and the purchase of unique areas.

The notion that people can question growth—and maybe do something about it—has only lately emerged from selected living rooms and meeting rooms as an important public issue. Just two years ago, the Nassau-Suffolk Regional Planning Board completed the first comprehensive look at development in the two counties. The planners said Long Island's urban sprawl was the "antithesis of a rational development pattern." They recommended channeling development into planned clusters, corridors, and downtowns. They foresaw a need for 400,000 new housing units, including 128,600 apartments and 76,000 public housing units over the next fifteen years. And they anticipated that by 1985 the population of the counties would increase to "at least" 3.3 million—100,000 more in Nassau and the remainder in Suffolk.[2]

Newsday, supporting the plan, summed up the issue: "The question is not: Will Long Island grow? It is: How will it grow?" Now, however, many Long Islanders are asking where those thousands of people will come from—and whether they must come at all.

On Long Island as elsewhere, citizens are more clear about what they don't want than what they do want. Usually, the undesirable is expressed in terms of communities Long Islanders believe they have escaped from. Nassau doesn't want to be like Queens, Suffolk doesn't want to be like Nassau, and the East End looks with horror at western Suffolk. Above all, no one wants to be like New York City. The reports of strife, crime, and welfare costs in the city reinforce citizen fears about what accompanies urban development.

Although officially (since November 1972) a Census Bureau standard metropolitan statistical area, Long Island continues to feel the special pressures of a largely white, well-off suburb outside a troubled, increasingly poor and black city. (Perhaps this explains the skepticism expressed more frequently on Long Island than in Florida, Colorado, or California about the genuineness of the citizen quest for quality. Some say it is little more than old exclusionary prejudices disguised in fashionable rhetoric.)

Several legal challenges to zoning and housing policies, now before the courts, attest to these pressures. The National Association for the Advancement of Colored People (NAACP) has initiated a suit against the town of Oyster Bay charging that zoning is being used to keep out the poor and the black. Their intention is to open up needed housing opportunities for low-income people already employed on Long Island as well as the ill-housed of the region. The Suburban Action Institute (SAI) is suing Nassau County, charging that it is violating federal law by permitting the development of 500 acres of county-owned land (a rare parcel made available by the obsolescence of Mitchel Air Field) without providing for any low-income housing. In another suit, filed in conjunction with the National Committee Against Discrimination in Housing, SAI is challenging the right of the Internal Revenue Service and the General Services Administration to locate a revenue service office in the town of Brookhaven without ensuring the availability of housing for its lower income employees.

None of these suits directly pits ecology against housing for the poor. Nevertheless, the problem the suits attack is local exclusion, which is typically defended in part on environmental grounds. Hence, there is suspicion in some quarters that ecology is just another code word.

Advocates of slowed growth insist, though, that poorly thought-out plans to accommodate low-income people could lead to the creation of new slums, which would not help the poor. They point out, too, that their opposition to development is far broader than simply being against low-income housing. In support of their claims of evenhanded resistance to growth, they cite the case of an environmentally oriented developer whose plan to construct costly homes on a 230-acre estate was blocked by local citizens.

Although Long Island communities are rejecting growth as an

42

*"[As for] growth, I think I can only say that you never really have a feeling of permanency. And so you wonder what's going to happen. You can't say everybody stop; you can't stop people from moving here. I just envision the whole place being like Queens in another fifteen years. I don't know if I would still be happy."*

automatic economic boon and discounting the old argument that more taxpayers will result in lower tax burdens, it is not clear how deeply convinced the citizens are, nor how long and how hard they will resist the powerful forces that promise jobs, industry, and homes to the Island. The attitude of Suffolk businessmen is "schizoid," John Keith, president of the Regional Plan Association, told a group of Long Island executives in June 1972. They put out the welcome mat for business, he said, but then join the feverish resistance to its trappings.

But even the skeptics agree that much has gone wrong with the way Long Island has been permitted to develop. Usually, Long Islanders have been "put down" by planners for not demanding anything better. They deserve what they have, runs the argument. Whatever the inconsistencies in their outlook, though, Long Islanders have higher expectations for the future and a new awareness of the kind of development policies that will *not* give them what they want.

## Colorado

In November 1972, in Denver and across the state, Colorado voters rejected the arguments of powerful economic interests and barred the use of city and state funds to support the 1976 Winter Olympic Games, pulling in a welcome mat that had been out for twenty years. The outcome was expressive of a new mood in Colorado. In May 1970, several thousand supporters greeted the Denver Olympics Committee on its arrival from Amsterdam with a bid for the winter games. Both the Denver City Council and the state legislature supported the effort.

But the people of Evergreen, to the west of Denver, protested proposed bobsled and cross-county ski runs through their community. Property owners organized POME (Protect Our Mountain Environment) and MAP (Mountain Area Planning) and were successful in forcing changes in site planning. It turned out, however, that there were Evergreeners everywhere.

In January 1971, another citizens' group opposing the Olympics was formed: Citizens for Colorado's Future (CCF). After the International Olympics Committee reconfirmed Denver as the 1976 Olympic site, CCF collected 77,000 signatures statewide—26,000 more than required—to put the motion for ending state tax support of the games on the ballot. A similar motion was placed on the ballot in Denver to stop city funds.

Protesters contended the games would bring tourists, development, permanent residents—and more pollution and more land abuse. Other citizens, concerned about rising property taxes, joined with the environmentalists in opposition. They insisted that, on balance, the costs in public dollars alone would far outweigh whatever revenues were generated. One CCF bumper sticker warned, "Don't Californicate Colorado." Another pleaded, "Save Our Mountains and Our Money." The vote in November brought an abrupt end to Colorado as a site for the Olympics, but not to the underlying tensions about growth that had turned citizens against the games.

Whether refugees from an eastern city or natives raised on a multi-acre ranch, Coloradoans are an environment-proud people. Many feel strongly about the piecemeal despoliation of their state by mining, recreation, industrial, and subdividing interests. Long-time residents of Denver remember when they daily enjoyed breathtaking views of the Front Range of the Rocky Mountains. On many days now, that mountain view all but vanishes in a haze of smog, one of the more visible results of the urbanization that stretches along the east side of the mountains to the north and south of the mile-high city.

The state's population increased 26 percent from 1960 to 1970—from 1.75 million to 2.2 million people, most of whom were newcomers. Major industrial employers have located in the state, finding that employees will accept the psychic benefits of climate and scenery in lieu of higher wages in less desirable locations. "Space to Live and Space to Breathe" proclaimed a Colorado State Commerce Department promotional publication mailed to entice out-of-state executives. The magnificent mountain slopes, too, draw millions of vacationers each year to an area now regarded as a prime national playground.

The overwhelming majority (80 percent) of the 2.2 million persons in the state live in the thirteen counties along the eastern side of the mountains in the so-called Front Range Corridor. Most of this population, 1.2 million people, is concentrated in the five-

*"I was hung up about the same thing. Get out of the city. Move to a nice little piece of land [where] you get a house and a piece of green grass so that your kid can grow up in a pretty nice suburban area. But the community really grew uncontrolled. People started to realize what was taking place. They were in a community, but they had no say."*

county Denver metropolitan area. If present trends were to continue, the state's population would almost double by the end of the century, with 70-80 percent of that growth expected in the Front Range Corridor and 60 percent in the Denver metropolitan area. (As of 1971, lands in approved subdivisions totaled between 1.5 million and 2 million acres. If allowable densities were applied to existing subdivisions, Colorado could be home to 14 million people in less than a century.)

Second to the fight over the Olympics, the liveliest debate over growth is taking place in Boulder, where, sparked by two local no-growth organizations, citizens considered the first referendum in the nation on limiting population size. Although the referendum was narrowly defeated, Boulderites did pass a building height limitation and directed their officials to conduct a study of "optimum" population size.

Colorado politicians unresponsive to concerns about growth now risk being replaced. Long-time U.S. Representative Wayne Aspinall, identified as a spokesman for development interests, was defeated in the 1972 primary election by Alan Merson, a law professor at the University of Denver who ran his primary campaign on environmental issues. Merson lost in November, but his campaign had ousted one of the most influential members of the U.S. House of Representatives.

In the state legislature, whose members also campaign specifically on growth-control issues, debates on extending state powers over land use have been going on for several years. In 1970 the legislature approved the Colorado Land Use Policy Act. Although not so strong as the more recent Florida legislation, the act, by establishing the Colorado Land Use Commission, provides a mechanism for a comprehensive response to environmental concerns. The commission's major responsibility is to develop a statewide land-use plan by December 1973. By April 1973, it had already issued a two-volume interim plan that formed the basis for public and legislative debate over the components of a comprehensive land management system for Colorado.

## California

If citizens on Long Island are living under the shadow of New York City, and residents of Boca Raton look askance at Miami, there is one place which is everyone's archetype of rapid growth and unrestrained development—California, the home of Los

Angeles, itself a symbol to many of how urbanization should not take place. (Before 1885, 90 percent of the 36 square miles of Los Angeles was considered rustic and thousands of acres in the western portion of the city were uncultivated. In less than a century, 2.8 million people had come to reside on the city's 464 square miles of land.)

Twenty million people now live in California. Everything in the state seems gigantic: ocean, mountains, redwoods, traffic jams, smog, land development profits. That California is home to more environmentalists than any other place in the country, which certainly seems to be the case, is undoubtedly due both to the pace of urbanization and to the magnificent setting, which gives a special poignancy to any diminishing of nature.

Not surprisingly, Californians are taken back by the speed with which damage is being inflicted on their state. Thousands of acres of prime agricultural land succumb to urbanization each year. Logging, forest fires, cuts and fills from housing and road construction, and wasteful agricultural practices result in the unnecessary loss of millions of cubic yards of topsoil every year. Groundwater, fossil fuels, wildlife, and other resources are being depleted or destroyed. Nearly 50,000 acres of estuarine habitat were lost to dredging and filling between 1950 and 1969.

A few important steps have been taken to control urbanization. Since 1965, the state has encouraged the preservation of farm lands by enabling counties to grant tax abatements to farmers who agree to keep their lands in active agricultural use for specified periods of time. Fourteen million acres are under such interim protection. Nevertheless, substantial acreages of farmland continue to be lost to urban development. And if the experience of other states with temporary contract zoning to protect agriculture is any guide, the preferential tax assessment procedure may be little more than a holding action.

Backed by more recent state legislation, several counties in the path of urbanization have been reviewing the zoning of their open farm and timber lands and reclassifying them into large-lot land-use categories that conform to present uses. Marin County, for example, recently rezoned two-thirds of its agricultural land, primarily in use as dairy farms, into lots of 3 to 60 acres, with the majority in 60-acre units.

The California Supreme Court handed down a legal decision in September 1972 of major importance. Initiated by the Friends of

Mammoth, a local citizens group protesting a large-scale multi-story housing and recreational community in the Mammoth Lakes region, the suit provided the first test of the California Environmental Quality Act of 1970. The decision confirmed that environmental impact statements must be issued for significant private as well as public developments.

California is probably the only state where concerned private citizens have produced a comprehensive plan, *The California Tomorrow Plan,* edited by Alfred Heller, to chart the course of future growth and provide alternatives to the development plans of federal, state, and local agencies. The plan allocates large amounts of open farm, desert, mountain, and forest to conservation, agricultural, and "regional reserve" uses.

If environmental awareness and citizen activism for change are increasingly effective in California (as evidenced by the recent approval of strong state and regional regulations to control coastline development), the citizens in San Diego and San Francisco have led the way. San Diegans elected one of the first mayors in the country who specifically promised to manage growth, and San Francisco Bay Area residents have literally saved their bay by supporting a regional grouping of separate but crucial decision-making agencies.

San Diegans are separated from Los Angeles by only 125 miles and a large military reservation, but they sometimes seem willing to die in defense of this buffer to the sprawl creeping southward.

San Diego's own growth statistics suggest one cause of the concern. Since 1940, the population of San Diego has more than tripled. Despite this, much land in the city as well as in the surrounding county is still vacant. There are magnificent natural environmental barriers—the ocean to the west, mountains and desert to the east. To the south is the Mexican border.

Driving northeast on Interstate 8, one would find it hard to believe that the highway follows a river valley which fifteen years ago was designated a recreation area. The road was built for motorists, but development soon followed. A shopping center with a large department store was the first. Then other sizable developments. A few years ago, the car dealers haphazardly filled in the spaces that were left. Citizens call it Los Angelization, a symbol of the free rein given to developers, especially after economic stagnation in the early 1960s jumped San Diego unemployment rates to 10 percent. Now, strip development lines the major freeways in the area, subdivisions leap-frog, and air pollution reached levels exceeding state standards on 176 days in 1971.

The city, however, has recently decided to slow growth. Mayor Pete Wilson was elected in 1971 on a platform that called for "clear authority and the tools needed to permit the city, rather than the developer, to determine the timing and location of new development." Environmental forces and community planning groups helped elect a sympathetic majority to the city council.

San Diego has gone well beyond rhetoric in its efforts to get a grip on growth. Long-standing city support of a multi-million-dollar flood-control channel in the Tia Juana Valley was withdrawn, partly to protect an estuary deemed of great ecological significance. The city has also served notice that heedless subdivision sprawl is over. The site of this battle was Mira Mesa, an area to the north of the city to which development had leap-frogged and where areas of tract housing were being built despite inadequate schools and services. (Following the threat of a building permit moratorium, the builders agreed to fund needed schools, street improvements, and other services.) Zoning in many parts of the city has been substantially tightened, too. In some instances, high-density apartment zones have been changed to single-family use.

The new mood toward growth is particularly apparent in one of the nation's most physically blessed, environmentally aware, and rapidly growing metropolitan areas, the San Francisco Bay Area. The Bay Area embraces nine counties with ninety-four cities and several hundred local and multi-jurisdictional special districts. It covers 7,000 square miles and contains 4.6 million people—a population greater than the total population of California in 1921. Here, as in the rest of the nation, the greatest impact of population growth has been in the suburban areas surrounding the city.

Such growth has consumed land at a staggering rate. In 1950, San Jose had a population of 95,000 in 17 square miles. Today, its population is 446,000 in a 136-square-mile area. Present zoning permits further massive population increases.

The Bay itself is actually composed of six bays, two straits, five rivers, and forty creeks. Two of the rivers, the Sacramento and the San Joaquin, account for 40 percent of all fresh water flowing in California. A little more than a century ago, the Bay's water surface was 700 square miles, and clam digging and swimming were popular activities. Now, the Bay's surface area is only 400 square miles, and the water is unfriendly to fishlife and people. Alarmed by the diminished size and deteriorated quality of the Bay as landfills made space for development, citizens of Berkeley (itself partly constructed on a fill) formed Save San Francisco Bay Association in 1961. The tenacity of citizen efforts resulted in the creation, in 1965, of the San Francisco Bay Area Conservation and Development Commission (BCDC) as a temporary three-year commission. After one of the biggest battles conservationists have ever fought and won, state legislation established BCDC in 1969 as an independent regulatory agency authorized to control all development along the Bay's shores. It has not only denied permits requested by powerful interests, but has also, by its very existence, slowed the rush to develop miles of shoreland and further fill in the Bay.

In November 1972, California voters empowered the state to take a similar approach to regulating all development along the California coastline, in most instances 1,000 yards inland from mean high tide. The bitterly fought Proposition 20 provided for the establishment of a state coastal zone conservation commission and six regional commissions to grant permits, review environmental impact statements, and prepare, within three years, a comprehensive coastal-use plan for consideration by the legislature. The regional commissions are expected to draw heavily on the experience of BCDC in drawing up the coastal regulations, and BCDC's executive director and chairman have been appointed to comparable posts in the new state coastal agency.

## Environmentalists—The New Mood Catalysts

This new mood stems directly from the pioneering, persistent efforts of those in the preservation-conservation-environmental movement who were the first to take on such battles and who still represent the hard core of the protest. Not too long ago, theirs was a lonely, almost instinctive fight against man's mismanagement of the earth's resources. Now, their fights, and their organizations, are changing. Their numbers have grown and their goals and tactics have shifted. Militancy, politicization, and scientific data have sharpened their arguments, their effectiveness, and their appeal.

There are several hundred environmental groups in the areas visited. There are vocal but numerically small groups solely interested in population limits, like Lesser San Diego and Zero Population Growth, and others that work only for building height limitations or reduced densities in beach areas. There is Save the Otters Society, now battling the abalone industry in California. There are more traditional groups like the Sierra Club, the League of Women Voters, and the National Wildlife Federation. There are confederations like the Long Island Environmental Council.

The change in environmental organizations is typified by the evolution of a major association in San Diego, Citizens' Coordinate for Century 3, known locally as C-3. When the organization was formed in 1960, its primary focus was The City Beautiful. Three years ago it was reorganized in response to the marked increase in environmental concerns. Now, C-3, primarily concerned with air and water pollution, goes into courtrooms and legislatures to make its points.

The Nature Conservancy, with headquarters in Washington, D.C., and a branch in San Francisco, is another group that has evolved in response to new needs. The Conservancy grew out of a committee formed in 1917 to acquire natural areas for scientific research. Today, it devotes itself entirely to land preservation and the conservation of threatened ecosystems. Recently, the Conservancy purchased 67 acres of crucial wetlands in Suffolk

*"I just get particularly concerned about the recreational second home business. Big in California, big in other states too. Those developments have shown little or no concern for the environment they're moving into."*

County and immediately leased them to the state, which will buy them when funds are available.

## The Movement Broadens

The political successes in the 1972 elections, especially in such populous states as California and New York, indicate that what was formerly a conservation movement has exploded beyond traditional boundaries. In California, the coastal initiative, Proposition 20, carried in most coastal and urbanized counties, drawing considerable support among working-class voters despite the opposition of many labor unions. It squeaked by in highly conservative Orange County (an unexpected victory) and was supported by blacks and Chicanos at about the 55 percent victory margin it received statewide. In New York, the environmental bond issue carried by a two-to-one margin. In Florida, the vote on the bond issue for purchasing endangered areas was overwhelmingly favorable. Virtually every precinct in Dade County backed the bond issue, including those made up primarily of blacks (although the margin of victory was narrower in Cuban and Spanish neighborhoods).

"The movement is sweeping the country," observed Professor John DeGrove of Florida Atlantic University, chairman of the University's new Center for Environmental and Urban Studies. Although the environmentalists were the catalyst, they alone do not account for the movement's force and intensity.

The new mood has become an umbrella for diverse—and not always consistent—dissatisfactions and hopes. There is anger. "The people have been outraged by what they see," says Professor DeGrove. And weariness. "They're tired of everything—the whole array of urban problems. They want the pressure off," says Arthur Marshall, head of the University of Miami's Division of Applied Ecology and co-chairman (with DeGrove) of the 1971 land-use task force that developed the comprehensive new state law. There is, too, distrust of growing urbanization, accompanied by nostalgia. "There is a great concern for the quality of life," says Dade County planning director Reginald Walters, "for ideal things—little congestion, green spaces, good schools, and low taxes—for life as they believe it used to be." And there is pure self-interest, the desire to preserve from any change personal benefits already gained.

Powerful groups whose economic livelihood is threatened by

land and water mismanagement have gotten under the new mood umbrella, too. In Florida, for example, they include shrimpers, crabbers, hunters, sportsfishermen, and, sometimes, the many people who cater to tourists.

The implications of this broadened movement cannot yet be fully appreciated, but it is clear that the impact of decisions taken in the name of quality radiates beyond the geographic areas in which they occur. Actions taken to limit growth in Florida may affect the choices of the citizens of New York or Chicago who intend to retire there; decisions taken by Delaware to exclude oil refineries could affect the cost and perhaps even the availability of fuel and energy to the citizens of Philadelphia and Pittsburgh; a decision by the people of Boulder or Boca Raton to limit population size could result in a decreased supply of housing that would eventually mean higher prices. Conversely, the failure of state and local governments to preserve their environmental assets diminish the opportunities of us all.

## Charges Against the New Mood

There is uneasiness about what the new attitudes mean and where they will lead us. Some question whether the effort is simply an escape from the unpleasant realities of underemployment, violence, and inadequate housing. Cynics call the movement a modern "bread and circuses" calculated to draw public attention from such divisive issues as poverty and racial discrimination. But perhaps the most serious charge is that public policies developed in response to these new attitudes would impose their heaviest burden on the least advantaged members of society.

It is true that many new mood policies are aimed at lessening people pressures. If Boulder or Boca Raton takes measures to limit its population, for example, the price of land and homes may be driven up, thereby pricing out the poor, and probably many of the middle class as well.

If sewage overload calls for low-density development, or if large tracts of open spaces or wooded areas are to be preserved, a possible effect, whether intended or not, could be to close off potential housing sites. If development is curtailed, there is apt to be a slowdown in building, and a consequent loss of jobs. (Several labor unions oppose the Florida building moratoriums and new coastal regulatory measures in California because of their potential threat to jobs.)

These issues are not easy to resolve, particularly since the environmental movement, which gave the new mood its boost, began as a concern of the "haves." Although the movement has broadened considerably, in many areas it still has not shed its white middle-class image. Some new mood activists in the areas surveyed were troubled by their inability to attract more blacks and Chicanos to their meetings. C-3, for example, the large San Diego conservation organization, reports that members can be sorted by zip code: affluent La Jolla is heavily represented; the ghetto area in southeastern San Diego, minimally. Spokesman for poor people have claimed that environmentalists are more sensitive to the plight of wild ducks than of people.

A few issues have transcended economic and social barriers. The use of pesticides is one. Transportation is another. New roads have often been cut through poor neighborhoods, destroying decent housing and communities without any plans for relocation or rejuvenation. Now, civil rights groups and environmental organizations are pushing the alternative of mass transportation in a combined effort to cut down pollution and to preserve neighborhoods.

But other issues remain standoffs, with poor and minority groups suspicious that new mood policies are aimed at them.

On Long Island, Nassau County has acquired over 4,000 acres of open space in the past five years; Suffolk County has acquired 6,000 acres. This policy, widely supported locally, was criticized by an NAACP official, who claimed, "They build parks next to parks."

Beach use, severely restricted on Long Island, is another area of contention. Towns jealously guard access to beaches and parks by setting high entrance fees and limiting parking places. Not only are blacks from the center city kept out but people from other Long Island towns as well. This restrictive use is now being attacked by citizens and in the courts.

But the issue that is generating the most tension is housing. All the areas visited have long-standing needs for subsidized housing. In Marin County, California, the Housing Authority has estimated that 17,000 people in the county need housing assistance. On Long Island, the Nassau-Suffolk Regional Planning Board calculated that 76,000 subsidized housing units would be needed in the next fifteen years. In South Florida, a local expert described the need for housing as "astronomical." In all cases, estimates were based on internally generated need, that is, on housing required for people already in the communities.

For both economic and environmental reasons, planners' usual answers to the need for more housing, and especially subsidized housing, is clustered, large-scale development. In the absence of master plans, growth policies, or local officials they trust, however, many citizens embrace what they believe to be most desirable—the single-family home and low-density development, which seems to ensure them some control over the size, and, to a certain extent, the residents of their neighborhoods. Those fearful of large-scale projects and increasingly aware of what a continuation of piecemeal low-density development entails in destruction of open space and other environmental assets often select the simplest course: fight development wherever it rears its head.

Claire Stern, Long Island Environmental Council director, believes that a major barrier to working out housing problems is lack of confidence in local land-use policies. Although she believes blacks need more housing opportunities on the Island, she says that "until better land-use decisions are made, I'll stand in opposition to density development, although my gut feeling is that this is arbitrary and wrong."

A few communities have taken the first steps to mitigate the possibly exclusionary impact of growth-slowing policies. Palo Alto, California, for example, at the same time that it has sharply limited development in its baylands and foothills, has adopted a series of policies to increase the supply and geographical distribution of low-income housing in the city.

But in many communities, citizens react against the kind of development they have witnessed by turning inward. It is easier to think in terms of stopping development and preserving what they have than of considering what desirable change might entail or grappling with the difficult issue of how the unmet needs of others are to be satisfied. While these reactions are understandable, the tensions they represent will have to be dealt with forthrightly in the future if the needs of all are to be met.

## Policy Responses to New Mood Pressures

Many would argue that the new mood is neither new nor, despite the vote in the 1972 elections, widely shared. Or, if it is, that it will be ephemeral, like so many earlier citizen movements.

We are aware of this possibility. Yet, in the places we surveyed, in the increasing sophistication about the nature of the problems and in the commitment and energy we found, we perceived the mood as powerful and the attitudes as deeply held. *We are convinced that, although the mood expresses a range of anxieties and discontents, it can be used as a lever to achieve changes in land-use planning and control that will make possible a qualitatively different future for us and for American generations to follow.*

What might some of these changes be? How are the different levels of government responding to pressures for no growth, lessened growth, or, at the least, managed growth?

Obviously, governmental responses can, and do, take various forms. The choices of local governments are perhaps the most difficult, for at the local level development is visible and must be dealt with in fact, not in theory. As pressures against growth mount, local officials who want to stay in office may conclude that they had better meet them, even if it means reversing a long practice of giving developers pretty much what they want. At the local level, stopping growth altogether may seem perfectly reasonable: people can always go somewhere else.

At the state level, the problems are more subtle and complex. Rare is the state where no growth is a realistic option, and more factors must be taken into consideration in a decision for or against development. Most states where new mood pressures are strong are beginning with systems for decision-making that will provide an institutional apparatus for reconciling conservation priorities with developmental needs. Right now, processes are getting more play than plans.

Proposals for land-use reform in Congress favor putting federal weight behind state assumption of responsibility for controlling growth with regional significance, leaving specific decisions to be worked out at lower levels. The federal message, too, seems to be that systems for decision-making are the first step in urban growth management.

In the following pages, we present responses to growth pressures in the city of Boulder, Colorado, the state of Florida, and the federal government. What is happening at these three levels of government indicates two possible directions land-use reform and urban growth controls may take. If local governments are allowed to have the last word in determining how many people they will accept, more and more will probably follow

Boulder's example and try to put a lid on population size. If the states enter the field, we can probably expect all kinds of approaches, with the emphasis on establishing a framework for decision-making, as in Florida. If pending federal legislation on land-use reform is enacted, we can expect federal guidance and money to bolster state efforts—and more states to take an active role in determining how their land is to be developed.

### Boulder, Colorado: A City Tries to Limit Growth

Called by civic leaders "the nicest town in America," Boulder is a well-off community of 73,000, including 21,000 students at the University of Colorado. Since 1950, the population has almost tripled. In the past decade, it nearly doubled. Every one of the city's major employers except the university has located in Boulder since 1950.

But citizens complain that life in Boulder is not as good as it used to be. There are reports of street crime on the campus. Taxes are climbing. "Denverization" threatens, especially on the days when Denver's smog creeps 30 miles to Boulder itself.

Citizens of Boulder have long cared about their city's development, from early in the century when landscape architect Frederick Law Olmsted, Jr., was retained by the local civic association to lay out a city plan to recent years when architect-planner Victor Gruen was asked to prepare a design for "Boulder Tomorrow." So it is perhaps not surprising that a report by the American Society of Planning Officials recently described Boulder as "probably the farthest along of any city in the country when it comes to a public consciousness that growth can be controlled or significantly affected as a matter of public policy."[3]

In 1967, the voters of Boulder approved one of the nation's first locally financed greenbelt programs and agreed to a sales tax increase to finance open space purchases. In 1971, its citizens chalked up another first when they voted on a charter amendment to set a maximum population limit on the city. Although this initiative was narrowly defeated, voters did approve a publicly financed study of optimum population size and set a general height limit of 55 feet to future buildings.

Boulder's compelling natural setting is fertile ground for the new mood. The city lies in a natural basin bordered on the north and south by mesas. Immediately to the west rise the mountains, first the foothills and then the great Rockies. To the east stretch the Great Plains. Boulder's neighborhoods have an ambience that greatly pleases the residents. Modest houses and stunning architect-designed homes line tree-shaded streets. The university provides a cultural and intellectual stimulus rare in a city of Boulder's size.

The growth issue emerged in 1970, when the Boulder Valley Comprehensive Plan was jointly adopted by both the city and the county. The plan anticipated that the population in the 58-square-mile area in and around Boulder would double again in twenty years to 140,000. This projection jolted local citizens into thinking about "optimum size," and by 1971 an active community debate was on. The local Zero Population Growth (ZPG) group prepared an analysis of the costs and benefits of previous growth in Boulder and, not unexpectedly, came up with a negative balance. Another group, People United to Reclaim the Environment (PURE), conducted an opinion survey and found over 70 percent of the respondents in favor of a stabilization of population "near" 100,000. ZPG went on to collect the legally required number of signatures to place the proposition for the population limit on the ballot in November 1971.

Although the amendment was defeated by a margin of six to four, 70 percent of the voters supported the resolution sponsored by the city council directing the government to "take all steps necessary to hold the rate of growth in the Boulder Valley to a level substantially below that experienced in the 1960's" and to conduct a study that would recommend an optimum city size.

The council selected a citizen group to produce a preliminary study, which was completed in early 1972. In the spring, a full-scale growth study commission was launched, with a budget of $100,000 for one year—two-thirds from the Department of Housing and Urban Development's "701" planning assistance money (the first federally aided growth-control study) and one-third from the city. The commission, focusing on a 375-square-mile area that covers about half of the county, including the foothill mountains to the west, will report in late 1973 on the physical, social, and economic effects of different growth strategies and on the citizen, business, and governmental actions each would entail.

Both the city council and the planning office have meanwhile taken specific steps aimed at slowing growth. The council has passed new land-use regulations and is discouraging the location of additional employment generators in the city. The chamber of

*"They discovered a minor loop hole in the city council ordinance, so you have this 13 story monstrosity over here. Before, all the buildings had been limited to 3 stories. And the presence of a single high rise is usually good excuse for a second."*

commerce has responded by no longer soliciting employers from out of the state.

Boulder's planning director, Bill Lamont, has backed such growth-slowing policies as the levying of a number of charges—utility fees, park dedication and improvement fees, public improvement fees—on commercial and industrial developers, and his department has promulgated stiffer requirements for subdivision improvements. The sewer hookup charge for a single-family home has been raised to $450; the charge for connecting water, to $950. The costs are still low, say city officials, who figure supplying water alone costs the public, annually, $1,400 per home. (The question of what limits water places on numbers of people that can be accommodated is a matter of some dispute in Boulder. The city must purchase all its water from surface supplies. Population estimates thus range from the present 73,000 to 30 million, if water now used for irrigation of land were instead used for people.)

The notion of a height limit on buildings, emotionally supported by citizen groups but questioned by local architects and businessmen, emerged from a series of heated local confrontations. One concerned plans for a major shopping center, complete with a highrise profiled against the mountains. Another, generating the biggest furor, revolved around plans for an expanded downtown, which citizens feared would have blocked the very mountain backdrop they were assiduously preserving through their greenbelt program.

In September 1971, after two years of study, the city council limited building height in dense areas to 140 feet. Many citizens successfully pressed on for a stricter charter amendment. The maximum height limit of 55 feet, narrowly approved by less than 11,000 votes, can be increased only by another popular vote. (In low-density residential areas, a 35-foot maximum has been set by the council.)

"This was not primarily a growth issue, but rather one of preserving the view, of keeping development in human scale," says Ruth Wright, a lawyer, local political leader, and environmentalist who activated Boulder's campaign against the highrise. Some, however, did see height as a growth generator, as well as an aesthetic blight.

Opposition to the height limit came from businessmen and developers and some planners and architects who criticized it as a too-rigid solution to Boulder's problems. The latter insisted that some of the handsomest buildings in town were higher than the citizen-mandated limitation.

Such governmental actions as fixed population maximums and height limits are very new, and their legality has been pondered. Beyond their legality, the implications of such policies for the future of Boulder, and their prospects for delivering what Boulderites want, are also difficult to assess at this early stage. For one thing, it is not quite clear what Boulder citizens want. According to one observer, a member of the preliminary growth study commission, the vote on the population limit was "a visceral response, a 'damned-if-we-want-urbanization' response." In this view, a generalized reaction to loss of amenities was strengthened and focused by ZPG and PURE. He questioned, however, how widely the no-growth attitudes are shared by the city's population at large.

Boulder citizens complain about pollution and traffic and demand an improved public transit system. But observers question whether such policies as height and growth limits are consistent with an economically viable public transit system.

Some citizens have considered what such limits imply in terms of housing for the less advantaged. Boulder has more subsidized housing than many of its neighbors, and the city council, in 1968, passed a resolution supporting a regional fair-share program for low- and moderate-income individuals. Still, the city has few minority citizens (2 percent nonwhite) and far fewer low- and moderate-income people than any fair-share program would allot the city. "The policies should not be exclusionary of anything except sheer numbers," says Lamont, who also points out that rapid growth in the past decade inflated housing and forced lower income people out of the city.

A move such as Boulder has taken is thus the impetus for considerable civic introspection. In its preliminary report, the growth study commission expressed a need for Boulder to define its purpose: "Limiting or managing population growth is not in itself a long-term goal: It is a way of gaining other benefits. . . . The city needs to be clear as to what kind of community it wants to belong to and be."[4]

Perhaps a more far-reaching question is to what extent Boulder can and should be making these decisions for itself. County planning director Vince Porreca believes the city of Boulder is shirking its regional responsibilities in a way that will frustrate its own goals as well. According to Porreca, too many variables are interconnected for isolated community planning to be successful, either for the community or the region. Growth limits make Boulder more desirable, and, ironically, may well increase overall growth pressures in the region, which must then be borne in adjacent areas. "You can't fence out the smog," says Porreca. "There has to be a strong regional concern or what Boulder wants won't happen for Boulder either."

### Florida: A State Turns to Land-Use Regulation

Not so long ago, decisions about land use were viewed ex-

*"I go to school ten miles inland. All that area used to be marshland. They keep on building and building and building. I imagine there has to be a point where they will stop."*

clusively as matters of local concern. Reflecting this attitude, states had few mechanisms, personnel, or funds to deal effectively with land-use issues. If someone said, "Let the state do it," the hidden message was often, "Let's not do anything." Proposals for regional decision-making were dutifully made and regularly ignored.

Yet state actions did affect land utilization and growth, enormously. Consider highway route location decisions. Although their effects on land use probably exceeded all other public works decisions, highway policies were rarely coordinated with the activities of other agencies. Now, that is changing.

The most remarkable turnaround is taking place in Florida, a state whose very discovery was impelled by the search for gold, and where a hungry race for profits—in land—has marked most of its history. Citizens in South Florida, alarmed about water crises, loss of mangroves, and a pace of change that appeared to victimize, not improve, communities that accommodated it, demanded action—and, to the surprise of many, the state responded.

There seem to be three reasons why the new mood in South Florida has resulted in fundamental change at the state level: first, people came to believe that they were up against governmental mechanisms that could not or would not help them; second, reapportionment led to a basic political realignment that increased the responsiveness of the state to urban problems; and third, a water crisis dramatized resource mismanagement.

Dade County's new mayor, John B. Orr, promised citizens in his campaign, "As metro mayor, I'll work for zoning that protects the people and put an end to the kind of variances that ruin our beautiful land. You the people can rely on that." He struck a responsive chord. People in South Florida are angry at the builders and developers who demanded rezonings to accommodate more units and at the local officials who caved into them. Dizzingly profitable deals have rested on "understandings" about rezoning, dredge-and-fill permits, sewer hookups, and scandals have received wide attention in the press and on television.

"It was all a brotherly relationship," says State Senator Robert Graham, the prime sponsor of the new state legislation. "The local governments were snowed. It was not necessarily illegal." Others do, however, talk of illegalities. "It was well known here. A zoning lawyer got $300 for just taking the case, $3000 if he got you the variance. We always assumed money was changing hands." The results? Developments that spewed sewage into inland canals, state lands that somehow came into private hands, high-rise buildings that blocked ocean views, publicly supported roads that seemingly joined nowhere to nowhere until a builder arrived at one end with a bulldozer.

Meanwhile, the whole character of the legislature was being altered. Reapportionment made "more of a change here than anywhere else. Florida had the distinction of having the most malapportioned legislature in the country, in both houses," says Professor DeGrove.

Reapportionment brought strong urban and suburban voices —both Democratic and Republican—to the legislature. Into this revitalized atmosphere came a governor with a "hard-nosed concern for environment" who made it respectable to question growth. "He didn't dream he could get this response," commented DeGrove.

As is often the case, it took a crisis—in this instance the drought of 1971—to dramatize the mismanagement of the South Florida floodplain and rally enough support for basic change. Signs in Boca Raton were posted announcing "water unfit for drinking." Alligators lost their crucial water holes. For over twenty days, and for the first time in its history, South Florida's drinking water came from Lake Okeechobee instead of underground aquifers. With storage reservoirs a geologic impossibility in this area, the drought moved people in a way no issue had.

Governor Reubin Askew called together 150 experts in a crisis conference on water management in South Florida. What began as a water management issue soon became interrelated with the environment, since the problems were not merely a mishap of nature but a direct result of man's misuse of nature. The conferees called for the state to develop a comprehensive land and water policy and went on to link "allowable population increases" to a quality environment.

A governor-appointed task force took over from there. By February 1972, it was ready with a package of legislation whose key component was a land management bill patterned after the model land development code of the American Law Institute. The following April, the legislature approved four bills: The Environmental Land and Water Management Act, the Florida Land Conservation Act, the Florida State Comprehensive Planning Act, and the Florida Water Resources Act.[5] The substantial bi-partisan majority that approved all the bills is a measure of the wide support the measures had throughout the state. The final votes obscure, however, the depth of opposition by most builders and developers, and some very close interim votes that whittled down important provisions. Its backers are nevertheless convinced that the package of laws that emerged represents one of the most significant advances in state land-use legislation in the country. The aim, according to Senator Graham, is "to balance growth with a high level of preservation."

The Environmental Land and Water Management Act—the

state's most important tool—sets up two categories for state supervision: "areas of critical State concern" and "developments of regional impact." In both categories, the state's role is focused on those land-use decisions that would have a substantial impact outside the boundaries of the local government in which the proposed development is located. Each category would be administered somewhat differently, although, for both, the language of the law preserves the old rules of local zoning at the same time that a regulatory role for the state is introduced—or recaptured, as many would have it.

State officials have been moving carefully in developing the specific policies that flow from the broad concepts in the legislation. Their initial efforts focused on getting past two hurdles set in place by opponents during the legislative battles.

The first was the environmental bond issue for $240 million for the purchase of environmentally endangered lands. Since citizen approval of this bond issue was a prerequisite to the state's administration of "areas of critical concern," its overwhelming

*"You can move into a house like this and in six months have it a wreck if you don't take care of it. You have to have a certain amount of pride in ownership. I would like it to stay this way—rural, no sidewalks, free from pollution."*

*"There were about 400 people in this little city hall making all sorts of noise. One of them came up to Springfield—he's a hunter and really likes the outdoors—and said, 'You know, if you build in this place, I'm not going to be able to go there anymore and watch birds.' Jim looked at him like that was the damnedest argument he'd ever heard for a zoning fight. The guy made the argument publicly and used the word ecology. That was the first time I heard the word in a public fight—in 1968."*

passage by a large vote in November 1972 considerably heartened officials. The interagency apparatus for purchasing the lands has been set up, and $50 million set aside in the governor's budget for land purchases in 1973.

The next hurdle was the setting of "guidelines and standards" for regional developments. After extensive consideration and public hearings, developments to be included in this provision were identified: mines, power plants, shopping centers, airports, large subdivisions, energy plants, and so on. For each, thresholds were specified to indicate the size that activates state involvement—for example, shopping centers of more than 40 acres or 400,000 square feet or 2,500 parking spaces; industrial parks or plants on sites larger than one square mile or with more than 1,500 parking spaces. For residential developments, the size varies from 250 to 3,000 dwelling units, depending on the size of the county. The guidelines were adopted by the governor and his cabinet in March 1973, and, if approved by the 1973 legislature, will go into effect July 1.

As the state agencies develop overall land-use policies, several compromises made in the legislative rough-and-tumble will hamper them somewhat.

First, the state does not have the power of eminent domain to condemn land for environmental purposes. All purchases must be negotiated at market, and land comes high in Florida and goes higher whenever public purchase is rumored. State officials are thinking about techniques short of purchase—flowage rights, development rights, tax abatements, leasing for public purposes—but they will have to face a deep-seated wariness about anything short of outright purchase.

Second, although the legislation specifically respects existing property rights, it does little to clarify what these rights are. Must a community go ahead, as it always has in the past, if a developer has bought land with the "understanding" that rezoning would follow? If the builder has his rezoning permits, and has, perhaps, for years, and the community is sorry, must it live with the mistake? Says Elliott Messer, counsel for the Arvida Corporation, one of the few large developers that supported the new legislation, "I don't believe a municipality is locked into traditional concepts or patterns of zoning, but its actions have to be justified to protect health and welfare. It must be responsible within the context of a growth plan. A solution to the problem must involve a fair balancing of the public interest and private property rights."

(Up against a local growth limit, the Arvida Corporation filed suit in December 1972 charging that Boca Raton's growth cap, as the housing unit limit is locally known, is unconstitutional. Arvida's first difficulties with Boca Raton arose when the city refused to zone for townhouses and garden apartments on a 2,300-acre parcel of land the corporation planned to develop. The city insisted instead that the area be completely developed in single-family dwellings. Now, the growth cap will further lower the number of single-family homes permitted on each of Arvida's acres.)

The law is not clear either about who prevails in the event of a clash between the state and local governments. Says Earl Starnes, director of the newly expanded state planning division, "We are not sure yet how the local police power applies to local decisions. We will have to be pragmatic about the interposition of state authority."

Remaining in the law are many potentially far-reaching

provisions whose translation into policies depends on the level of administration in Tallahassee, the continuing support of citizens and the legislature, and a rapprochement between regulating officials and builders and developers.

"We'll have to develop a track record first," says Senator Graham, "with nuclear plants and airports." There is a general consensus that these have to go somewhere, but local governments do not want the onus of giving their assent. Water and sewage, too, are relatively noncontroversial issues—in the "first circle of regulation," as Graham put it.

At some point, however, state officials know they will have to tackle the more controversial issues—where growth should and should not be encouraged, what criteria should be used to judge proposed new communities, where sizable developments for low-income housing should be placed. They worry about the citizen mood in South Florida that brought the new legislation into being.

Will the citizens who supported moratoriums also support policies dealing with the management of growth? To preserve sensitive areas, to provide mass transit, to fight air pollution and call a halt to excessive roadbuilding, all key environmental goals, planners and developers say that development must take place in less space, that is, with higher density and in larger planned communities. But this runs counter to the consistent rallying theme of citizens: single-family homes.

The state will have to grapple with what quality is, and what public policies foster it. If zoning has not brought quality, and most agree it hasn't, what takes its place? "Planned unit development ordinances [ providing flexible standards subject to review of overall project plans] are needed as an incentive for a higher quality product," insists Graham. But the distrust of builders and developers is widespread. Juanita Green, environmental editor of the *Miami Herald,* expressed a widespread fear. "If you put flexibility in a plan, then crooks take advantage of it. It's greed. There's so much money in it."

According to Messer, the development industry "can live with reasonable restraints. It is reasonable for government to delay development until traffic is worked out, for government to slow up because of sewage inadequacies. But only as long as those who impose that burden recognize it's a burden. It's when they don't give a damn that we get upset—when their attitude is, 'I slew another business today.'" But others say that the builders and developers have been so accustomed to the rubber stamp that it will take time before they accept a state government that simply does its job.

Developers have meanwhile modified some of their practices. One major development corporation, for example, is moving into the development of new communities, with clustered development and open space preservation—but not in Dade, where it claims the land is too expensive. To a point, developers are finding profitable ways to operate within the new constraints. Other builders warn, however, that reserving huge tracts of land in their natural state may well impose an "astronomical" cost on the land that is left—a cost that developers alone should not be expected to bear.

Meanwhile, the governor's statements about growth reflect the complexity of the phase Florida is now entering in its attempts to control growth and be fair to developers: In a June 1972 speech to

*"I don't want anybody taking oil out of my ground. My property is the square that is on the surface of the earth and a cone shape to the center of the earth. Because of all my beliefs, I'm going to do all I can to protect that much of this earth."*

*"I have found that a piece of property like this should be shared. I don't believe in one person owning a piece of land along a beautiful coast like this. But try to find someone to give it to who feels the way you do about it. It is harder to give land away than to sell it. We tried for five or six years."*

the Environmental Land Management Committee charged with reviewing current land management policies and recommending new ones (a body which has real estate and developer-builder representation), Governor Askew said, "I'd like to emphasize that the purpose ... is not negative, but positive.... You are specifically charged to find ways of encouraging well-planned development."

In South Florida, the new state laws are viewed favorably, but with a distinct air of wait-and-see. There is concern that just as citizens are beginning to make a dent at the local level, the scene is being shifted upward. Some of the qualms come from the widely held belief that it is the sum total of little decisions at the local level that degrade the environment, rather than the few big ones that the state will focus on. And many of these small decisions remain solely under local control. But much of the skepticism stems from the unmistakable distrust and cynicism that are as much a part of the new mood as the more positive concern with the quality of life. In election after election in Dade, the incumbents are thrown out. "The lack of public confidence in public officials is the biggest problem we face," said Senator Graham.

## At the Federal Level: Moving Toward a National Land-Use Policy

The new mood is apparent in Washington, too.

In the past few years, ambitious laws to improve air and water quality and insert noneconomic environmental criteria into governmental decision-making have been enacted. Something approaching a consensus has evolved that air and water quality should be achieved and that the federal government can play the key role in setting standards and determining the timing for clean-up.

No such consensus has yet emerged at the federal level on land use. But a beginning was made with enactment of the National Environmental Policy Act (NEPA) in January 1970, setting forth federal responsibility to "use all practicable means . . . to preserve important historic, cultural, and natural aspects of our national heritage . . . [and to] achieve a balance between population and resource use which will permit high standards of living and a wide sharing of life's amenities."

NEPA further directed federal agencies to prepare detailed statements on the anticipated environmental impact of proposed federal actions significantly affecting the environment. The statements, to be made public, must include an indication of alternatives to the proposed federal action. NEPA also set up the Council on Environmental Quality in the Executive Office of the President.

Senator Henry Jackson, legislative author of NEPA, had scarcely concluded work on that act when he proposed a bill which would have provided federal money to states to undertake land-use planning and land classification outside major metropolitan areas. At the same time, the new Council on Environmental Quality was preparing its first annual report on the quality of the nation's environment, a report that included a chapter on land use and an important statement by President Richard Nixon. "The time has come," the President said, "when we must accept the idea that none of us has a right to abuse the land, and that on the contrary society as a whole has a legitimate interest in proper land use. . . . I believe we must work toward development of a National Land Use Policy."[6]

In his February 1971 environmental message to Congress, the President proposed a bill to establish such a policy. The bill had been developed by the Council, whose chairman, Russell Train, in legislative testimony, cited land use as "the single most important element affecting the quality of our environment which remains substantially unaddressed as a matter of national policy."[7]

The administration proposal, first known as the National Land Use Policy Act of 1971 (and currently pending as S. 924) would authorize federal funding for states to develop land-use regulatory programs to protect areas of critical environmental concern, to control development along major highways and around major growth-inducing public works projects (such as airports, highway interchanges, and recreational facilities), and to regulate all large-scale development. The bill would also require states to have a method for assuring that development needed by a regional or metropolitan population is not excluded or unduly restricted by local governments. Any state that failed to have the required program within three years after enactment would lose a portion of its federal highway, airport, and park funds to other complying states. In addition, federal agencies would be required to comply with state land-use programs that conform to the federal legislation.

In the course of congressional hearings and committee deliberations on the two land-use measures, Senator Jackson revised his earlier bill to incorporate the principal, regulatory features of the administration bill. The compromise bill, which passed the Senate in 1972 but failed to be reported out of the House Interior Committee, is now pending as S. 268.

The pending land-use legislation, although it responds to environmental concerns to halt bad development, or at least keep it away from critical areas, is balanced in its regard for the need to accommodate development, particularly the kind of development that local governments so often exclude on social or economic grounds. In its attempt to draw the line between development that truly affects a population beyond the borders of a local jurisdiction, and is thus appropriate to warrant a state override of local control, and developmental decisions that are of purely local impact (the vast majority of governmental land-use decisions), which would be left to local administration, the legislation attempts to conserve the best aspects of a system that has kept decision-making close to home, while reforming it in accordance with modern realities.

The legislative proposals, which draw heavily (as does Florida's land-use act) from the draft model land development code of the American Law Institute, make constructive use of the unprecedented opportunity created by changing citizen attitudes toward development. If either the administration proposal or the Jackson bill should pass, the future course of land-use planning and regulation will be profoundly altered, and important opportunities will exist in all states to consider new policies and techniques for affecting future growth.

# Chapter II
# But Grow We Will

The new mood has created, and will continue to create, opportunities for preserving natural areas and improving the quality of urban development. But part of the strength of the new attitudes has derived from the willingness of people to say no to development. This skepticism has been healthy, for it has forced developers and public officials to think through their proposals carefully and to consider the broad impact of projects to which people are objecting.

But citizen negativism could create untenable situations. People may lose sight of the critical need for a measure of additional development.

To those who think the solution to development excesses in the past lies in policies aimed at no growth or markedly slowed growth in the near future, the statistics bear little comfort. Although the Census Bureau projects a slowed population increase, buried in the data is a legacy of past population increases that will keep us growing for decades.

Whether we welcome or fight it, development is going to continue during the rest of this century in the cities and suburbs and exurbs of our nation. There will be more people and more households. And these people and households will (barring some unforeseen shift in the preference for low-density living) be spread out over much larger urban areas than we know today. More people, in vast urban regions, are what the future appears to hold.

There will be tension while we accommodate the new development we need without destroying the environmental and community values we cherish. Solutions will not come easily.

Knowledgeable authorities believe that the prevailing growth
trends put us on a collision course with nature and with ourselves
as natural resources run out, pollution builds, and social systems
collapse under the burden of stress caused by crowding. We do
not suggest that these authorities are right or wrong. We only say
that, looking at urban development needs, the die is cast: we must
provide for the people who are already here or whose birth is
foreseeable under all but the most cataclysmic scenarios of the
near future.

The case for more development is not based simply on
demography or projections of economic growth. There is also an
ideal involved, that of respecting the free choices of Americans to
move in search of a better job or a better life. Mobility has been a
traditional road to opportunity in America. Wholesale growth
restrictions, imposed by many communities, could block that road
for the many who still want to travel it.

The desirability and the inevitability of a measure of development must be faced in any responsible effort to achieve better
quality in urban growth. No growth is simply not a viable option
for the country in the remainder of this century. Stop growth here
and it will pop up there; slow it down over there and it will speed
up somewhere else, because people are not going to go away. We
do have many options, however, in where and how we accommodate that growth.

## The Demographic Future: More of Us

The American population will grow well into the twenty-first
century—even though there has been a substantial decline in the
number of children women are having and in the number they expect to have. Since 1960, the Census Bureau has reported (with
one exception) a continual decline in the fertility rate, the number
of annual births among women of childbearing age. The 1971 rate
was almost 31 percent lower than that of 1960. Based on a 1972
survey of birth expectations, the Census Bureau estimates that all
women eighteen to twenty-four "can be expected to complete
childbearing with an average of about 2.1 births."[1] (The Bureau
estimates a total fertility rate per women for 1972 that is even
lower—2.03 births.)

A 2.1 fertility level is that required (assuming no net immigration, which was almost 400,000 in 1970) for *eventual* attainment of
zero population growth (ZPG), the level at which we simply

*"We're glad you've moved here, even though we've been fighting increased population density."*

replace ourselves. The ZPG concept is commonly misunderstood, though. Attainment of the ZPG fertility rate does not mean that the population has stopped growing. What it does mean is that the rate, if maintained consistently over a long enough time, would ultimately cause the population to stop growing.

Today, because there are so many women of childbearing age and so many females already born who have not yet reached childbearing age, the fertility rate would need to remain at the ZPG level for about seventy-five years before population growth would actually stop. Even if the rate were to drop to 1.8 births per woman, a rate with "no precedent in American demographic history," according to the Census Bureau, our population would continue to rise at least until the year 2020.

FIGURE 1
**Population Projections**

millions of persons

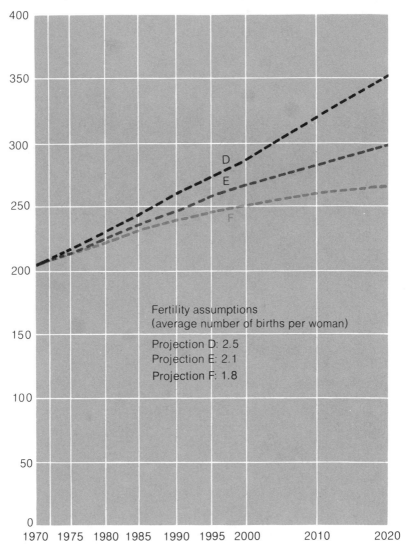

Source: U.S. Bureau of the Census, *Current Population Reports*, Series P-25, No. 493, "Projections of the Population of the United States, by Age and Sex: 1972 to 2020."

There is no guarantee that the fertility rate will remain even as low as its present level. If it does remain at approximately two children per family (and assuming a net immigration of 400,000 per year), the Census Bureau estimates that U.S. population in the year 2000 will be about 264 million, an increase of about 60 million over the 1970 level. (See Figure 1.)

The number of households is increasing even more rapidly than the number of people. During the 1960s, while total population increased by about 11 percent, the number of households increased by about 17 percent. The number of "primary individuals" (household heads with no relatives in the household) increased by almost 50 percent, indicating a greater tendency on the part of both young and old to live apart from their families.

Over the next two decades, households will be formed by the children born during the 1950s and early 1960s, when fertility rates were high. From now until 1985, over 27,000 new households are anticipated every week, equal to a city the size of Kalamazoo, Michigan. The expected rate of increase between 1970 and 1980 is one-third greater than the actual rate between 1960 and 1970. (See Figure 2.)

Since each new household requires a place to live, household formation translates directly into demand for housing and supporting facilities. Even without taking into account the need for replacement of obsolete housing, the next fifteen to twenty years will be a period of record housing demand. This demand is likely to be concentrated in the outer portions of existing metropolitan areas, particularly the larger ones.

### The Economic Future: More Money All Around

Growth in numbers of people and households explains only part of urban growth. Increasing affluence explains much of the rest. Higher incomes mean higher levels of consumption—automobile ownership, recreation, travel, and the purchase of bigger homes and even second homes. With affluence, people demand more services—airports, power plants, shopping centers, freeways, public parks. As a result, the amount of land in urban use has been increasing at a far faster rate than the size of the urban population or even the number of urban households.

The Commission on Population Growth and the American Future estimated that, by the year 2000, average family income will rise from the current $12,000 to more than $21,000 (in con-

FIGURE 2
**Household Formation to 1990**

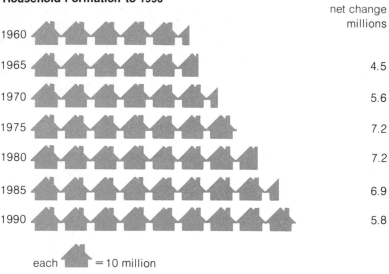

net change
millions

1960

1965        4.5

1970        5.6

1975        7.2

1980        7.2

1985        6.9

1990        5.8

each   = 10 million

Source: U.S. Bureau of the Census, *Current Population Reports*, Series P-25, No. 476, "Demographic Projections for the U.S."; Series P-20, No. 237, "Households and Families by Type, March 1972"; Series P-20, No. 233, "Household and Family Characteristics, March 1971."

stant dollars) and that per capita consumption expenditures will more than double, even with 3 children per family or a thirty-hour work week.[2]

Should population growth decline, economic growth (and, hence, growth of individual purchasing power) will still continue. In fact, the Population Commission estimated that per capita income in the year 2000 would be about 15 percent higher under a 2-child-per-family assumption than under a 3-child-per-family assumption, mainly because the 2-child rate would permit more women to enter the labor force.[3]

As in the past, much of the increase in income is likely to find its way into such land-extensive uses as airports and highways, big houses with large yards, and outdoor recreation areas.

A few trends have been projected. The Department of Transportation, for example, estimates that the number of motor vehicle registrations will increase 50 percent between 1970 and 1990 and that the number of vehicle miles traveled within urban

## FIGURE 3
### Power Plant Needs Through 1985 in the Western States

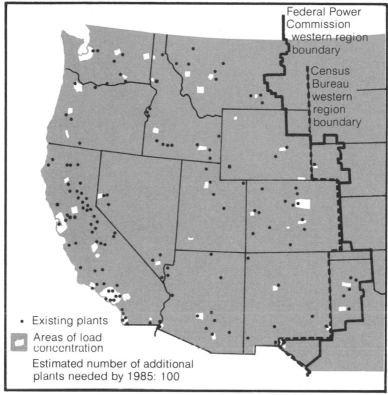

Federal Power Commission western region boundary

Census Bureau western region boundary

- Existing plants
  Areas of load concentration
  Estimated number of additional plants needed by 1985: 100

This figure is a gross simplification of a very complex problem. We have identified existing power plant sites without specifying size or type. The plants range from 20 to 10,000 megawatts in output and include conventional hydropower and thermal plants, nuclear plants, pumped storage, and peaking thermal plants. Taking into consideration line losses and loading factors (the actual time spent producing), we have assumed for the sake of simplicity that the new units would be of average size (1,000 megawatts) producing just over 4.5 million megawatt hours of electricity per year. We have further assumed yearly per capita consumption rates of 7,800 kilowatt hours in 1970 and 17,000 kilowatt hours in 1985. The resulting number of needed plants, roughly 100, might be reduced by building plants of greater capacity, clustering the plants, cutting energy consumption, or developing new methods of production over the rest of the century. However, the point we wish to make is that population increases and continued concentration will necessitate substantial increases in our energy-generating capacity, and those plants will have to be located somewhere. Although the Federal Power Commission's western region differs slightly from that of the Bureau of the Census (the Census Bureau western region includes Alaska and Hawaii; the FPC's does not) the population figures for 1970 are comparable, 34.6 million and 34.8 million respectively (excluding Alaska and Hawaii). The 1985 population projection of 43.5 million is based on the Census Bureau's low-fertility estimate (series I-E) for the western region (again excluding Alaska and Hawaii).

Sources: U.S. Bureau of the Census, *Current Population Reports,* Series P-25, No. 477, "Population Estimates and Projections." U.S. Department of the Interior, *U.S. Energy through the Year 2000.* Federal Power Commission, *1970 National Power Survey, Part III.*

areas will more than double. To serve this travel, the Department estimates a need in 1990 for approximately 18,000 miles of additional freeways and expressways within the boundaries of urbanized areas, compared with about 8,000 miles in 1968.[4] According to the Interior Department, per capita energy consumption will quadruple by the year 2000, resulting in the need for scores of sites for power plants and transmission corridors, and with a potentially far-reaching impact on the land from strip-mining, oil shale development, and the construction of extensive deep water ports and pipelines. (For a projection of energy needs in the western states, see Figure 3.)

## The Urban Future: Urban Regions

More people, with more money, following their expressed preference for low-density living in a metropolitan area can mean only one thing—bigger metropolitan areas. If past trends continue, 36 million of the 54 million population increase expected by the year 2000 will live in suburbs, more than moved there between 1950 and 1970. But metropolitan areas will not share this growth equally. Between 1960 and 1965, the Population Commission reported, the lion's share of metropolitan growth occurred in sixty metropolitan areas, many of them among the largest in the nation. (At the same time, eighty metropolitan areas lost population.)

Because of the regional concentration of the growing areas—along the eastern seaboard, the Great Lakes, the west coast, for example—anticipated outward expansion will cause many metropolitan areas that are currently separate entities to grow together into urban regions. "An urban region is not a single 'super city'," the Population Commission explained. "It is a regional constellation of urban centers and their hinterland. Although substantial portions are comprised of more or less continuous geographic settlement, the urban region offers ... a variety of residential settings within the functional sphere of a metropolitan economy."[5]

By the year 2000, five-sixths of our population is expected to live in urban regions. (See Figure 4.) And these regions are expected to occupy one-sixth of the land area of the continental United States, as against one-twelfth in 1960. From 200,000 square miles in 1960, urban regions are projected to cover almost 500,000 square miles in the year 2000. (See Table 1.)

Urban regions have resulted from two distinct migratory trends.

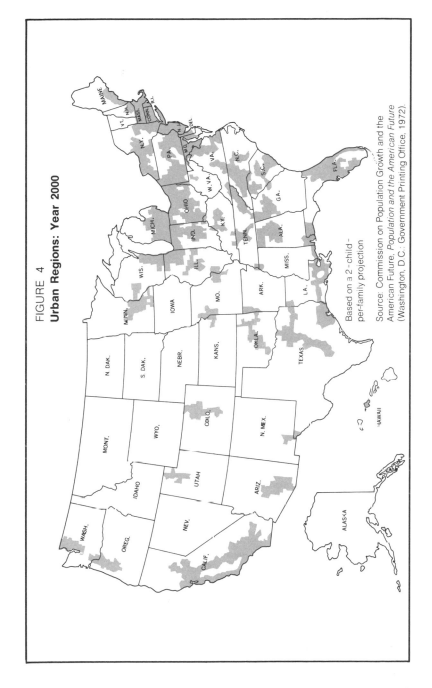

FIGURE 4
**Urban Regions: Year 2000**

Based on a 2-child-per-family projection

Source: Commission on Population Growth and the American Future, *Population and the American Future* (Washington, D.C.: Government Printing Office, 1972).

TABLE 1
**Population and Land Area of Urban Regions: 1920-2000**

|  | 1920 | 1940 | 1960 | 1980[a] | 2000[a] |
|---|---|---|---|---|---|
| Number of urban regions | 10 | 10 | 16 | 24 | 25 |
| Population | | | | | |
| *millions* | 35.6 | 53.9 | 100.6 | 164.6 | 219.7 |
| *percent of total U.S.* *population* | 33.6 | 40.8 | 56.1 | 73.4 | 83.1 |
| Land area [b] *sq. miles* | 60,972 | 94,999 | 196,958 | 395,138 | 486,902 |
| *percent of total* *U.S. land area* [c] | 2.1 | 3.2 | 6.6 | 13.3 | 16.4 |
| Gross population density *people per sq. mile* | 584 | 568 | 511 | 417 | 451 |

[a] Based on Census Bureau series E population projection (based on a fertility assumption of 2.1 births per woman)
[b] Excludes urban region of Oahu Island, Hawaii
[c] Coterminous U.S. excluding Alaska and Hawaii

Source: Jerome Pickard, "U.S. Metropolitan Growth and Expansion 1970-2000 with Population Projections," prepared for the Commission on Population Growth and the American Future at the Urban Land Institute, Washington, D.C., December, 1971.

The older is migration from rural areas and small towns into cities and metropolitan areas; the other, migration from urban centers into surrounding areas. In combination, the two trends have, first, concentrated population into metropolitan areas and, then, enlarged those metropolitan areas and decentralized population within them.

Migration into cities and metropolitan areas transformed America from a rural to a largely urban nation. By 1970, more than two-thirds of us were living in metropolitan areas. Now, the larger movement is from urban centers into surrounding areas.

From 1950 to 1970, when metropolitan areas, overall, increased their proportion of the total population from 63 to 69 percent, center-city populations typically remained stable, and all net growth occurred in the periphery. In those years, the proportion of people living in center cities declined from 36 to 31 percent, and the proportion living within metropolitan areas but outside center cities increased from 27 to 37 percent. (See Table 2.)

Might these two trends be slowed or even reversed in the

decades ahead? Governmental efforts to divert growth away from metropolitan areas and into "lagging" areas or to small towns have had little success. A report prepared for the Economic Development Administration of the Department of Commerce concluded that, of two hundred federal assistance programs, only a handful significantly altered patterns of population growth or of public and private investment. "Even with substantial modifications of priorities, fund levels, and administrative processes," the report concluded, "the capacity of these programs to alter—and particularly to reverse—geographic patterns of economic development is extremely limited."[6]

More ambitious policies aimed at stemming growth in the very largest urban areas and stimulating it in more remote areas have been tried in other countries, including Great Britain and France, but without much success quantitatively. Early efforts to keep the population of Moscow within planned limits did not even work very well (although now, with more coordinated control over migration, work permits, and industrial location—controls beyond any ever seen or desired in western nations—Russian planners apparently are doing better).

Perhaps the most important reason for thinking urban regions

TABLE 2
**Population by Place of Residence: 1950-70**

| | 1950 | | 1960 | | 1970 | |
|---|---|---|---|---|---|---|
| | Millions of Persons | % of Total Popula-tion | Millions of Persons | % of Total Popula-tion | Millions of Persons | % of Total Popula-tion |
| Total population | 151.3 | 100.0 | 179.3 | 100.0 | 203.2 | 100.0 |
| Metropolitan areas | 94.6 | 62.5 | 119.6 | 66.7 | 139.4 | 68.6 |
| Inside central cities | 53.8 | 35.5 | 60.0 | 33.5 | 63.8 | 31.4 |
| Outside central cities | 40.8 | 27 | 59.6 | 33.2 | 75.6 | 37.2 |
| Nonmetropolitan areas | 56.7 | 37.5 | 59.7 | 33.3 | 63.8 | 31.4 |

[a] Covers 243 standard metropolitan statistical areas as defined in 1970.

Source: U.S. Bureau of the Census, *Statistical Abstract of the United States: 1971.*

will continue to grow is that they offer what Americans say they want. Recent surveys have indicated a strong preference for small-town living, provided the small town is located within easy access of a large metropolitan center. A University of Wisconsin study team, for example, found that over 70 percent of its respondents preferred being within 30 miles of a center city, despite their actual locations (just over 50 percent lived within this limit). (See Table 3). People seem, in effect, to be looking for smallness and identity within a framework of bigness—something urban regions can provide. Quaint rural backwaters, pristine natural settings, small towns and villages—the urban regions will be large and varied enough to offer all of these without foreclosing the opportunity to work or play in the midst of a city with an hour or two of driving.

## The Character of Urban Regions

What will future urban regions actually look like? If we let growth go on as it has been, probably not too different from the way they look now, only on a much larger scale. Land will not be intensively developed, but a great amount of it will be built upon.

TABLE 3
**Preferences for Residential Location**
(based on a statewide survey conducted in Wisconsin)

|  | Percentage of Responses | |
| --- | --- | --- |
| Location | Respondents' Actual Location | Respondents' Preferred Location |
| *30 miles or less to central city* | 53.7 | 70.3 |
| Central city | 25.7 | 9.5 |
| Suburb | 8.7 | 11.7 |
| Medium-sized city | 7.3 | 11.9 |
| Small city or town | 4.7 | 16.0 |
| Rural | 7.3 | 21.2 |
| *Over 30 miles to central city* | 46.3 | 29.7 |
| Medium-sized city | 10.3 | 6.0 |
| Small city or town | 14.5 | 10.1 |
| Rural | 21.5 | 13.6 |

Source: James J. Zuiches and Glenn V. Fuguitt, "Residential Preferences: Implications for Population Redistribution in Nonmetropolitan Areas," paper read before the 138th meeting of the American Association for the Advancement of Science, Philadelphia, December 1971.

Job locations are likely to be more dispersed than they are now, with proportionately fewer high-volume travel corridors than at present and an increasing dependence upon private means of transportation. With more time for recreation, pressures upon environmentally attractive areas such as beaches and riverfronts will be great.

Older cities are likely to have a less significant role in the social and economic life of future regions than they do in the urban areas of today. And the degree of interdependence between center cities and suburbs will diminish as suburbanites find they need the city less.

If present trends continue, the expected decentralization within urban regions will make most of those who live in them even more dependent on the automobile than they are today. Urban regions could not have taken their present form without widespread automobile ownership and an extensive road network. Transportation investment, particularly for highways, brought huge amounts of formerly remote land within a few hours of major urban centers.

Continued low-density development will depend on an individualized, flexible form of transportation supportive of the diffused travel patterns expected (patterns sharply different from the concentrated corridor patterns that have traditionally characterized urban areas, and still do the larger ones). With today's technology, the automobile best meets these requirements. Urban regions are developing at densities too low to permit economical rail transit. Bus transit, which for most urban areas is the only reasonable form of public transit, has lost substantial numbers of riders over the past two decades, although buses, in conjunction with outlying automobile feeder services, probably offer the best mass transit option for serving the expected densities of future urban regions, especially in heavily traveled intra-metropolitan corridors.

Although we see a continuation of trends favoring decentralization within urban regions, some significant recentralization may well occur in smaller cities, present-day suburbs, and even center-city areas under the impact of: (1) the continued rapid appreciation of unimproved land in outlying areas, which is beginning to cause some developers to regard the economics of buying land in older areas where utilities and services are already provided as more attractive; (2) stronger state or regional land-use controls that encourage large-scale development or redevelopment of older neighborhoods; and (3) the provision of mass transit, highways, utilities, and other public facilities in selected growth areas, if state land-use agencies consolidate their authorities over transportation planning as pending national land-use legislation would encourage. In fact, college-educated Americans under thirty-five appear to be far more inclined than their elders to concentrate in center-city neighborhoods near friends, restaurants, and movie houses, suggesting at least the possibility that recentralization sparked by the young may occur in selected older built-up areas.

Beneath all calculations about the future is, of course, the very real prospect that a fuel shortage could enhance the attractiveness of more dense, self-contained communities where a long automobile trip is not necessary for the journey to and from work or for the trip to the supermarket.

### Mobility: An Option Worth Holding Onto

The discussion so far has been about why new development is inevitable. There are other reasons, transcending economics and demography, why new development is desirable. One principal reason is to assure continued opportunity for individual mobility. The American way of life is a way of movement and change, of going to a new town or state to take a better job, of trying a different climate, of making a new start a thousand miles away. This ability to move on is one reason why our sense of place is often shallow ("We'd get involved in the neighborhood association but we're moving to California next year.") Undoubtedly, such frequent moves contribute to the look of Instant City that characterizes many developing parts of the country. But any limitation on mobility, or on the development needed to accommodate a mobile population, would strike at one of the principal proven means that each individual has to control and improve his own life. The tradition of mobility is one we value highly.

The right of free travel, of unrestricted coming and going among the states, is considered a fundamental right protected by the Constitution. Although there is no specific constitutional language on the point, the right is entwined with our very beginnings as a nation and has been consistently confirmed in court decisions. Mobility has meant opportunity: to settlers who landed in America and took their separate paths to new lives in different

88

colonies; to pioneers who trekked westward; to immigrants who came to the cities in the nineteenth and early twentieth centuries; to rural whites who left depleted mines and obsolete farms; to poor blacks who took part in the great mid-twentieth-century exodus from the rural South; to those today who move from the center cities to outlying areas. To all, the chance to move has meant the opportunity to break away from traditional patterns in search of a better life.

This restlessness apparently runs deep in the American personality: the average American moves about fourteen times in his lifetime.[7] "Fixity of neighborhood status has been possible in the static societies of Europe," the late Charles Abrams observed, "but fixity of status is an illusion in most American areas. Industry is still on the move, settling freely where it wishes, drawing to the community the labor force it needs ... for in the long run it is the call of jobs which determines the flow of populations."[8]

For most of the nation's history, a national policy of encouraging migration has been matched by the eagerness of state and local governments to attract new residents. Now, however, growth restrictions are being considered in many areas—and implemented in a few. Some of these limitations are responses to the damage of past urbanization on the environment and to the quality of life. Some result from a belief that continued growth will mean rising taxes or degradation of an unspoiled landscape. Some seem but the latest trick to keep the "good life" to oneself. Some are transparent efforts to exclude specific groups of "immigrants."

With this mixture of purposes, it is not surprising that restrictions range from the clearly legitimate to the clearly illegitimate. Uncertainties about the evenhandedness of decisions—whether developments for better-off whites will win easy approval while developments for the poor or for nonwhites will be kept out—add further tensions. The following four cases illustrate the range and variety of mobility-limiting situations now arising, and likely to arise with increasing frequency as growth-limiting pressures intensify.

### Black Jack, Missouri

In the summer of 1970, a 2.7-square-mile piece of rural St. Louis County was incorporated as the city of Black Jack. Just a few

*Black Jack, Missouri, outside St. Louis, was recently incorporated by its residents to exclude a multi-family low-income housing project, which was kept out by an ordinance that permits only single-family residential units. ACLU and Justice Department lawyers are challenging the ordinance as discriminatory.*

weeks later the new city zoning commission recommended, and the city promptly adopted, a zoning scheme that excludes multi-family residential development from the corporate limits of Black Jack. During the same period of time, negotiations had been going on with the Department of Housing and Urban Development to obtain funds for a 210-unit multi-family housing project to be built in what was then unincorporated St. Louis County—but is now the city of Black Jack. That project, designed to provide homes for moderate-income families, is not allowed under the city's new zoning ordinance.

The drive for incorporation appears to have been motivated less by a desire for self-government than by the desire to control land use in the largely undeveloped areas. According to a newsletter circulated by the Black Jack Improvement Association just prior to incorporation, prime concerns in opposing the proposed housing project were the lack of employment opportunities, lack of transportation, devaluation of neighboring property, projected school tax deficits, and "crowding of low-income families into a close space [which] may result in disturbances that require more police support." More to the point, the letter suggested, "Remember, if this project is approved, it could open the door to similar projects being located almost anywhere in the North County area. By stopping this project, you would lessen the chance of one perhaps appearing in your neighborhood."

Black Jack is essentially an undeveloped area of rolling meadows and woodlands; what housing there is consists of single-family residences and a prize-winning apartment complex known as Whispering Lakes. The area, in northern St. Louis County, is on the edge of the St. Louis metropolitan area, with ready access (by automobile) to major industrial facilities such as those of McDonnell-Douglas Aircraft and the Ford Motor Company.

While there may well be some strain on community facilities if massive development occurs in Black Jack, as the report of the city zoning commission claims, it is not wholly clear that excluding all multi-family residential development will necessarily alleviate that strain. The predominant issue appears to be the movement of low-income families to Black Jack. Although the project was presented as a moderate-income complex of garden apartments whose rental rates would be comparable to the lower rents of other existing apartment units in the area, allegations that low-income subsidies would permit relocation of welfare recipients in the complex as well did much to stir up residents.

Lawsuits have been filed by American Civil Liberties Union (ACLU) and Justice Department lawyers challenging Black Jack's zoning ordinance. The principal complaints are that the lack of appropriate suburban rental units has resulted in substantial racial discrimination within middle-income classes as well as the virtual exclusion of low-income groups from the suburban job market.

*Ramapo, New York*

Located within commuting distance of New York City, the town of Ramapo is a largely residential community in historic Rockland County, New York. The semi-rural life of its inhabitants came to an abrupt end with the completion in the 1950s of two major transportation links with the city: the New York Thruway and the Palisades Parkway. The resulting demand for housing in Rockland County doubled Ramapo's growth rate in the 1960s. From a way-station on the Overland Road between Albany and New York City surrounded by farms and orchards, Ramapo found itself on the edge of an urban area expanding with a vengeance.

Faced with such growth pressures, Ramapo adopted a comprehensive plan followed immediately by zoning amendments. The development plan, issued in 1966, called for "every effort" to be made "to preserve those natural features of the town which

The town of Ramapo, New York, on the outer fringe of the New York metropolitan area, is hoping to retain its low-density character by limiting and controlling growth through phased development according to a con-

give it a pleasant, open setting and which serve as an attractive background to the more developed areas of the town." As the first stage in the implementation of this policy, the plan called for densities of two to four families per acre near the large villages, where urban services and some transportation services were available, with the bulk of the town projected for lower densities.

Next, Ramapo placed a moratorium on development with interim development controls. Then, the town amended the zoning ordinance to permit residential development only in accordance with an eighteen-year capital planning budget. Specifically, no property can be developed for residential purposes unless and until the developer can show that certain capital improvements are either available or will be—whether constructed by the town or the would-be developer—by the time the project is completed.

*trovercial oomprohcnaive plan. Development can occur only in areas where capital facilities are planned unless the would-be developer offers to build the facilities himself.*

Sewers, drainage, public parks, recreation facilities, major road facilities, and fire houses—all are scheduled in the capital planning budget.

To receive the necessary special-use permit to develop, an applicant must show that his project has accrued 15 "points." For example, a project is assigned 5 points if there are public sewers available, but only 3 if a package sewer plant must be constructed. Public parks, recreational sites, and school sites will attract from 1 to 5 points, depending upon their proximity to the proposed residential development.

Ramapo lost its first court test of the controversial system of development control, but in 1972 New York's highest court upheld the town in *Golden v. The Planning Board of the Town of Ramapo.*[9]

Under Ramapo's new ordinance, the building rate has been cut from approximately one thousand new dwelling units a year to roughly three hundred fifty a year. Critics claim that the development timing regulations work to exclude minority groups from the town's housing market. Proponents point to new public housing provided on scattered sites in relatively low-density garden apartments. Since first choice for the housing units goes to local residents, the public housing continues to reflect the racial and ethnic profile of the existing community.

## Martin County, Florida

Martin County, immediately to the north of rapidly growing Dade, Broward, and Palm Beach counties, was until recently a quiet rural backwater with orange groves and cattle ranches in the interior and old-fashioned summer cottages along the beaches. Now, virtually the entire coast (with the exception of Jonathan Dickenson State Park) is being developed for residential and commercial-recreational uses. The explosive growth is taking place principally along the coastline, where 85 percent of the county's population of approximately 40,000 presently live.

Projections of a 1972 comprehensive development plan, together with the reports prepared by outside planning consultants and an older (1965) comprehensive plan, suggest that a realistic population for Martin County by the year 1990 is 90,000 people. According to the new comprehensive plan, land zoned for uses permitting development would, if developed to the maximum presently permitted, result in a 1990 population of 400,000. (Some county officials predict 500,000 without a plan for controlled growth.)

The comprehensive development plan sets out a number of alternatives for the county with respect to development and population over the next eighteen years: regulated growth to 90,000 by 1990, unregulated growth, keeping things as they are, and what is called picturesquely "Fort Lauderdale North"—a rapid influx of people along the coast. The plan is extensively weighted toward the first alternative: regulated growth to a population of 90,000 by 1990.

The comprehensive development plan has been formally adopted by Martin County's Board of Commissioners. While there seems to be a general feeling that the first alternative is the preferable one, it is difficult to find any *official* statement reflec-

*Martin County, Florida, threatened by rampant development along its coastal area, has adopted a comprehensive development plan, set up strict subdivision regulations, and plans to revise its zoning ordinance to fix the number of housing units permitted in each section of the county.*

ting this choice. However, the county has already passed a series of subdivision regulations that it hopes will help control the patterns of growth and has plans for extensively revising its zoning ordinance, placing special reliance on density zoning. As explained in the comprehensive development plan, density zoning is conceived as setting a fixed number of housing units for each of several sections of Martin County, corresponding to a fixed number of dwelling units to be permitted per acre. A number of rezonings may be made to amend the county zoning map to correspond to the recommendations in the comprehensive plan.

*Land from the old Kilauea sugar plantation in Kauai County, Hawaii, has been the site of several plans for residential developments. Kauai County, which hopes to keep much of the land in agricultural use, has declined to approve any of the proposals.*

## Kauai County, Hawaii

In rural Kauai County, sugar plantations are going out of business, bringing large tracts of land on the market and creating substantial unemployment. One of these plantations was operated by the Kilauea Sugar Company. Since it ceased operations in 1971, the Kilauea plantation, as it is known, has been the subject of several land development proposals. So far, the county of Kauai, which has been asked to review the various plans informally, has approved none of them.

At the time of the first proposal for development, the county had no zoning ordinance and only a rather loosely worded subdivision ordinance. Initially, though, local land-use controls were of little importance since the plantation was classified by the state in the agricultural district—one of four categories in which all of

Hawaii is classified. Under that classification, only limited residential development is permitted. It is only when the state has classified land in the urban district that local (county) regulations become formally applicable.

The first proposal, made by a joint venture, was a plan to subdivide approximately 7,700 acres into 3-acre lots and about 1,040 acres into half-acre lots, all in accordance with existing state land-use regulations administered by the State Land Use Commission.

Of the total acreage proposed to be developed, about 4,350 acres have been termed "productive agricultural" by Brian Nishimoto, planning director of Kauai County. According to Nishimoto, the developers offered to give Metcalfe Farms (who had leased a portion of the plantation to cultivate sorghum) a lease of two to five years on the property they were using if the county would approve this proposal, which meant that any purchaser of the lot would buy subject to that lease. Kauai County officials informally turned down the proposal because they were concerned that the prime agricultural land would be subdivided when Metcalfe's lease ran out.

Representatives of the joint venture met again with the Kauai Planning Commission later in 1971, proposing to leave the prime agricultural lands un-subdivided and to subdivide the remainder into 3-acre lots and other land along the ocean shore into half-acre lots. Metcalfe Farms was to have a ten-year lease this time. While the planning commission agreed with the objective of providing Metcalfe Farms with a longer lease than previously proposed, it was still not at all clear what would happen to the prime agricultural land when the lease expired. The county concluded there was no substantial difference between the two proposals, and again rejected the plan.

The joint venture then pulled out of the land development business in the Kilauea Plantation area and sold off parcels of its property in "tax tracts" of between 10 and 1,200 acres. (A tax tract is an area used for many years by the state as the basis for levying taxes. Sale by tax tracts does not constitute a subdivision, so there is no requirement that a subdivision plat be filed before disposing of land in this fashion.) There were twenty-seven such tracts.

So far, the only investment group with firm plans to develop its parcel is an unnamed consortium represented by Theodore DiTullio. The parcel involved is roughly in the shape of an arrowhead, with the tip pointing out to the ocean. The tract contains approximately 203 acres, including the old Kilauea Plantation town. DiTullio's plans are to construct, initially, thirty-six units for the elderly (next to a clinic and a "small" neighborhood shopping development), followed by 250 HUD-subsidized homes, all on approximately 60 acres. He says he can sell such houses for about $25,000 each. He plans to ask that the state reclassify those 60 acres from their present agricultural classification (in which the smallest allowable residential lot is 3 acres) to urban in increments of land sufficient to develop fifty houses at a time. When he has completed the subsidized housing, he will then ask that the balance of the parcel be reclassified urban.

Even if DiTullio and company obtain reclassification from the state, they will have to deal with the county. Until the November elections, the attitude of the county was probably best exemplified by Ordinance No. 154, passed in December 1971, establishing a moratorium on the granting of approval for agricultural subdivisions for six months. Since agricultural subdivisions require a minimum 3-acre lot size, one can imagine the attitude toward higher density subdivision. But the mayor during whose term the ordinance was passed was defeated in November, and the new mayor is reputed to take a more favorable attitude toward development.

## The Right of Mobility

These cases only sample the issues involved in current efforts of local governments to establish controls on growth in their communities. Each represents a conflict between the accommodation of a mobile society and the desire to protect existing character and values. Individually, it may sometimes be difficult to quarrel with a community's attempt to preserve the remnants of a natural landscape in an urbanizing world. Communities must beware of prohibiting too much, though, for the right of mobility is clear not only in tradition but in law.

The Articles of Confederation, which joined the newly freed colonies after the American Revolution, explicitly established a right to travel freely among the states: "The people of each state shall have free ingress and regress to and from any other state, and shall enjoy therein all of the privileges of trade and commerce, subject to the same duties, impositions and restrictions as the inhabitants thereof respectively."

The Constitution, which superseded the Articles of Confederation and brought the former colonies together into a single republic, includes no such provision. Most scholars agree, however, that this right was so inherent in the concept of a federal union in the minds of the Constitution's drafters that they saw no need to specify it in the new document.

Supreme Court rulings recognize freedom of movement as a basic right. Decisions on the subject were few in the early years of the republic because attempts to abridge the right were few.

In 1867, an attempt to restrict interstate travel came squarely before the Court. Nevada had imposed a tax on persons leaving the state. The Court held it invalid, quoting Chief Justice Roger B. Taney in the 1849 *Passenger Cases* decision: "We are all citizens of the United States, and as members of the same community must have the right to pass and repass through every part of it without interruption, as freely as in our own states."

The depression of the 1930s raised the issue anew, as western states—particularly California—sought to discourage continuing immigration that was believed to aggravate unemployment. A California statute required persons seeking to enter the state to demonstrate that they had jobs. In 1941, the Supreme Court held this statute unconstitutional as an undue interference with Congress's power to control interstate commerce.

The issue surfaced again recently when states imposed residency requirements barring welfare payments to new residents. The Supreme Court, in holding these requirements unconstitutional, reiterated its recognition of the right to travel from state to state:

> This Court long ago recognized that the nature of our Federal Union and our constitutional concepts of personal liberty unite to require that all citizens be free to travel throughout the length and breadth of our land uninhibited by statutes, rules, or regulations which unreasonably burden or restrict this movement.[10]

The Court again considered the issue of mobility as part of another great social movement of the period—the development of civil rights legislation. In *United States v. Guest,* the defendant had been indicted for conspiring to intimidate black citizens from exercising the right to travel freely to and from the state of Georgia. The Court upheld the validity of the indictment and set forth what appears to be the prevailing constitutional doctrine of mobility: "Freedom to travel throughout the United States has long been recognized as a basic right under the Constitution."[11]

The Court's statements and rulings constitute clear warning to any community or state that seeks to stop growing.

State court warnings are even more specific, notably *Appeal of Kit-Mar Builders, Inc.,* an influential decision of the Pennsylvania Supreme Court invalidated local controls that failed to take into account the impact on surrounding communities. Said the court:

> It is not for any given township to say who may or may not live within its confines, while disregarding the interests of the entire area. If Concord Township is successful in unnaturally limiting its population growth through the use of exclusive zoning regulations, the people who would normally live there will inevitably have to live in another community, and the requirement that they do so is not a decision that Concord Township should alone be able to make.[12]

Clearly, the courts are going to be asked to draw, with some precision, the line between legitimate protective regulations and improper restrictions on growth and mobility. The line they draw—and the responsive measures adopted by governments as that line becomes clearer—will have a major influence on how and where we grow.

## Influencing the Future

The issue is not whether there will be urban regions but what form they will take, for we are convinced that the urban region is a fact of life—that the vast majority of Americans will continue to live, not predominantly in cities as we have known them, but in suburbs and exurbs that will be contiguous in many areas. Even though many trends now point toward a continuation of sprawl, destruction of critical environmental areas, and racial and economic segregation, the development process could be altered to inhibit these tendencies of uncontrolled (or in some cases over-controlled growth by exclusionary local governments) without denying valid development needs or asking Americans to change preferred life styles.

Within the framework of urban regions there is enormous scope for directing the way in which those regions develop, for determining how our land is to be used, and by whom, for influencing the quality of life. There is no need for people or their governments to accept a future of blanketing urbanization in which individuals and communities lose their identity. Nor is there need to put up with some of the suburban barriers that limit the mobility of people of modest means. Nor is there need to accept development stretching endlessly along the edges of roads and sprawling across scenic hills and valleys, forests and farms. There is opportunity, in short, to have urban regions that contain natural beauty, to have new and renewed urbanized areas that are more varied and satisfying than those we are familiar with. The needed quantity of urban development can be provided consistently with our environmental, social, and economic values. Whether or not it is depends on what we demand of the development that is going to take place in the final quarter of this century.

# Chapter III
# Protecting What We Value

England and Wales, although approximately the same size as North Carolina, have nine times as many residents. Yet, as a North Carolinian recently observed, the English countryside seems more spacious than rural North Carolina. Why should this be so?

No doubt, because the British take open spaces as seriously as developed areas, actively protecting them as positive features of the environment, not dismissing them as voids urbanization has yet to reach, lands "unripe for development," "undeveloped," "unurbanized," the terms so used often to describe our rural land.

But open spaces are receiving more attention in the United States. Several states have enacted laws to protect agricultural land from development and have increased their acquisition of land for recreation. If federal funds become available to states for planning and regulatory programs for the protection of "areas of critical environmental concern," as they will if the national land-use policy act becomes law, state governments will face important decisions about what to protect, and what techniques to employ.

When a developing region is viewed as a whole, some parts unquestionably should be left as they are. Several sorts of open land and water areas perform especially valuable functions—biologically active wetlands, aquifer recharge areas, coastal dunes, forests that reduce floods or prevent erosion of steep slopes, very productive agricultural land. Open spaces are needed, too, for recreation (both regional and neighborhood in scale), to assure freedom from hazards (as on floodplains and steep slopes subject to landslides), and to provide visual relief—a respite from hard surfaces and regular forms—between communities. Open space designations can also powerfully influence the form and timing of urban growth.

The sheer good sense of open space protection becomes all the clearer when we look at our cities. Almost all have acreages of vacant land—land not occupied by buildings, their surrounding lots, or by streets or other rights-of-way—and some have very substantial amounts. Most of the vacant areas are useless remnants in inappropriate places, unwanted leftovers of development. Their existence gives extra plausibility to the demand that vacant parts of future regions be grouped where they can do the most good.

Substantial undeveloped areas undoubtedly will exist in future urban regions. In the Atlantic Region, for example, even in a projection of low-density sprawl, 50 percent of the region's 104-county core is estimated to be vacant or in parks by the year 2020. For the 214-county region as a whole, the vacancy estimate is 75 percent.[1]

When we think of open spaces, we think first of public parks, national seashores, recreation areas, and forests. Americans are using them more now than ever, and we will have even greater need for them in the future, as population, leisure time, and mobility increase. Not all open spaces need be public open spaces, though. In fact, they cannot be. We will do well to meet the recreation needs of an increasingly leisure-oriented people by budgeting enough public funds for parks. It is unthinkable that the nation could ever buy all the scenic vistas and wetlands, beaches and dunes, farms and forests that it is desirable or necessary to protect. But we should not have to.

Privately owned open space can serve many of the same functions that public open space does, save that the public may not have access. In fact, land kept open for purposes other than recreation is, we believe, best left in private hands and regulated to prohibit uses inconsistent with the conservation of scenic characteristics or ecological processes.

The critical area of opportunity for state and local governments lies in conserving privately owned open space through careful planning and firm regulations. Other techniques are important, to be sure—governmental purchases of partial interests such as scenic easements or development rights, for example, techniques that ensure against development while leaving ownership in private hands. But most governmental agencies, given their limited money for land purchase, are going to ask first, "Do we have all the recreation areas we need?" If the answer is no, then parks will be the first priority, and the protection of a privately owned riverbank will be set aside.

It need not be. The park could be purchased and the riverbank zoned for conservation. But most state and local governments are too timid to use the police power with which critical privately owned lands could be protected. How often are citizens seeking protection of scenic lands put off by county and city attorneys with the argument, "You can't expect us to change the zoning on that land. We would have to pay Jones if we did that, or the court would overturn the zoning."

If we do not take the opportunity to conserve privately owned open space, though, we must all be prepared to give up much of what we treasure in America. Although the aggregate amount of open spaces may be ample even in the year 2000, getting those spaces in the right places will require stronger planning and regulations than most state and local governments now employ.

Historic areas need protection, too. Many communities have important or unusual historic buildings or whole streets and neighborhoods with historic integrity, where the buildings, by their age, design, and scale, form a unit of visual continuity and character. Such areas may already be registered historic districts, as in Charleston, Boston, and Santa Fe, or they may be stylistically varied areas lacking any significant single buildings but forming units of pleasing proportion and providing a sense of the past. Such historic properties are vulnerable to the same threats as open space, and their preservation often poses the same buy-it-or-lose-it dilemma to local authorities. We see historic districts and buildings benefiting from the approach and many of the techniques we recommend for protecting privately owned open space, an approach based primarily on regulation, not purchase.

## What to Protect

Because of the pioneering work of Stuart Chapin, Phillip Lewis, Ian McHarg, and others in inventorying land according to its suitability for development, it is now possible to be more precise about which lands need protection for which reasons. The categories of land which, all other things being equal, ought to be kept natural, or at least free of development, include:

105

1. *Areas of critical environmental concern,* areas with important cultural or natural characteristics that development would interfere with. Types of land include: coastal and inland wetlands; beaches and dunes; estuaries and shorelands; floodplains of rivers, lakes, and streams; areas of unstable soils and high seismic activity; steep slopes and ridgetops; rare or valuable ecosystems; valuable forests and related land; and historic districts.

2. *Areas required for future public recreation.*

3. *Areas that would serve as buffer zones between urban areas* and would have a strategic significance in controlling the pattern of future development.

4. *Unique and highly productive farmland,* which might also perform the buffer-zone function.

To promote a consensus about land protection and to spare every state and local government from having to set up its own classification system, we believe the federal government should establish and disseminate open space classifications. Obviously, any level of government can formulate classifications. Obviously, too, decisions about buffer-zone spaces will have to be made at a lower-than-national level and apart from any scientific classification system. But national classifications could at least set out general constraints on development. Federal agencies such as the Soil Conservation Service and the U.S. Geological Survey have the experience and facilities to establish and disseminate the standards. Once issued, they could become as influential and useful as the agricultural soil classifications that evaluate land productivity.

*We believe there is an enormous opportunity for the federal government to encourage open space protection by formulating, mapping, and publicizing a set of advisory national open space classifications for consultation by federal agencies in the planning of development projects, for use in support of state and local plans and regulations, and for consultation by private land buyers and sellers.*

We need broadened classifications for historic areas, too. Since 1966, historic structures and districts have been systematically classified in *The National Register of Historic Places.* A listed property is accorded special review and consideration if a federal or federally assisted project threatens to destroy or impair it. The criteria for listing are that the area possess integrity of location, design, setting, materials, workmanship, feeling, and associations *and* represent a significant and distinguishable entity (even if the components lack individual distinction). These criteria are broad enough to qualify an area like Williamsburg or a simple street of nineteenth-century merchant shops in North Adams, Massachusetts.

But the insistence upon integrity of design, feeling, and workmanship discriminates against areas where organic growth has produced a stylistic mixture. Because of the variety in physical structures, these areas can often support a varied rent structure and provide a refreshing diversity of uses and people. *We urge that urban neighborhoods characterized by a mix of uses, a vitality of street life, and a physical integrity be given recognition on the National Register as "conservation areas."*

## Public Open Spaces

The public open spaces most needed are recreation spaces. Between 1950 and 1970, acreage in state park systems increased by over 80 percent while attendance increased more than 300 percent. For the National Park System, acreage increased by about 29 percent while total number of visits jumped more than 400 percent. (See Figure 5.)

The situation is expected to grow more serious as increasing leisure and affluence among a growing population put even more demands on recreation areas. Hundreds, perhaps thousands, of miles of coasts, waterfronts, and other suitable parkland need to be acquired and opened to public access. Acquisition, in short, will have to match the scale of the urban regions themselves. (There have been responsible proposals for such acquisition, one, for example, to acquire 10,000 square miles of new parkland in the Appalachian Mountains at a cost of a billion dollars or more.)

Increasingly visible strains are resulting from the shortage of recreation land. Some communities are excluding nonresidents from their parks and public beaches or are accomplishing the same result by imposing prohibitive fees for admission or parking. Private property owners report growing difficulty in excluding trespassers, particularly from private beaches. Even in some national parks, stringent restrictions and limitations on the number of park visitors (and the machines they bring with them) have become necessary.

With the natural supply of prime recreation spaces limited, demand would undoubtedly outstrip supply in some regions even

FIGURE 5

**Visitors and Acreage of State and National Parks**

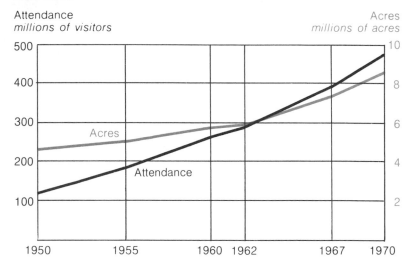

State Parks

Attendance
*millions of visitors*

Acres
*millions of acres*

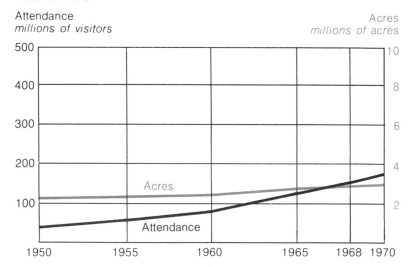

National Parks

Attendance
*millions of visitors*

Acres
*millions of acres*

Note: Number of state agencies reporting varies from year to year.

Source: U.S. Bureau of the Census, *Statistical Abstract of the United States: 1971.*

108

FIGURE 6
**State Park Expenditures**

millions of dollars

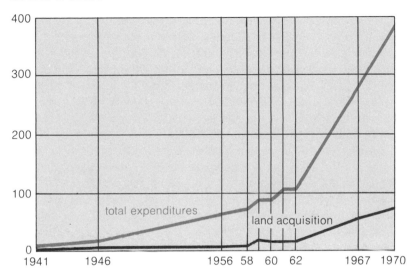

Source of Funds Received By State Park Agencies

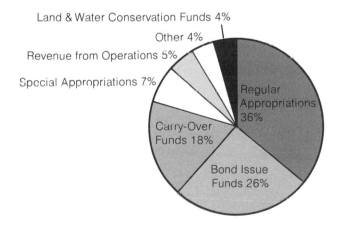

Source: *State Park Statistics,* (Washington, D.C.: National Recreation and Parks Association, 1970).

if the entire supply were acquired and made accessible to the public. Under the best circumstances, recreation areas will have to be carefully managed, probably with restrictions on use and number of users.

But what if only a small fraction of the natural supply were publicly accessible? The resulting problems could well be socially divisive. The residents of fortunate localities as well as other privileged minorities would be increasingly differentiated from the excluded majority. A conflict of growing bitterness would surely ensue, a conflict that has already appeared in some urban areas where citizens have gone to court to contest recreation permits and fees for nonresidents.

We believe that such a conflict can and must be avoided, especially in the areas now being developed for the first time. *Especially in newly urbanizing areas, we see both recreation and social needs best served by establishing as public policy that the limited natural supply of prime recreational open spaces, particularly beaches and other waterfront areas suitable for recreation, should, to the maximum feasible extent, be acquired by government, preserved, and made publicly accessible.*

*Crowded beaches such as this one are an indication of the increasing need for more recreational areas that are easily accessible and open to the public.*

Of the many ways to acquire public open spaces, purchase is by far the most important.

## Purchase: Buy As Much As We Can, As Soon As We Can

How much of the needed open space is in fact likely to be purchased? The answer depends less on need than on the quantities of public funds that can be pried loose for land purchase. Although we would hope that governments at every level would contribute to purchase programs, success in a task of this magnitude obviously requires major funding at both state and federal levels.

A number of states are budgeting significant amounts for open space acquisition, some aided by voter-approved bond issues. Between 1960 and 1970, state expenditures for parkland acquisition increased more than fourfold. (See Figure 6.)

Federal open space outlays increased in the late 1960s, too. Between fiscal 1966 and fiscal 1970, the National Park Service, the Forest Service, and the Bureau of Sport Fisheries acquired more than 820,000 acres at a cost of over $240 million.

*Federal spending for open space acquisition should be maintained at levels commensurate with needs. We see particular merit in continuing to extend the network of parks, seashores, and lakeshores that are owned and managed by the federal government itself. States, many of which are currently enjoying budgetary surpluses, should also adjust open space acquisition plans to rising needs, particularly with respect to areas where urban growth is anticipated and where waterfront land is beginning to appreciate as a result of pollution-control activities.*

No matter who the purchaser, the effectiveness of open space purchase programs is threatened in many areas by rapidly increasing land prices. Unless price rises are dampened, land acquired will be needlessly expensive and the quantity purchased will be needlessly reduced. (Needlessly, because if land is regulated for open space early enough, developmental expectations will thus be reduced.) None of the measures we propose is intended solely to reduce land price increases. But several recommended measures—those which would maintain property in low-density private uses—would incidentally affect prices. We regard these incidental effects as an additional public benefit should it become necessary for the government to purchase for recreation use land protected for its scenic or agricultural value.

111

## Asserting Neglected Rights

Even under the best foreseeable circumstances, no combination of federal, state, and local land purchases is likely to acquire enough open spaces to satisfy demand. Other techniques must be used as well.

The assertion of long-neglected public rights to certain lands is one such technique. Established public use of accessways across privately owned beachfront properties, for example, may lead to property easements.

Executive or judicial action may be necessary in some cases to assure that public rights and laws providing for access are respected. The best example of this approach is Oregon's vigorous reassertion of the rights of the public to use the state's beaches, including those in private ownership. Similarly, in 1972, Senator Henry Jackson introduced legislation that would have directed the federal government to assert its full range of powers over coastal waters to ensure public access and use. (Federal jurisdiction extends to the upward limits of tidal flow and thus takes in a portion of beachland.) Such measures are not alternatives to acquisition programs, but they can add to the stock of public open spaces and prevent the government from purchasing what the people may already, in effect, have access to.

Federally aided projects also present opportunities for promoting public access. The federal share in beach erosion-control projects, for example, is determined by the degree of public access to the beach. Of the more than 9 miles of Dade County beachfront to be protected and restored by the U.S. Army Corps of Engineers, less than 2 1/2 miles are in public ownership. Dade County is negotiating to obtain public access to more of the privately owned beachlands to increase the approximately 30 percent federal contribution to the project.

*State and local governments should assert and protect often neglected public rights in beaches and other recreation land. Similarly, the federal government should exploit its full range of powers, including its permit authority and public works activities, to promote protection, public access, and use.*

## Voluntary Donations

When sufficient money is not available to purchase needed land, what alternatives are available? One possibility is voluntary donations. Gifts can be a more important source of public open lands than is generally recognized. The Regional Plan Association in New York has estimated, for example, that one-third of the public open space in the New York metropolitan area was acquired by donation.

Federal income tax provisions, by generally permitting the deduction of charitable gifts from income during the five years after donation, and by generally excluding appreciation in the value of donated property from the donor's taxable income, provide significant incentives for many donations. If profits from land sales were to be taxed more heavily than at present, the incentives (and, of course, the cost to the federal treasury of each donation) would be increased still further.

Federal estate tax laws, however, fail to provide a donation incentive that exists in Great Britain and elsewhere. To clear estate tax liabilities, the federal government insists on receiving cash. As a result, large tracts ideal for public use can be lost to subdivision. In 1971, the owners of the 480,000-acre Vermejo Ranch in New Mexico were willing to transfer part of the property to the federal government to meet estate tax obligations, but the government declined to accept the land.

*Federal estate tax laws or regulations should be amended to permit the transfer to the federal government of land determined by the Secretary of the Interior to be of national significance, with the fair market value of the land offset against federal estate tax liabilities.*

Catalytic action—sometimes by governments, sometimes by charitable organizations—is often needed to bring about donations. The catalytic role consists of matching a willing donor and a suitable recipient. The possibility of donation may be explained to a landowner who simply never thought of it. Or explanations may be given of the relatively low cost of donations, of the usefulness of donations when a seller is unable to locate a buyer in a sluggish market, or of available safeguards to assure that donated land is in fact preserved and not later used as a cheap site for a governmental building.

Such charitable organizations as the Nature Conservancy make major contributions by serving as conduits, temporarily holding land while government agencies proceed with appropriation and acquisition, and also as permanent holders of land slated for preservation.

*Governments at all levels should actively solicit open space donations and should facilitate the work of responsible private organizations, such as the Nature Conservancy, by granting them charitable status for real estate tax purposes.*

Finding a willing donor is only part of the problem. Over the years, offers to donate land have been turned down by local governments unwilling to pay for maintenance or to take land off the local tax rolls. A would-be donor may be asked to set up an endowment to finance maintenance and management. If he does not, or if an alternative financing method cannot be arranged through the city, offers are frequently turned down.

At the state level, the difficulties of maintenance problems and lost property tax revenues are frequently compounded by the lack of a mechanism to accept and administer easements and donations of land. In Virginia, for instance, the Open Space Foundation established by the legislature several years ago, remains without funds and is thus unable even to respond to the more than three hundred Virginia landowners who have written to the state requesting information about procedures for donating easements or land to the state.

*States should establish and staff offices to solicit and receive environmentally significant land. Such offices should furnish technical advice and assistance to donors on the tax advantages of donations and on means of conveying easements and other partial interests consistent with public open space objectives.*

## Dedication by Developers

In hundreds of communities, donations by land subdividers and developers are a principal source of public open spaces. Most of these dedications are mandatory; a few are voluntary. Two kinds of local land-use regulations generate such donations.

One kind of provision permits land subdivision only if a portion of the subdivided acreage is dedicated for park use or if money is contributed for purchase of parkland elsewhere. An ordinance might, for example, require dedication of anywhere from 100 to 2,000 square feet of parkland for each permitted dwelling unit. Or it might require dedication according to a sliding scale of density.

A second type of provision, often called a planned unit development provision, authorizes developers to "cluster" permitted development on part of their land if the remainder is set aside as open space. (Instead of dividing a 100-acre tract into one hundred

1-acre lots, for example, the developer might create one hundred half-acre lots and have 50 acres of open space.) Under some of these provisions, any designated open space must be dedicated to the community. Under others, the developer need only provide sufficient guarantee (perhaps by dedicating easements or development rights) against future development of the open space; the land itself may (or, sometimes, must) be retained or transferred to a homeowners' association.

We see no inequity in requiring developers to dedicate parkland before subdivision or development. At a minimum, demand for recreation space is surely increased when additional dwelling units bring more people into a community, and it is reasonable for the community to satisfy that demand through a public park system. Moreover, the occasion of subdivision and development is the only appropriate strategic moment for doing so.

The chief issue in this approach is who should pay, the taxpayers at large or the residents of the new dwellings that create the added recreation demand. Municipalities are often unable or unwilling to buy parks at the expense of general taxpayers. If parks are to be provided, then, the costs must normally be borne by those who benefit most. The easiest way for them to bear those costs is to have the developer include park costs in the price of the homes he sells. Mandatory dedication accomplishes this result.

The added housing costs resulting from required park dedications appear to be small relative to total housing costs. In some cases, the open space is practically "free." The value of land to the residential developer is determined not so much by its acreage as by the number of dwelling units that can be built on it. With clustering, that number need not change. Similarly, the homeowner gains in common open space what he may be giving up in private open space, assuming the same density of development.

What, then, is the cost of mandatory dedication? Where a cluster regulation is in effect, the permitted number of units are simply built closer together. Mandatory dedication of leftover open space then costs very little. In the absence of a cluster regulation, the mandatory dedication will reduce the number of permitted units, just as a zoning change might do. Once the requirement is on the books, however, developers will take it into account in determining what they can afford to pay for land.

115

*Mandatory dedication requirements can be an equitable and inexpensive way to provide essential urban open space. We believe the requirements should be used even more widely than they already are.*

Nevertheless, we note two related limitations on their effectiveness. First, the *size* of the acquired open spaces is limited by the size of the developer's project. Since most projects have relatively small acreage, and since most regulations require only a small fraction of that acreage to be dedicated, the regulations are seldom a source of extensive open spaces. The provisions prove useful mostly to secure small urban parks.

Second, the *location* of the open spaces is restricted by the location of the development. If farm A is being subdivided, the dedicated space must normally be located within farm A. This remains true even if a park plan shows that the park might better be located on farm B next door.

How can these limitations on size and location be overcome? The simplest way to preserve more open space, of the right size and in the right place, is to encourage large-scale development: if a single project includes both farm A and farm B, it can more easily provide larger open spaces in the right location. (We deal later with ways of encouraging scale.)

Or a fund can be established for purchase of parkland, with developers required (or permitted) to contribute cash instead of dedicating land. In concept, this more flexible approach seems better suited to getting open spaces of the right size in the right places. It also assures that a contribution is made even by small developers whose projects are not large enough to include a park. In practice, however, many cash-contribution requirements are not equivalent to dedication requirements because the required cash contribution is very small. Cash-contribution requirements have been legally challenged (as have mandatory dedication requirements), although their legality has been maintained in California.

*In newly developing areas, developers should contribute open space, or cash for the purchase of open space, sufficient at least to satisfy the reasonable needs of the residents of their developments. Local governments should adopt regulations requiring such contributions, preferably in connection with cluster provisions. States should authorize and encourage the adoption of these local regulations or should adopt similar state regulations.*

The need to assure appropriate dedication is particularly acute when waterfront land is subdivided or developed. Even in states where beaches themselves are lawfully available for use by the general public, the public right can be meaningless without access routes across adjoining property. A 1972 California law requires local governments to condition the approval of subdivisions adjacent to beachfront land upon a finding of "reasonable public access by fee or easement . . . to land below the ordinary high-water mark on any ocean coastline or bay shoreline." *State legislation and local regulations should assure that adequate public accessways exist before allowing the subdivision or development of private property adjacent to public beaches and waterfronts.*

## Just Because No One Lives There Doesn't Make It the Place for a Highway

Even when open lands are in public ownership, they need to be protected against avoidable diversion to other public uses. Parks and public forests attract highways and public buildings because the lands can be used without displacement of people, without the inconvenience of taking over many small parcels of land, and, in some jurisdictions, without payment of compensation to the public agency whose land is taken.

Present provisions to protect public open spaces against diversion vary widely. Portions of the Adirondack Forest Preserve in New York, for example, are required by the state constitution to be kept "forever wild." The extent of protection within a single state may depend on the type of public open space affected and public construction proposed.

Because of relatively strict federal provisions, federally aided projects are often more respectful of public open spaces than state or locally financed projects. Before the taking of parkland for a transportation project can be approved, for example, the Transportation Secretary must determine that no feasible and prudent alternative to the taking of the park exists and that efforts will be made to mitigate adverse impacts on the park. Such protective provisions are less often found in state and local laws, a matter of concern now that federal funds are to be made unconditionally available through revenue-sharing.

The enactment of revenue-sharing makes it all the more urgent that states provide comparable procedures to discourage diversion of parks. *At a minimum, states should provide that (1) alterna-*

tives to the diversions of parks for other uses be formulated with full opportunity for public comment; (2) any open space taken be replaced by other open space that will, wherever possible, meet similar public needs; (3) additional procedural protections be established to ensure careful evaluation of proposals by one agency to condemn open space under the jurisdiction of another agency; and (4) methods for determining the value of open space be improved so that any open space may be replaced by land of at least comparable monetary value.

## Private Open Spaces and Historic Properties

Public acquisition cannot, and need not, be the whole answer to the problem of open space and historic conservation.

In the first place, funds for land purchase are limited. It is unlikely that they will be sufficient even to buy all the land that should be accessible to the general public, and it is inconceivable that the nation would allocate funds to acquire all the vast areas that ought to be left in natural or agricultural or historic condition. The sums would be prodigious. Legislatures in many states are reluctant to invest extensively in land, a reluctance that has only recently begun to yield to the growing strength of the conservation

movement. Even among land needs, open spaces and historic preservation may not receive highest legislative priority. Land for future airports, highway rights-of-way, communities, or waterfront sites for ports or power plants probably would rank higher.

In the second place, and at least as important, public acquisition of many areas should not be necessary. For many farms and natural areas, the principal open space objective is achieved when urban development is excluded; neither governmental management nor access by the general public is required. There are important reasons, cultural as well as economic, for leaving these open spaces in private hands. Acquisition of these lands would be excessive as long as a suitable alternative method exists, or can be devised, to prevent urban development.

*Since it is neither feasible nor acceptable for governments to acquire the vast agricultural, natural, and historic areas that ought to be protected within future urban regions, mechanisms to protect privately held open space and historic properties are essential. Without such mechanisms, even moderate objectives of protection programs are unlikely to be achieved.*

The land market, as it operates today, stacks the deck against effective protection of private open spaces. Land simply is more

highly valued for urban development than for agriculture or any other open use. Sound conservation policy requires that development be spread unevenly over the surface of a region. If the entire region were in single ownership, this clustering of a fixed number of units—with development concentrated here and open space over there—would make relatively little difference in the owner's total land value.

In fact, regions are divided into thousands of small holdings, and our traditions of unplanned urban growth convert each of these holdings into a kind of lottery ticket in a grand urbanization drawing. The holder's risks and uncertainty are great, but the prizes—if he draws a site for a gas station, say, or a shopping center—can be very high. If a holding is irrevocably committed to open space, however, the holder loses out because there is no longer an expectation of possible development. As a result, he has an economic incentive to avoid any voluntary open space commitment. If regulations designate his land as open space, he has a strong economic incentive to resist them by raising legal objections, exerting political pressures, and seeking to influence administrators. The same forces work against the preservation of historic districts.

### Regulations to Keep Private Land Open and Preserve Historic Buildings

Numerous local governments, using their general zoning powers, have for years established agriculture or conservation districts where urban development is prohibited. The best known state program is in Hawaii, where agricultural and conservation districts are among the four classifications into which the entire state is divided.

In California, where large amounts of rural land are urbanized every year, three coastal counties (two near San Francisco)—Marin, Santa Cruz, and Monterey—recently reduced permitted densities.

Of Marin County's 300,000 acres, 200,000 were placed in an agricultural preserve in 1965, and one-half of that area has since been placed under preservation contract, with local governments authorized to reduce property tax assessments to landowners who contract to retain their property in agricultural use for a fixed period of time. In late 1971, land in the agricultural preserve was rezoned from one dwelling per 3 acres to much larger parcels.

*Surrounded by modern buildings, Boston's Old City Hall now provides private office space in a graceful nineteenth-century historic structure.*

Sixty thousand acres, the majority of the county's agricultural land, now is zoned for 60-acre-minimum lots.

Santa Cruz County, where 65 percent of total acreage was unclassified and unzoned as recently as two years ago, and where agricultural yield is particularly high, plans to zone up to 148,000 acres of agricultural lands (about half the county) into lots no smaller than 20 acres, with many 40-acre lots. Monterey County has about 396,000 acres (one third of the county) now zoned for 40-acre lots. An additional 219,000 acres have long been zoned for 10-acre-minimum lots.

Essential to the political and legal durability of any such ambitious scheme of protection is a first-rate planning process to assure that lands protected are carefully selected and truly merit protection and to make sure that reasonable development needs are planned for and met. At the local level, the difficulty of maintaining a high level of planning competence and the risk that protective measures will be used arbitrarily to exclude new residents increase.

121

We see protective regulations—agricultural, natural areas, or floodplain zoning; conservation restrictions; protective orders; and so on—as an essential first line of defense to keep private space open. Relative to other protection measures, regulations can be applied to large areas rapidly and at low cost. Their reliability and permanence will vary state by state and community by community. Nevertheless, even in jurisdictions where courts have not tended to uphold them, regulations may serve to keep development forces at bay when they threaten environmental values, providing time for the establishment of more permanent defenses. In areas where judicial attitudes toward regulations are more favorable, the regulations themselves may provide the permanent defense needed.

Who should enact and administer regulations? Although varying conditions from place to place make a national prescription impractical and unwise, we hold the view that great opportunities lie with the states, perhaps with details of administration and implementation left to local governments. The open space regulator must have a broad territorial perspective and be able to protect open spaces effectively and fairly. Many local governments can meet this test, but many more cannot, because of a limited perspective or ineffectiveness or the taint of exclusionary intent. Most regional agencies lack both authority and a strong political base and, therefore, the effective power to divert development pressures.

The states have the power, but must overcome a tradition of inactivity. The proposed national land-use policy act and the draft model land development code of the American Law Institute can be of immense help in creating state willingness to act for protection. So, within the state bureaucracies themselves, can the new environmental agencies, not yet tranquilized into the passivity that afflicts so many older agencies.

How much control should states assert, and what kind? The answers depend primarily on what is politically and legally possible in each. A few states are still unreconciled to protective regulations even to safeguard magnificent mountain ranges and seashores. At the opposite extreme, a few may be ready to follow the comprehensive Hawaiian pattern. Most, we believe, and certainly most of the states where development pressures are greatest, will increasingly be willing and able to regulate at least their most critical areas.

*State as well as local governments should establish protective regulations to prevent development that would be incompatible with open space needs in critical agricultural and environmental areas.* Where protected areas are carefully selected through comprehensive planning, states should authorize and encourage, in appropriate cases, very low-density zoning, including, for example, requirements for 50 or more acres per dwelling unit. Enactment of the pending national land-use policy act is urgently recommended to encourage state and local regulation in a balanced framework that is respectful both of conservation and development priorities.

For historic preservation, as for open space protection, the first requisite is a framework for regulation, preferably a statewide system for registration of historic districts and properties and a clear policy favoring preservation. *States should enact appropriate legislation to implement the Model State Guidelines for Historic Preservation recommended by the Council of State Governments among its 1972 suggested legislative proposals. Such legislation would establish a state institutional structure for the review and regulation of historic sites, structures, and districts and would enable local governments to take special measures to assure that the integrity of historic areas is protected.*

Protective regulations, though urgently needed, are unlikely to be sufficiently protective in all cases. At the local level, the effectiveness of open space regulations has been limited by the tendency of legislators and administrators to repeal or relax them as development pressures intensified. Even if the legality of such regulations is firmly established, political and administrative pressures to alter them will remain. Because of the impact of regulations on land values, landowners have strong incentives to exert those pressures. Unless measures are found to reduce or remove those pressures, it seems likely that they will continue to be virtually irresistible in many areas as the time of potential development nears. As a result, realistic local administrators often regard agricultural or conservation zoning as a temporary measure, useful until development pressures become overwhelming and perhaps helpful then to make rural-urban transition a bit more orderly.

It is too soon to tell whether state regulations will suffer from the same infirmities. Recent cases involving attacks on state land-use regulations show a tendency on the part of courts to look more favorably on land-use restrictions imposed by state governments as a result of careful planning. There is no reason to suppose, however, that the enormous pressures placed on local officials will not also be placed on state officials, especially by large landowners and developers whom access to state officials presents no problems. Nothing in the administrative traditions of many states suggests that conservation officials will be able to hold out for long.

It is for these reasons that we believe regulations in many areas must be strenghtened and supplemented by other forms of public action. The three essential supports are those of policy, law, and incentives. ⚹

## Policy Support for Protective Regulations

Forceful policy measures supporting protective regulations are the key to modifying the profit expectations that now so fundamentally influence the thinking not only of landowners but of legislators and judges as well, for it is expectations of profit that ultimately break down protective regulations. (Ironically, the very absence of such measures in the past encourages profit expectations for the future, even for land whose natural physical characteristics make it more suitable for open space than for development.) Owners expect less of land that physically *cannot* be developed (quicksand, for example). What is needed is a comparable modification of expectations for land that *should not* be developed.

Land whose development would be hazardous may be the place to begin. Surely it should be possible to develop a national consensus that profits from the residential development of a floodway are the moral equivalent of profits from selling tainted meat. Beyond this, though more slowly, it should be possible to develop an equivalent consensus with respect to land where development would damage valuable and irreplaceable resources or significantly interfere with natural processes.

The owner of steep slopes or important wetlands must come to accept these features as a speculative "bad break" much as he resigns himself to the decision to build a proposed expressway interchange 15 miles away instead of next door. The speculative buyer must be persuaded to avoid important open spaces by the knowledge that development permission will be especially hard, if not impossible, to obtain.

How are these modifications in expectations to be created? Local regulations have not created them in the past. Speculative expectations are so widely shared that the regulations, not the expectations, have tended to give way. Nevertheless, we believe that more widespread adoption of local open space regulations can help. The more that localities recognize the need for such regulations, the more commonplace they will become, and the more widespread their acceptance by all concerned.

State regulations, especially if enacted by a number of states, should be even more effective. Vermont has gone the farthest in making the protection of environmentally valuable areas general policy. Its ambitious land-use law, passed in 1970, prohibits a district commission from granting a development permit unless it finds that the development:

(1) Will not result in undue water or air pollution.

(2) Does have sufficient water available for the reasonably foreseeable needs of the subdivision or development.

(3) Will not cause an unreasonable burden on an existing water supply, if one is to be utilized.

(4) Will not cause unreasonable soil erosion or reduction in the capacity of the land to hold water so that a dangerous or unhealthy condition may result.

(5) Will not cause unreasonable highway congestion or unsafe conditions with respect to use of the highways existing or proposed.

(6) Will not cause an unreasonable burden on the ability of a municipality to provide educational services.

(7) Will not place an unreasonable burden on the ability of the local government to provide municipal or governmental services.

(8) Will not have an undue adverse effect on the scenic or natural beauty of the area, aesthetics, historic sites or rare and irreplaceable natural areas.

(9) Is in conformance with a duly adopted development plan, land-use plan or land-capability plan [statewide plans required by the law].

(10) Is in conformance with any duly adopted local or regional plan.[2]

## Utilities Decisions: A Special Policy Tool

One reason for designating an area as open space may be the difficulty or expense of supplying it with sewer and other public services. Even where that is not the case, decisions on the location of sewers and other utilities can serve as powerful backups for open space designations. For the same reasons, inappropriate decisions on utility locations can make the designations hard to defend. ("Mr. Mayor, there's a trunk sewer not 300 feet down from that meadow you've got zoned for one family every 50 acres.")

One factor making utility decisions so important is their impact on development costs. As distance from utilities raises the costs of development, the desirability of the open space for development declines, and so does the pressure placed on public officials to let it be developed. In addition, land-use regulations may provoke angry responses from the same people who concede the local government broad discretion to decide on the number and location of expensive trunk sewers and treatment plants.

More and more communities are recognizing the handiness of utilities decisions as tools to carry out planning policies. Too commonly, however, utility decisions are still stimulating development of land planned for low-intensity use. New statutes and ordinances may be needed in some places; in others, the need is simply to assure that the consequences of utility decisions are carefully considered and that location decisions are coordinated with open space plans.

*Decisions to construct sewers and to provide other public services should be taken only after careful consideration of whether those decisions will stimulate or discourage the development of designated open spaces. Plans for the location of federally assisted sewers should be in accordance with a comprehensive land-use plan.*

### Legal Support for Protective Regulations

Uncertainty about the constitutional and statutory validity of highly restrictive regulations inhibits many governments from adopting such regulations and from adhering to them as pressures mount. The possibility of expensive litigation and fear that the courts might require governments to pay compensation where they have stringently restricted development are especially intimidating. Because of their complexity and special importance, legal problems are considered in Chapter IV.

### Incentives Supporting Protective Regulations

Open space regulations often need the support of incentives and related measures. This support is particularly important where openness is dictated more by planning than by the physical characteristics of the land itself. Aided by a growing policy consensus, regulations alone may force respect for important natural features, but the nation is still far from any comparable consensus

126

that would enable regulators to resist indefinitely pressures for development within a greenbelt set aside only to provide breathing space between communities.

The search for incentives should concentrate on measures that satisfy two minimum requisites. The first is proper location of the preserved land. The second is permanence of protection.

The requirement of proper location, while essential, is in one sense unfortunate. Many supporters of incentives are discouraged realists who recognize the widespread failure of regulations and other mechanisms that rely on case-by-case judgments by public administrators. These supporters have turned to incentives as a more nearly "automatic" way to achieve sound decisions in a larger proportion of cases. To them, location criteria are unwelcome because the variables are so numerous that careful planning is needed to apply them.

Nevertheless, location criteria are essential. Just as some land areas are most suitable for protection, others are needed for immediate development. Protection incentives could prove detrimental if applied extensively to lands that ought to be developed. *At a minimum, major protection incentives for open space conservation ought to be available only for land designated by carefully prepared regulations or plans as appropriate for permanent protection.*

Pressures to grant incentives for protection in the wrong places do arise, however, and should be anticipated. In Hawaii, for example, favorable tax treatment originally accorded to farms in the state's agricultural district was later extended also to farms in the urban district where, presumably, the state had decided that urban development should occur.

Why focus on measures that provide permanent conservation? There is more precedent for temporary measures, such as deferring some taxes until the land is sold for development. (Since deferred taxes seldom amount to more than a small fraction of the sale price, deferrals will rarely deter ultimate sale for development in an area where immediate development would be profitable). And it is clear enough that temporary protection can be in the public interest—to alleviate personal hardship for working farmers, for example, or to prevent premature subdivision of land for development, or even to hold land open while governments or charities try to raise money to buy it.

The reason for seeking permanence is that temporary protec-

127

tion falls so far short of meeting open space needs. Since we see little likelihood of massive public acquisition of farms and other nonrecreational open spaces, or some states being able to stand up for long against owners' pressures for rezoning, permanent protection measures are imperative. Half-way measures, by appearing to solve the problem, may actually delay the more fundamental reforms needed.

What makes a measure permanent when applied to private land? Since conditions can change in unforeseeable ways, even the most permanent restriction may some day have to give way to new needs. Protection measures therefore must include some flexibility to permit modification in future decades and centuries.

To achieve as much permanence as is reasonable, the protection mechanism should insulate protected open spaces as completely as possible from the market forces that now inexorably press them into development. This may be difficult unless owners of protected open spaces give up part of their property rights. There is ample room for experimenting with the form these property changes might take. Easements, deed restrictions, development rights, and land tenure changes all appear promising. In time, we believe, ownership of open spaces without urbanization rights should become as commonplace as ownership of land without mineral rights.

The key question remains: What could possibly cause property owners to give up these rights? What should government offer in exchange for them? Finding the right answers to these questions—finding the mix of incentives that can preserve open spaces without needless public costs—is the key to permanent open space conservation.

Because incentives involve a trade-off—offering the landowner something in return for a desired response—care must be taken to assure that public benefits are commensurate with public costs.

*Preferential Tax Assessments for Agricultural Lands:*
*A Temporary Measure at Best*

Measures that grant partial relief from real estate taxes on farms in urbanizing areas, but provide no effective protection, can be worse than nothing at all. These measures, in force in about half the states, respond to concerns that rising property taxes in urban fringe areas "drive the farmer off the land," or at least contribute to his decision to sell out to a developer or speculator who can offset the tax payments against other income. Authorizing farmers to pay real estate taxes only on the agricultural value of their land, with remaining taxes on the difference between agricultural and urban land value deferred until urbanization, provides some relief. In some states, however, the additional taxes are simply waived, not deferred, even where future urban use is not barred. The practical effect of such measures can be merely to reduce speculators' holding costs while the development opportunity ripens.

The preferential farmland assessment laws of Maryland and Florida illustrate the misuse of such incentives. In both states, it is enough that land be in agricultural use for property tax reductions to be available. That the benefited owner may be a corporation engaged in land speculation or real estate development, or even that the farmland is part of a registered subdivision plat, does not affect the property owner's eligibility for tax relief. Nor do the laws in these states authorize public recapture of past taxes when the owner finally sells the land at prices reflecting its value for urban development.

Preferential farmland assessment laws in California and New Jersey provide for recapture of taxes under a deferral theory whereby the property owner at time of sale is required to pay back to the taxing authority the taxes he avoided by having his land classified as agricultural.

The 1965 Williamson Act authorized California counties to designate special agricultural preserves and to accord favorable property tax assessments to owners of farms of 100 or more acres who contracted to retain their land in a "use not incompatible with agriculture." California provides for a recapture of 12.5 percent of the market value of land sold from under a preferential assessment contract. Moreover, specially assessed farmland is to be under contract for a minimum of ten years, with contracts automatically renewable annually in the absence of notice.

The Williamson Act and its administration have been much criticized. Ralph Nader's study group report on land use in California, *Politics of Land,* attacked the substantial subsidy the act provides to major landholders, the lack of state supervision, and the failure of local governments to protect the very agricultural land that the act was intended to keep open—farmland at the urban fringe.

The situation is worse in New Jersey. The state reclaims in

taxes benefits conferred during the last three years before sale of the land. According to one authority on the New Jersey law:

> The three-year rollback usually amounts to a tax of up to 10 percent of the market value. Since land is often selling for prices that have risen 1000 percent in ten or fifteen years, the buyer is quite willing to throw in the extra 10 percent. Frequently, the rollback is payable years after the sale has taken place, when a developer is ready to change the use of the property and finds 10 percent a tolerable expense when large capital gains are in sight. If really potent rollback taxes were required, most farmers and speculators would stay out of the program.

In one New Jersey county a major beneficiary of property tax benefits is a public utility that is seeking an industrial buyer for the acreage it now maintains in agriculture. A New Jersey committee reporting to Governor William Cahill last year recommended that the law be amended to require that a significant proportion of gross income be attributable to farming as a condition of eligibility for the beneficial assessment.

A new and potentially effective measure aimed at providing property tax relief to farmers and at the same time discouraging speculation in land has been proposed by the recently elected governor of Vermont, Thomas P. Salmon. The governor's pending legislation provides that a farmer's property tax not exceed 5 percent of his total farm income. The state's loss of revenues from this measure would be offset through a state capital gains tax on land sales, scaled (to discourage short-term speculation) from a 29 percent tax on profits in land held for one year or less to nothing on land held for ten years or more.

*Tax reduction or deferral should be re-examined to assure that the public benefit in open space protection warrants the very substantial expense that reduced taxes entail. Provisions that grant reductions in the absense of permanent restrictions should be regarded as half-way measures, justified only when political processes will not accept permanent restrictions.*

*Noneconomic Incentives: Stewardship and Neighborhood Protection*

Many owners are willing to donate their land to governments and charitable organizations. Even more owners, we suspect, would be willing to donate urbanization rights. The concept of land stewardship, preached for many years by a hearty minority, is very much alive. Although this attitude can change dramatically if development nears and land prices skyrocket, it can be nurtured, often simply by an indication that government (or charity) cares enough for an area to be willing to protect it. A program in which many neighbors join ("Only a sucker would give away these rights if the others are going to sell for development") can be even more effective.

This possibility has been amply demonstrated in Massachusetts. Under the 1965 Massachusetts Coastal Wetlands Act, the commonwealth has, with landowners' consents, placed permanent restrictions on more than 26,000 acres of private coastal wetlands without a cent of compensation being paid. Protective orders are issued only after on-site inspections, discussions with landowners, public hearings, and, if requested, appeals. A record of only twenty appeals in several thousand cases attests to the success of such a personalized effort.

The desire to protect against urbanization of neighboring land can be an additional incentive for a group of neighbors to donate rights. Land trusts among neighbors are another alternative. A trust agreement between several landowners ensuring perpetual restrictions on development are becoming increasingly common in New England and the Midwest.

The outright purchase of land by citizens who wish to maintain the natural character of an area offers special opportunity. Where local zoning authorities do not share the buyer's interest in conservation, the stimulus to donate urbanization rights to some entity that will not exercise them may be especially strong.

*Governments and charitable organizations have a significant opportunity to protect open space by providing owners with a just and convenient method of donating urbanization rights and then persuading owners to use it. State and local land-use agencies should determine which lands qualify for permanent protection to assure that voluntary donations are not encouraged to protect property better allocated to development. A mechanism for periodic reconsideration of the lands placed in preservation trusts may be necessary to guard against abuse of the device.*

*Economic Incentives: Tax and Partial Purchase*

Reduced real property tax is one appropriate reward for giving up urbanization rights. At most, the property should be assessed at its restricted (natural or agricultural) value. Conceivably, it could be assessed at some still lower value. As long as real estate taxes remain such a small fraction of the potential development value, however, it seems unlikely that reduced assessments will tempt many owners to give up urbanization rights. Any potential incentive is diminished still further in states that continue to grant reduced assessments for all farmland, restricted or not.

Federal tax laws also create powerful incentives and disincentives for protection of private land, albeit often unintentionally. Modifying federal income and estate tax laws could help to achieve permanent protection of some private open spaces, in the right places, without excessive public cost. (The pending environmental protection tax act is one promising proposal. It would provide for a more favorable federal tax treatment of donations of partial land interests and would deny favorable depreciation and certain other deductions to those whose developments destroy coastal wetlands and historic sites.) Nevertheless, avoiding inequity in any such modifications (which typically favor high-income taxpayers) appears exceedingly difficult. Any scheme that leaves estate owners in full possession of their properties, and confers what amounts to a public subsidy, may appear to many to be compensating the affluent for doing what they already have the incentive and means to do on their own.

If federal funds must be spent to preserve privately owned open land, the most straightforward approach is public purchase of part of the property rights in the land itself. The role of this technique in a protection strategy depends on answers to several questions:

—What kinds of legal interests should be acquired?

—How much will acquisition of these rights cost? Supporters of this technique cite cases where costs were very low; critics argue that costs can approach the cost of the property itself. It seems that cost ought to depend largely on the seller's estimate of the imminence of development, but experience is too limited and varied to permit confident prediction. The National Park Service, in its acquisition of scenic easements, suggests that 20-25 percent of the full value is a realistic rule of thumb where owners cooperate with Park Service objectives. But the service has had to pay up to 90 percent of full value.

—Where costs are high, as on the edges of developed areas, what critiera should be applied to decide whether to buy the limited right, buy the whole property, or just conclude that the area has been "lost" to development?

—Would widespread purchase of development rights from some owners reduce the willingness of others to donate rights free? Would it reduce public acceptance of uncompensated conservation regulations? Would legislatures be likely to require payment of unnecessary compensation? (Consider the federal legislation requiring payment of compensation for removal of billboards along interstate highways, even in states where the courts have permitted mandatory removal without compensation.)

—Given the competing claims on public funds, when is it wiser to buy limited rights in open space instead of, say, buying recreation spaces or rights in land needed for new towns or other uses?

To answer such questions, we need experience and, we have concluded, a new institution that can guide and support open space preservation.

### Greening Urban Regions: The Need for a New Institution

Given the scale of growth expected in the next fifty years, we need an entity that can evaluate open space needs and plan on a grand scale, the scale of the urban regions themselves. The reservation of open spaces in and around urbanizing areas now could assure that the settled regions of the future are relieved by significant open and forested lands, providing outdoor recreation opportunities to millions and giving shape and coherence to urban settlements. We need, in short, a new institution with the vision to direct the course of urban growth on a regional scale.

But, it may be argued, the vision is meaningless without the means to bring it about, and the American experience with resisting urbanization is one of successive lost battles. The British, though, have had considerable success in maintaining much of their countryside in open space, and their experience suggests what might work for us.

#### The British Experience

Through a system of greenbelts and country parks, 28 percent of the land of England and Wales is conserved as open space. (See Figure 7.)

The greenbelt plans became possible with passage of the Town and Country Planning Act in 1947, which introduced noncompensable land-use regulations as the principal means of controlling urban growth. Land for the London greenbelt was based on the Greater London Plan of 1944, which proposed a contiguous

FIGURE 7
**Greenbelts and Parks in England and Wales**

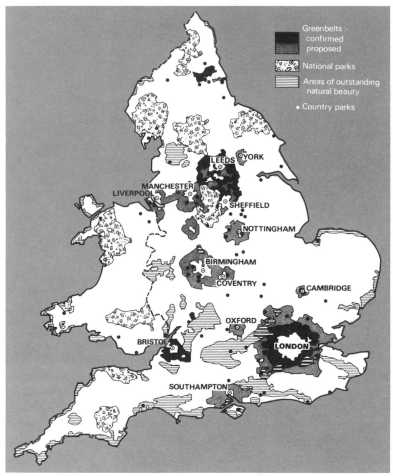

Source: Countryside Commission Department of the Environment, Ordnance Survey, reprinted in *The Economist,* January 13, 1973.

zone of up to 10 miles surrounding London. Most of the greenbelt land is in private ownership, with less than 10 percent in industrial, commercial, mining, and residential use (much of this predating the greenbelt). Within the greenbelt are numerous towns and villages, many of which were allowed to "round off" their boundaries. Approximately 1.4 million persons live in the greenbelt area, including those in the towns and villages.

What is remarkable about the London greenbelt is that it came into being without extensive public acquisition or compensation in a region that was experiencing rapid population growth.

Similar, if less spectacular, successes have been achieved in the other English cities to which the greenbelt concept has been applied. Through non-compensable regulation, vast quantities of land also have been incorporated in national parks, country parks, and areas of outstanding natural beauty. These parks are substantially in private ownership, but the government, through payment of a small "consideration," encourages private landowners to permit public access to the land.

Peak District National Park, located in the west midlands between Manchester and Sheffield, is one example of such a reconciliation of public interest and private ownership and use. Created in 1951 out of parts of five counties and covering 542 square miles, the park has 40,000 permanent residents, but well over 5 million visitors a year. Since its boundaries are 50 miles or less from Birmingham, Derby, Leeds, Liverpool, Manchester, Nottingham, and Sheffield, whose combined urban populations approach 17 million, it is no wonder that the development and tourist pressures on the park are intense.

Almost all of the park is in private ownership, but access agreements have opened 73 square miles to the public, much by means of public footpaths and trails. Nevertheless, a good deal of private economic activity takes place within the park, including some heavy industry and mining, and, of course, agriculture and grazing.

The park is governed by a Peak Park Planning Board consisting of representatives from the five county councils and the Department of the Environment. The board sets land-use policy in the park, an unusual arrangement; land uses in other national parks are governed by the county council and other local authorities in whose jurisdiction they happen to fall.

## A Greenspace Program

The relevance of the British experience to American circumstances is not the greenbelt form that the protection program has promoted but the demonstration of the effectiveness of a mix of protection techniques, with primary reliance on non-compensatory controls. *Techniques in the United States should include public acquisition of land and of development rights in strategic* land parcels, such as those located along highways, directly adjoining urbanized areas, and along waterfronts. Such a system, based on non-compensatory controls and supplemented by other techniques, appears to present the only realistic hope of achieving the permanent protection of critical open spaces, including buffer zones between urbanized areas. A congressional mandate for the establishment and support of state-controlled greenspaces could have a significant influence on local and judicial attitudes to such a program.

The major role in the planning, designation, and regulation of regional greenspaces cannot be federal but must belong to the states, which alone possess the police powers necessary to limit land use. Major urban greenspaces could be established as part of state efforts to develop land-use programs for identifying and protecting critical environmental areas.

But the institution to assist and coordinate such an effort should be federal. A federal or federally chartered agency could best highlight the national urgency of the effort, coordinate the efforts of contiguous states, publicize successes in greenspace conservation activities, advertise the advantages of donation of land or partial interests in land located in greenspace areas, and, by coordinating the recreation programs of federal agencies within greenspaces, assure that such areas offer ample public recreation opportunities.

We see the need for a National Lands Trust to assist public bodies, particularly state land-use agencies, in the designation, planning, and conservation of extensive greenspaces in and around major urbanizing areas. The National Lands Trust would advise on regulatory and acquisition measures and make funds available for acquisition of full or partial interests in strategically located lands within greenspaces. For this purpose, federal funding of $200 million should be made available annually on a matching basis with a 75 percent federal share. The goal would be the conservation of significant, predominantly private open spaces in urban regions to give coherence and form to the patterns of urban growth, provide buffer zones between urban areas, and assure that countryside is easily accessible to residents of urban regions. The primary technique for controlling land use would be regulation and related measures short of full public purchase. Affected states would be encouraged to coordinate their land-use programs with greenspace programs by designating greenspaces as "areas of critical environmental concern."

It should be emphasized that $200 million is relatively little in view of the needs; acquisition funds would be made available *only* for selective strategic purchases to support state and local programs that rely primarily on non-compensable regulations. A new "Greenspaces for America" effort, with primary emphasis on urbanizing areas, could be an appropriate way to celebrate the national bicentennial in 1976.

The trust should be established either by federal charter or within the Department of the Interior, where it could be administered as a part of the Department's Land and Water Conservation Fund. With the Department's jurisdiction over national parks, wildlife refuges, and historic sites, and its designation as administering agency for pending land-use program assistance to the states, it could be equipped to coordinate a greenspace strategy. In any case, however, legislation is needed, either to grant a charter or to expand the Land and Water Conservation Fund and direct support for a greenspace program.

The impact of the greenspace program on the land market and on real estate values would depend very much on the scale at which it is implemented. The principal economic impact would be on the spatial distribution of urban land values, with resulting implications for housing and urban development costs.

Under existing conditions, urban development value is distributed widely over the land surface of metropolitan areas; if it were added up, the total would constitute more value than is potentially realizable from development. Potential development value is a "floating value," which can be determined only when the float settles on sites actually selected for development.

The effect of a regulatory program such as the greenspace program would be to provide more certainty as to where the "float" would settle by removing expectations of development from those areas included in the program. In doing so, it would "shift" land values without destroying them, since the total demand for development would not be materially affected.

This shift would not alter the aggregate quantity of private land values; it would simply redistribute them in a spatial sense. Nor would the greenspace program as described here stifle needed urban development. Although in the short run it might lead to cost increases, in land available for development in the long run, it would probably offer higher economic and environmental values.

In sum, the greenspace program would have two major economic advantages. It would protect for future use and enjoyment natural assets whose social value is likely to increase steadily and perhaps quite rapidly. It would also offer potentially significant savings in the costs of public facilities through its impact on the location and organization of urban development.

## Clustering and Density Transfer

The cluster principle can also provide an incentive for the preservation of private open space. Under the cluster principle, the designation of open space within a project causes no reduction in the total quantity of urbanization rights: the same quantity of rights is just grouped together on a portion of the tract. If regulations allow 100 dwelling units on a 100-acre tract, the developer need not lay down one unit on each acre. He can instead set aside 20 (or 10 or 98) acres as open space and put all 100 units on the remaining 80 (or 90 or 2) acres. The cluster principle works best in large projects, where there are more rights to spread around and more space to spread them in.

But why cluster only within one project? If one owner would be permitted to cluster within a single project of 100 acres, why not permit several owners to cluster when the same 100 acres have been cut up into several tracts? Why not, in other words, enable adjoining owners to pool and redistribute urbanization rights, perhaps applying pooling concepts like those used when several adjacent landowners discover they are sitting on top of one large pool of oil?

"Density transfer" is one possible mechanism to permit just this sort of pooling of urbanization rights. In effect, it would permit the cluster principle to operate across lot lines. Suppose, for example, that the same 100-acre tract on which regulations permitted 100 dwelling units had been subdivided years ago into two parcels, one of 80 acres and one of 20 acres. And suppose that a community plan showed the entire 20-acre parcel as open space. Under density transfer, the owner of the 20-acre parcel would end up with 20 units of "leftover" density credits which, though he could not use them on his own land, he could transfer (i.e., sell) to the owner of the 80-acre parcel. After buying those rights, the owner of the 80-acre parcel could build all 100 permitted units on his tract. The purchase price paid to the owner of the 20-acre parcel would become his "compensation" or "incentive" to retain his land as open space.

Density transfer is already being used on an *ad hoc* basis. New York City's Historic Preservation Ordinance, for example, utilizes the transfer scheme as a fundamental tool for saving historic buildings. Developers are permitted to transfer development "rights" from a site occupied by an officially designated historic landmark to an adjacent site under development. The first use of this mechanism was approved by the city's Historic Landmark Commission in December 1972. Approximately 20,000 square feet of development rights were transferred from a small mid-nineteenth-century residence on Manhattan's East Side to the site of a nearby apartment and office building, increasing the scale on the latter site beyond that which applicable zoning would have permitted in the absence of the transferred credits.

Other detailed schemes have been proposed to establish more extensive transfer systems for historic preservation as well as for open space protection. A detailed plan to help preserve Chicago's numerous landmark structures, for example, is now in the works.

Obstacles to the establishment of a workable density transfer system on any significant scale are truly formidable. Nevertheless, if a market could be created for the transferable rights, the remaining obstacles could probably be overcome. But no healthy market can be created so long as regulatory authorities persist in granting new rights free through zoning changes or bonuses or variances. Why buy from your neighbors what the zoning board gives away free? The value of transferable rights, like the value of taxicab medallions, depends in part on a governmental willingness to establish a limited number of rights and then hold to them. Regulatory authorities have not yet been willing to do this.

Clustering rights within one project will remain much easier than pooling of rights among several projects. For the time being, the most efficient way to obtain the benefits of clustering is probably just to encourage large projects.

Nevertheless, the technique of density transfer could be important. On a regional scale, for example, it might be used to reduce the effective cost of open space: unused development rights in regional parks, instead of being effectively extinguished at taxpayers' expense, might instead be sold to owners who wished to develop other property in the region more intensively. For this and other purposes, *we think the concept of density transfer worthy of experimental application.*

# Toward a Top-Down Theory of Development Rights

Density transfer, or any measure that separates ownership of land from the rights to build on it, raises a question with far-reaching implications: Where do development rights come from in the first place?

Historically, Americans have thought of these rights as coming from the land itself, "up from the bottom" like minerals or crops. As a result, land-use regulations have been viewed as restrictions on each landowner's pre-existing rights rather than as grants of rights he did not have before. If a regulation permits construction of one dwelling unit for each 50 acres of land area, the owner of a 500-acre tract thinks, not that he has been granted a right to build 10 units, but that he has been deprived of a right to build more than 10.

But land planning must look not only "up from the bottom," from the vantage point of each land parcel, but also "down from the top," from the vantage point of the region or community as a whole. From this second perspective, a quantity of needed development is agreed upon and then spread, unevenly, over the community or region.

American land-use regulations, starting with bottom-up assumptions, have had great difficulty in applying top-down limits. The cluster principle, however, even in its routine application to set aside open space within a single project, starts with a top-down limit. Take the 100-acre tract on which 100 dwelling units are permitted. Where did that 100-unit limit come from? Just because all 100 units are built on 80 acres, why should more units not later be built on the 20 acres reserved as open space? The limit did not come from an inherent inability of the tract to hold more than 100 units. If it had, clustering would presumably be impossible. Rather, the 100-unit limit represents a decision that 100 units are that tract's share of the total quantity of development planned for the community (or region or block.).

Clustering, which is being used to obtain open space in "planned unit developments" all across the country, illustrates the usefulness of changing—in whole or in part—to a different way of thinking about where urbanization rights come from. With such a change, land planning and regulations would come to be seen as giving out rights created by society rather than as restricting or taking away rights that come from the land itself. Present land-use regulations would then be seen as parceling out rights unevenly, with land in some zones getting a bigger share than land in other zones, and with many exceptions made for individual parcels within each zone (an invitation to corruption). The present allocation of shares would be seen as a give-away by society (with

*Columbia, Maryland, a planned community, has clustered residential "villages" separated by open spaces of parks, trees, and lawns. Almost one-fifth of the total land area of Columbia has been preserved in open spaces.*

*"God's country? Well, I suppose it is.*
*But I own it."*

no cost to the landowner) of rights that often virtually determine
property value.

Density transfer, from this standpoint, would appear as a helpful mechanism to smooth out differences in land values caused by
the uneven allocations of development shares. Its result would be
a more nearly uniform distribution of rights among landowners,
with the owners of historic buildings and open spaces receiving
some of the cash benefits of development by transferring their
unused development rights to others.

If a workable system of density transfer can be devised, it may
eventually be considered preferable to tax incentives and less-
than-fee acquisition, since those incentives would be seen as
arrangements to pay for recovering rights that the government had
previously given away.

Yet density transfer may be only a halfway measure, more
equitable than the present approach to land-use regulation but

still less equitable than one in which development rights are sold by government. Density transfer would allocate development rights more evenly among landowners but still would not allocate them among those members of society who did not happen to own land. Some might compare it to dividing up the whole pool of rights to operate television stations only among those people who happened to own transmitting equipment, with those who actually got broadcasting franchises paying some compensation to those who lost out.

*We think it highly likely that in forthcoming decades Americans will gradually abandon the traditional assumption that urbanization rights arise from the land itself. Development potential, on any land and in any community, results largely from the actions of society (especially the construction of public facilities). Other free societies, notably Great Britain, have abandoned the old assumption in their legal systems and now treat development rights as created and allocated to the land by society.*

For now, when we need incentives to back protective regulations for open spaces and historic preservation, the old assumption remains very much in force. Today's incentives must be fashioned to be workable with today's attitudes. Noneconomic incentives can do some of the job. Density transfer may prove workable enough to do part, as well. Tax and other economic incentives, despite their cost and possible inequity, may be useful in some circumstances.

None of these incentives, though, is likely to be sufficient to protect the amounts of open space or the numbers of historic sites that would be ideally desirable. What is needed is a changed attitude toward land, not simply a growing awareness of the importance of stewardship, but a separation of commodity rights in the land from urbanization rights.

# Chapter IV
# Adapting Old Laws
# to New Values

*...nor shall private property be taken*
*for public use, without just compensation.*

Known to lawyers as the "takings clause," these few words from the Fifth Amendment to the U.S. Constitution protect one of the most fundamental of individual rights: the right to private property. Like other guarantees of the Bill of Rights, the takings clause establishes a basic principle that must be continually interpreted and applied by lawmakers and judges. In many situations, the interpretation of the clause has long been settled. In others, judges and scholars continue to search for sound, consistent interpretations that respect both public and private rights.[1]

One of the most difficult issues of interpretation arises out of judicial rulings that regulations restricting the use of private land can, if sufficiently restrictive, amount to a "taking" of the land itself for which compensation must be paid by the public. In thousands of cases, courts have had to determine whether a particular restriction went too far to be sustainable without compensation. Decisions and rationales have been widely divergent. The result is uncertainty about how far restrictive powers can go before expensive compensation must be paid.

This uncertainty, if it remains unresolved, promises to become increasingly troublesome in the years ahead. For the protection of critical environmental and cultural areas will require placing tough new restrictions on the use of private land. These restrictions will be little more than delaying actions if the courts do not uphold them as reasonable measures to protect the public interest, in short, as restrictions that landowners may fairly be required to bear without payment by the government. The interpretation of the takings clause is therefore a crucial matter for the future of land-use planning and regulatory programs.

Our examination of the takings issue has persuaded us that there are two principal problems involved. The first stems from the many judicial precedents (including some from the U.S. Supreme Court) that date from a time when attitudes toward land, natural processes, and planning were different than they are today. Many precedents are anachronistic now that land is coming

*Connecticut, seeking to preserve the Great Salt Meadow, one of the largest virgin salt marshes that line the coast, has denied the Rykar Industrial Corporation's request for a permit to fill a portion of the marsh for*

to be regarded as a basic natural resource to be protected and conserved and urban development is seen as a process needing careful public guidance and control.

The second principal problem is widespread misunderstanding of the constitutional language and its interpretation. Ignorance of what higher courts have actually been willing to sustain has created an exaggerated fear that restrictive actions will be declared unconstitutional. Such uncertainty has forestalled countless regulatory actions and induced numerous bad compromises. The popular impression of the takings clause may be even more

*an industrial site. Rykar has charged that the denial of the permit constitutes a taking. The case is typical of controversies arising over state wetlands legislation.*

out of date than some court opinions.

The takings issue involves apportioning the rights and obligations of society, on the one hand, and the individual acting in his capacity as landowner, on the other. Since there is no "pure" position on these matters, the law draws a line at some point along the spectrum of views about the rights and obligations of society and of property owners. Courts have always applied the takings principle in light of their understanding of current conditions. The effort to develop a satisfactory resolution of the issue adequate to our own time and needs entails drawing the line differently from where it might have been drawn in other times.

The takings issue can arise in almost any situation in which land use is severely restricted, from wetlands protection to historic preservation, from phased development planning to open space protection. To sample the range of situations, and the varied court stands on takings, we present four cases in which landowners are challenging land-use regulations as violating the takings clause.

## Great Salt Meadow in Stratford, Connecticut

Approximately 600 acres remain of the Great Salt Meadow in Stratford, Connecticut. This expanse of yellow marsh grasses, salt hay, and numerous other plants is bordered by Lewis Gut, a tidal estuary winding from the edge of Bridgeport airport southwest to Long Island Sound. For much of its length, the Gut is bounded by a popular public beach. Important portions of the remaining meadow are in private ownership, and one owner, Rykar Industrial Corporation, is currently proposing an industrial facility and related upland construction for a 277-acre parcel of marshland adjoining the Gut.

The meadow is one of the few remaining undeveloped sites that might be suitable for such a facility in the industrial corridor between Boston and New York City. Local zoning regulations have permitted industrial development in the area since 1927. Rykar, which has held this land and adjoining parcels for over twenty years, has made substantial improvements in anticipation of development, including construction of a new railroad spur.

But recent Connecticut legislation to protect coastal wetlands has stymied Rykar's proposal to dredge and fill their marsh. In September 1970, the property was designated a protected "ecological unit," making a state permit mandatory for virtually all development. Rykar's application for a permit was ultimately denied on several grounds—that the property is in fact a tidal wetland subject to flooding, hurricane, and other natural disasters; that it benefits marine fisheries; and that the dredging would destroy shellfish grounds and endanger the adjoining beach. Rykar has alleged that the ruling results in an unconstitutional taking of its property, and the issue is now before the Superior Court of Hartford County, Connecticut.[2]

How is the takings clause to be interpreted in this case? What precedents apply?

Connecticut courts have approved substantial restraints on land uses through zoning, even though property values were thereby reduced. According to the state's highest court, "The maximum possible enrichment of a property owner is not a controlling purpose of zoning."[3] But the same court has on different occasions indicated that laudable purposes, including protection of a salt marsh, are insufficient basis for depriving a landowner of all uses of his land without compensation.

Two Connecticut cases are cited in opposition to the wetlands regulation—*Dooley v. Town Plan & Zone Commission of Town of Fairfield* and *Bartlett v. Zoning Commission of the Town of Old Lyme.*[4] In the *Dooley* case, land recently assessed with a $11,000 special levy for a sewage district was then placed in a floodplain zone where no improvements were permitted on the land. The court overturned the zoning ordinance as applied to that land. In the *Bartlett* case, tidal wetlands restrictions were invalidated when they permitted only limited water-related uses and prohibited filling or destroying the wetlands.

Other states, balancing the interests involved, have sustained wetland regulations. The Supreme Judicial Court of Massachusetts approved a town floodplain ordinance somewhat similar to the one rejected in Connecticut's *Dooley* case, saying: "Although it is clear that the petitioner is substantially restricted in the use of the land, such restrictions must be balanced against the potential harm to the community from overdevelopment of a flood plain area."[5] (The applicability of this holding to tidal wetlands is unclear if the connection with public safety, a key element in the Massachusetts decision, is not as strong.) In *Candlestick Properties, Inc. v. San Francisco Bay C & D Commission*, the Court of Appeals of California sustained regulations that prohibited the filling of San Francisco Bay. Applying a balancing test, the court concluded that protection of the Bay justified an uncompensated exercise of regulatory power.[6] The importance of the Bay played a key role in this determination.

### Grand Central Terminal in New York City

Built in the first decade of this century, Grand Central Terminal was designed as the hub of a $180-million redevelopment project by the New York Central Railroad to reclaim space occupied by midtown rail yards. A team of architects headed by Whitney Warren designed a spectacular office, hotel, and railroad complex stretching from 42nd to 50th streets, with the trains feeding Grand Central running two levels under the buildings and Park Avenue.

Now, only the cavernous main concourse and the south facade of Grand Central remain. The New York City Landmarks Preservation Commission designated Grand Central Terminal a landmark in August 1967, terming it "a magnificent example of French Beaux Arts architecture . . . [and] one of the great buildings of America."[7] All exterior improvements of the terminal now require a "certificate of no exterior effect" issued by the city before any construction can begin.

An application for such a certificate was made in 1968 by UGP Properties, lessor of the air rights over the terminal, and Penn Central Railroad, owner of the terminal, requesting permission to construct a 55-story skyscraper in the air space above Grand Central. UGP and Penn Central first proposed a building that, they claimed, would not physically destroy the exterior of the terminal. The Landmarks Commission disagreed. They and the property owners then investigated other alternatives, including demolition of all but the main concourse for a 59-story structure (the Landmarks Commission objected) and construction of the office tower on an alternative site (the property owners objected). After failing to reach an agreement, UGP and Penn Central took their case to court, arguing that their property had been taken by the city.[8]

The principal obstacle to the UGP-Penn Central plan was the city landmarks ordinance and related zoning provisions. The Landmarks Commission evaluates the historic or landmark value of a structure, weighing it against the economic burden of maintaining the landmark privately. Since only the exterior is protected, the commission is empowered to help the owner find alternative paying uses for an uneconomic landmark, which may include alteration of the interior. If the property is found

Grand Central, one of the great classic railroad stations, has been declared a landmark under New York law. Penn Central Railroad, which owns the station, proposed to build an office tower in the air rights above the building, a proposal denied by the Landmarks Commission. In a case typical of controversies arising over historic preservation laws, Penn Central has challenged the law as a taking of its property.

uneconomic, the city must acquire an interest in it through eminent domain or must grant permission to alter or destroy it.

UGP and Penn Central asserted that depriving them of "the privilege to make millions of dollars per year, and at the same time [forcing] Penn Central, which is bankrupt, to maintain an aging and deteriorating terminal at a deficit, is a regulation which undeniably goes so far that it amounts to a taking for which compensation must be provided."[9] The trial was held in spring 1971, but the judge has yet to issue a decision. The proof at trial went beyond narrow theories to weigh the whole protective regulation and the benefits accruing from preservation against the burdens borne by the landowner.*

In this case, both sides could cite supporting precedents. UGP and Penn Central relied on *Keystone Associates v. Moerdler,* a New York case denying the city the right to withhold permission to demolish the old Metropolitan Opera House during a 180-day holding period.[10] Quoting a turn-of-the-century case, in the *Moerdler* decision the court stated: "All that is beneficial in property arises from its use and the fruits of that use, and whatever deprives a person of them deprives him of all that is desirable or valuable in the title and possession."

On the other hand, the New York courts that have examined the landmarks preservation ordinance have had little difficulty accepting it as constitutional. In *Trustees of Sailor's Snug Harbor v. Platt,* a lower court said: "We deem certain of the basic questions raised to be no longer arguable. In this category is the right, within proper limitations, of the state to place restrictions on the use to be made by an owner of his own property for the cultural and aesthetic benefit of the community."[11] The court skirted the takings issue, however, remanding for additional evidence. But in an earlier case involving a residential property, another lower court upheld landmark designation where the owner failed to show that either the marketability of his building or the return on his investment had been impaired by designation.[12]

Courts in other states have upheld preservation ordinances, although in most situations their objectives were more narrowly phrased. Design controls in New Orleans' historic Vieux Carre have been accepted in the Louisiana courts for many years.[13] Illinois appellate courts have accepted regulations preventing commercial uses in a district surrounding the Lincoln residence in Springfield.[14] A New Mexico court upheld restrictions on window size in certain districts of Santa Fe to preserve the districts' character.[15]

---

*Both the issue of economic return on the existing terminal operation and compensation for the unused air rights are extremely complex. For example, the city argues that a provision authorizing transfer of unused density rights to other property must be considered when testing the reasonableness of this regulation.

152

## Fleur Du Lac in Lake Tahoe Basin, California

With winter skiing and summer water sports, the Lake Tahoe Basin is extremely attractive to second-home buyers. Already, demand for land in the basin has contributed to a regional development boom. In the words of the California Supreme Court:

> [T]here is good reason to fear that the region's natural wealth contains the virus of its ultimate impoverishment. A staggering increase in population, a greater mobility of people, an affluent society and an incessant urge to invest, to develop, to acquire and merely to spend—all have combined to pose a severe threat to the Tahoe region. Today, and for the foreseeable future, the ecology of Lake Tahoe stands in grave danger before a mountainous wave of population and development.[16]

To deal with the development boom, the states of Nevada and California formed the Tahoe Regional Planning Agency (TRPA), which has instituted areawide controls.

The owners of Fleur du Lac, a retreat of the late Henry Kaiser on the western shore, finding their application to build sixty condominium units blocked by the controls, filed a claim with the TRPA, alleging $4.5 million in damages.[17] Their claim is the first of more than $150 million of filed claims to reach court.

Fleur du Lac occupies 17 acres between a two-lane state highway and the lake. Most of the land is heavily wooded with twelve or thirteen older buildings already on the site. The proposed development included correction of drainage problems and maximum protection of trees and other vegetation.

After examining the developer's engineering studies, however, the technical advisory committee of the TRPA concluded that the land would not support 3.5 units per acre and the land was reclassified for lower density. In evaluating development applications, the TRPA considers two factors. The first is based on traditional zoning criteria, an evaluation of "the appropriate interrelationships of land uses, transportation, utilities, public services, existing development, recreational opportunities, and population."[18] The second is based on an engineering test of the physical capability of land to bear development, measured in terms of land coverage. Land is then placed in a capability class.

The Fleur du Lac property had tentatively been placed in a relatively high capability class. On the basis of those reports and further investigation, which indicated drainage problems and

*Fleur du Lac in Lake Tahoe Basin, California, was to be the site of sixty condominium units. The Tahoe Regional Planning Agency rejected the application for a building permit on the basis of its land capability plan, which showed that the site could not adequately support the planned development. In a case similar to those arising over restrictive development plans, the landowner has challenged the ruling as a taking.*

potential seismic instability, a portion of the land was moved to the lowest land capability class.

The landowners argue that TRPA engineering conclusions are inaccurate and that the present classification of their land amounts to an unconstitutional taking requiring compensation. Their case illustrates what will probably become an increasingly difficult issue for the TRPA and similar planning agencies. The use and density restrictions imposed by the TRPA are based on what the owners characterize as an engineering judgment involving a value judgment about the most desirable overall population level for the basin. Insofar as the limitations on the use of their property are the result of a public decision to maintain the land at an artificially low development density, the owners claim they must be compensated.

The TRPA can draw from a variety of precedents to defend its land-use ordinance. *Younger v. County of El Dorado* is one among many cases indicating sympathy for comprehensive environmental protection.[19] In *McCarthy v. City of Manhattan Beach,* the California Supreme Court approved an ordinance that restricted beach land to exclusive recreational uses.[20] (In addition to dangers to residential development on the beach land, the court found that the property owner had not exploited the possibility of operating the beach for commercial recreational uses.) Another case, *Consolidated Rock Products Co. v. City of Los Angeles,* approved stringent zoning regulation of gravel removal.[21] A more recent appellate case, *Turner v. County of Del Norte,* approved a floodplain regulation, concluding that the regulation simply formalized the natural and practical realities applying to the land.[22] In the *Candlestick Properties* case, the court approved the application of strict legislative standards by a regional agency to deny permission to fill lands in San Francisco Bay.

If this list of cases seems to remove all doubt, it should not. Recent cases such as *Turnor* have been careful to acknowledge the takings problem.[23] *Breidert v. Southern Pacific Company* set standards for public takings not connected with zoning and planning.[24] And courts in other states have invoked the takings clause to reject some regulations that result in clear public benefit. Cases such as *State v. Johnson* in Maine, which found that stringent regulation charged the individual landowner with more than his fair share of the cost of the resulting benefit, are not uncommon.[25]

Even though California has not tied such regulation to compensation, the takings question will undoubtedly recur in the varying factual circumstances that result from the TRPA investigations of basin development proposals.

## The Foothills of Palo Alto, California

Foothills to the west and south of Palo Alto flank the city with a vast reserve of undeveloped land. These hills, characterized by grassy meadows, chaparral, and woodland, are used mainly for outdoor recreation, with quarries, a Christmas tree farm, and some pastures the only commercial uses.

*Foothills to the south and west of town constitute the last major area of open space within the limits of Palo Alto, California. After a planning study recommended retaining the hills as open space, the town passed an ordinance to permit only residential estates on 10-acre lots in the area. One landowner with plans for subdivision in smaller lots filed suit alleging a taking of his property. This case is representative of those involving the preservation of open space in increasingly congested areas*

157

Approximately seventeen owners control the 7,500 acres comprising the foothills. Annexed by the city in the late 1950s, the lower foothills contain large tracts of prime land that have been the subject of development proposals since the mid 1960s. City planning studies originally proposed cluster development for the area, and the city extended public utilities, but successive development moratoriums prevented further action.

A final study prepared during the last moratorium reversed its predecessors, suggesting that acquisition of the land would be a less expensive alternative for city taxpayers than development. This study, prepared by Livingston and Blayney of San Francisco, recommended preservation of the land as open space. A cost-revenue projection of development over a twenty-year period indicated that the aggregate cost of various development alternatives to the city of Palo Alto, particularly for school services, would substantially exceed revenues from taxes, municipal services, and other sources at both high and moderate densities. On the basis of these and other findings, the city adopted an open space ordinance and classified the foothills land as open space.

The owner of one 22-acre parcel in the meadows of the upper foothills is contesting the classification, arguing that there has been a taking of his property for public use.[26] His two applications for subdivision approval were both denied in 1971. The landowner claims that he purchased the property in 1961 expecting to subdivide the land, that he spent considerable sums for professional services to prepare the property for subdivision, and that the city cannot deny permission to develop after the annexation and extension of water and sewer lines. The central issue is whether the rezoning resulted in a taking, especially since the former zoning permitted low-density development not beyond the city's capacity to service or the land's inherent adaptability for development.

Cost-revenue studies evaluating the burden of new development on municipal resources, when used to justify withholding permission to build, have had a mixed reception in the courts. *Padover v. Township of Farmington,* a Michigan case, affirmed the right of a town to channel development to minimize burdens on the local school system and other facilities.[27] (The town must prove a reasonable relationship between existing conditions and the public welfare.) In other cases, the courts have perceived a direct conflict between the right of a municipality to regulate growth and services and its duty to provide them. *National Land and Investment Co. v. Kohn* states, "Zoning is a means by which a governmental body can plan for the future—it may not be used as a means to deny the future. . . . Zoning provisions may not be used . . . to avoid the increased responsibilities and economic burdens which time and economic growth bring."[28]

Growth restrictions may also be ruled as a taking, as happened when Fairfax County, Virginia, tried to concentrate development in one area of the county ostensibly because of the availability of municipal services.[29]

In the foothills dispute, Palo Alto is expected to rely on traditional California cases, such as *Clemons v. City of Los Angeles,* which accords great weight to legislative actions establishing zoning regulations.[30]

The *Consolidated Rock* case also contains strong language in support of regulatory powers:

> The very essence of the police power as differentiated from the power of eminent domain is that the deprivation of individual rights and property cannot prevent its operation, once it is shown that its exercise is proper and that the method of its exercise is reasonably within the meaning of due process of law.[31]

Subsequent cases have made it clear that the burden is on the landowner to show that land-use regulations do not further public health, welfare, or safety and therefore do not constitute a valid exercise of regulatory powers.[32]

## The Development of the Takings Issue

The proper relation between public authority and private rights in land is a recurring theme in Anglo-American history, a theme that has greatly influenced our legal traditions.

In medieval times, the English system of land ownership involved a hierarchy of land tenures under which each nobleman "held" land "of" a superior nobleman, the highest of whom "held of" the king himself. The right to hold land conveyed the right to its profits and the right to exercise certain governmental functions over it. The noble, for his part, pledged loyalty to the king and his next-superior lord and agreed to perform specific services and obligations, principally to provide knights (or money) for the defense of the realm.

As Norman England became steadily more secure, these obligations were considered more onerous by the nobles. Resentment against seizure of lands, the penalty for failure to honor the obligations, finally stirred the nobles to revolt. The resulting *Magna Carta* was the first of many compromises between crown and nobility as the landholding lords consistently and successfully sought to convert their possessory rights over land "held of their lord" to absolute ownership. Article 39 of *Magna Carta* provided that "no freeman shall be ... deprived of his freehold ... unless by the lawful judgment of his peers and by the law of the land."

Out of the conflict between nobles and king a principle became established, at least by the seventeenth and eighteenth centuries, that was widely recognized both in England and her colonies—that a man's private property should not be taken by his government without compensation. By the beginning of the seventeenth century, the noted jurist Edward Coke was able to say in his *Institutes of the Laws of England* that Article 39 of *Magna Carta* insured "that lands, tenements, goods and chattels shall not be seized into the King's hands contrary to this great charter, and the law of the land."[33] Sir William Blackstone, in his Commentaries on the laws of England went further and derived from the doctrine a right of compensation: "The legislature alone can ... compel the individual to acquiesce [in a taking of his land] by giving him a full indemnification and equivalent for the injury thereby sustained."[34]

It was from these seventeenth and eighteenth century English legal traditions that the United States derived many of its constitutional principles, including the takings clause of the Fifth Amendment. At the time the takings clause was adopted, the draftsmen were concerned about the actual physical taking of property by the government.

The English law from which this constitutional provision was drawn permitted extensive regulation of the use of land. Such regulation was never thought to violate the principle that takings should be compensated because no one thought of a regulation as a taking. In 1589 for example, Parliament passed a statute placing all unincorporated areas under restrictions that sound remarkably similar to modern large-lot zoning:

> For the avoiding of the great inconveniences which are found by experience to grow by the erecting and building of great numbers and multitude of cottages, which are daily more and more increased in many parts of this realm, be it enacted ... that ... no person shall within this

realm of England make, build, or erect . . . any manner of cottage or habitation or dwelling . . . unless the same person do assign and lay to the same cottage or building 4 acres of ground at the lest . . . being his or her freehold and inheritance lying near to the said cottage to be continually occupied and manured therewith so long as the same cottage shall be inhabited.[35]

Four years later, Parliament passed a further statute that resembles the currently popular moratoriums on building permits. It not only placed limits on the construction of new residential buildings in London and Westminster, but also the conversion of existing large residential buildings to multi-family use:

For the reforming of the great mischiefs and inconveniences that daily grow and increase by reason of the pestering of houses with divers families . . . and converting of great houses into several tenements or dwellings, and erecting of new buildings within the cities of London and Westminster and other places here thereunto adjoining, whereby great infection of sickness and dearth of victuals and fuel hath grown and ensued . . . and divers remote places of the realm have been disappointed of workman and dispeopled . . . [No person] shall from henceforth make and erect any new building or buildings, house or houses for the habitation or dwelling within either of the said Cities, or within three miles of any of the gates of the said city of London [except for certain limited additions to existing houses and gardens]. . . . [No person] shall at any time hereafter convert or divide any dwelling house or other buildings now erected and builded, or hereafter to be erected and builded within the Cities and places aforesaid or any of them into divers and several habitations or dwellings for several and divers families [with certain exceptions and for certain assurances].[36]

The act was "to endure for seven years."

Land-use regulations were also imposed in the American colonies. In Pennsylvania, shade trees were required by a 1700 law:

Every owner or inhabitant of any and every house in Philadelphia, Newcastel and Chester shall plant one or more tree or trees, viz., pines, unbearing mulberries, water poplars, lime or other shady and wholesome trees before the door of his, her or their house and houses, not exceeding eight feet from the front of the house, and preserve the same, to the end that the said town may be well shaded from the violence of the sun in the heat of summer and thereby be rendered more healthy.[37]

Fences were required in rural areas, with a fine for failure to keep them in good repair. If the fences were not properly maintained, the landowner could not collect damages for animals wandering at large.

After the great fire in Boston in 1679, a series of laws was passed requiring the use of brick or stone in buildings. No dwelling house could be built otherwise, and the roof had to be of slate or tile upon penalty of double the value of the building. A 1692 act declared any building that did not meet these standards a common nuisance and ordered its demolition.

The Fifth Amendment takings clause refers only to takings by the federal government, not to takings by the states. Although the constitutions of most of the original thirteen states required that property not be taken without due process of law, eleven of the thirteen did not explicitly require payment of compensation for state take-over of property. Some state courts nevertheless ruled that constitutional provisions or common law required compensation for state appropriation of land, but others did not. In these states, there was for a time no legal right to compensation even for the physical taking of property by a state or its instrumentality.

At first, the U.S. Supreme Court saw no federal constitutional objection to uncompensated physical takings by the states. In 1857, the Court decided in *Withers v. Buckley* that if a state constitution did not require the payment of compensation for the taking of a property right, then neither did the Fifth Amendment.[38] The Fourteenth Amendment, added to the Constitution at the close of the Civil War, bars the states from taking property without due process of law. As late as 1877, in *Davidson v. New Orleans,* the Supreme Court ruled that even this provision did not guarantee compensation.[39] But by the close of the nineteenth century, the Supreme Court had reversed itself. In *C.B. & Q. Railway v. Chicago,* it held that the requirement of "due process of law" as expressed in the Fourteenth Amendment required the states to compensate for a taking.[40]

It thus took the Supreme Court until the end of the nineteenth century to decide that physical takings by state governments required compensation. No one would question this requirement today. It is actions that limit the use of property, while leaving it in private ownership, that are now causing differences of opinion about the need for compensation.

Shortly after the Civil War, the Supreme Court held that an impairment of the use of property that significantly reduced its value, while not a taking for public use, could violate the takings clause. In *Pumpelly v. Green Bay Company,* the Court held that the directing of water on private land as a result of a state statute authorizing construction of dams for flood control constituted a taking for which compensation must be paid. Responding to the argument that there had been no real taking, the Court said:

> It would be a very curious and unsatisfactory result, if in construing a provision of constitutional law, it shall be held that if the government refrains from the absolute conversion of real property to the uses of the public it can destroy its value entirely, can inflict irreparable and permanent injury to any extent, can in effect, subject it to total destruction without making any compensation, because, in the narrowest sense of that word, it is not taken for the public use.[41]

In cases that followed, however, a checkered pattern appeared. In *Transportation Company v. Chicago,* the Court denied compensation for acknowledged damages incurred while the city built a tunnel under the Chicago River, noting that "acts done in the proper exercise of governmental powers, and not directly encroaching upon private property, though their consequences may impair its use, are universally held not to be a taking within the meaning of the constitutional provision."[42] The case limited the *Pumpelly* rule to situations in which there had been a permanent direct encroachment. Similarly, in *Bridge Co. v. United States,* the Court held that Congress could require substantial modification of a bridge over navigable waters without payment of compensation.[43] In a vigorous dissent, Justice Joseph Bradley, arguing that compensation was necessary, voiced a position that was to surface with increasing regularity at the close of the nineteenth century.[44]

Without abandoning direct encroachment as a standard for measuring a taking of land, the Court turned increasingly to the takings issue in examining state regulation of commercial activity, particularly of railroads.[45] Although never denying the government's right to regulate property, the Court frequently displayed a distrust of regulation by striking down the procedures adopted. In 1885 it stated, "Under pretense of regulating fares and freights, the State cannot require a railroad corporation to carry persons or property for public use without just compensation, or without due process of law."[46]

It was the era of railroad expansion in the United States, and many states attempted to deal with railroad excesses both before and after the federal government entered the field in 1887 with the creation of the Interstate Commerce Commission. The cases are legion, and the Supreme Court's policy of laissez faire toward railroads, and much other industrial activity is clear.

Among the regulations struck down by the courts as a taking of railroad property without due process of law were: a Minnesota railroad commission order requiring a railroad to install weighing scales in other than a selected few stations; a Missouri statute enacted to prevent discrimination in the erection of grain elevators along a right-of-way; ratemaking in North Dakota, and Kansas; a Nebraska attempt to require the installation of switches

*"I'll tell you what else in there deserves to be protected: $744,000 of mine!"*

near grain elevators.[47] The law continued to favor railroads despite strong public reaction, especially among farmers. Robert Hunt, in *Law and Locomotives,* even claims (with case citations to back it up) that the Illinois state courts, in lawsuits for property damage caused by locomotives discharging ashes, held that landowners were required to keep property adjoining the railroad free of weeds or other combustibles to avoid a charge of contributory negligence.[48]

As a result of these decisions, railroads were transformed by the courts from a common nuisance, required by law to compensate housewives for dirtying the wash on their lines, to a privileged user of property subject only to a limited degree of governmental regulation.

Even though courts would decide many of the railroad cases differently today, the decisions remain important because they illustrate how the courts have adapted constitutional language to meet what they saw as society's needs. In an era of manifest destiny, the courts viewed occupying and developing the nation as a goal of pre-eminent importance, and they read the Constitution with this goal in mind.

There were other cases, however, in which the Supreme Court adopted a much stricter construction. In *Mugler v. Kansas,* a Kansas law prohibiting the manufacture of alcoholic beverages was challenged by a brewery owner as a taking of his property. The Court upheld the law as a valid exercise of the police power even though it destroyed the value of the brewery.[10]

Similarly, in *Hadacheck v. Sebastian,* the city of Los Angeles had passed an ordinance zoning brickyards out of certain parts of the city. A brickyard owner challenged the ordinance, alleging that it reduced the value of his land from $800,000 to $60,000. The Court rejected the allegation that the ordinance constituted a taking and upheld it as a valid exercise of the police power:

> It is to be remembered that we are dealing with one of the most essential powers of government, one that is the least limitable. It may, indeed, seem harsh in its exercise . . . but the imperative necessity for its exercise precludes any limitation upon it because of conditions once obtaining. . . . To so hold would preclude development and fix a city forever in its primitive conditions. There must be progress, and if in its march private interests are in the way they must yield to the good of the community.[50]

Throughout this period, the Supreme Court wavered between

strict and broad construction of the takings clause, apparently unable to establish a consistent policy. Then, in the early 1920s, a crucial case came before the Court. At issue was the validity of Pennsylvania legislation forbidding coal mining that would cause the surface of the land to subside under homes, streets, or public buildings. Pennsylvania argued that the legislation was necessary to prevent buildings from sinking into abandoned mine shafts; the mining companies claimed that they had obtained the right to mine the land without being required to compensate the landowner for damages to the surface, and that it was an unconstitutional taking of property to disturb this relationship. In *Pennsylvania Coal Company v. Mahon,* the Court decided that, despite the social desirability of the legislation, the only constitutional way to accomplish its purpose was for the state to buy the coal company's interest. Since the legislation authorized only regulatory control, it was struck down. In the Court's opinion, Justice Oliver Wendell Holmes wrote:

> The general rule at least, is that while property may be regulated to a certain extent, if regulation goes too far it will be recognized as a taking. . . . We are in danger of forgetting that a strong public desire to improve the public condition is not enough to warrant achieving the desire by a shorter cut than the constitutional way of paying for the change.[51]

Justice Louis Brandeis in dissent argued that the scope of the police power was sufficiently great to reach cases where the facts demonstrated an important public need:

> Every restriction upon the use of property imposed in the exercise of the police power deprives the owner of some right theretofore enjoyed, and is, in that sense, an abridgment by the State of rights in property without making compensation. But restriction imposed to protect the public health, safety or morals from dangers threatened is not a taking. . . . The property so restricted remains in the possession of its owner. The State does not appropriate it or make any use of it. The State merely prevents the owner from making a use which interferes with paramount rights of the public.[52]

The next major case to reach the Supreme Court began just about the time *Pennsylvania Coal* was decided. In November 1922, the village of Euclid, Ohio, adopted a comprehensive zoning ordinance. The Ambler Realty Company, which was holding large tracts of land as potential industrial sites, found some of its land restricted to residential use.

At that time, zoning was becoming popular, but the state courts had given varying opinions on its constitutionality. Ambler brought suit in the federal court, seeking an injunction against enforcement of the ordinance. Among its allegations was a claim that the ordinance constituted a taking of its property because the value of its land was reduced from $10,000 to $2,500 per acre.[53] The trial judge, relying on *Pennsylvania Coal,* held the ordinance invalid, but the Supreme Court upheld the ordinance in an opinion by Justice George Sutherland in which both Justice Holmes and Justice Brandeis joined.[54] However, the Court never addressed the takings issue, saying only that it would be time enough to deal with the application of the ordinance to particular property as the cases arose; the Court merely upheld the general principle of zoning, leaving the application of the principle for case by case determination.

Two years later, the Supreme Court took another zoning case. In *Nectow v. Cambridge,* the owner of land zoned for residential use showed that he had a contract predating the zoning to sell his land for industrial use for $63,000. This time, the Supreme Court found that the loss in value to the property owner outweighed the value to the community and held the particular zoning classification invalid.[55]

In the same year, however, the Court reviewed a Virginia statute requiring the destruction of red cedar trees without compensation to the owners because they produced a cedar rust that damaged apple orchards. Citing cases such as *Mugler* and *Hadacheck,* the Court upheld the validity of the requirement against the charge that it constituted a taking.[56]

In summary, the Supreme Court set out a "diminution of value" test for a taking in *Pennsylvania Coal,* considering the economic burden placed on the affected landowner, with compensation payable if the regulation is judged to go too far. The Court then showed that the test could operate to favor the public in *Euclid* and the landowner in *Nectow.* Read in conjunction with *Mugler* and *Hadacheck, Pennsylvania Coal* has subsequently been interpreted by many state courts as establishing a balancing test for determining whether a regulation amounts to a taking, with courts "balancing" the importance of the public interest served by a regulation against the economic loss it entails for an affected property owner.

The Supreme Court then retired from the field. Since the *Nectow* decision, the Court has only rarely taken cases involving the regulation of land, preferring to leave these subjects to state courts. The one notable exception is *Goldblatt v. Town of Hempstead,* in which the Court upheld a regulation prohibiting the operation of a gravel pit in an urbanized area.[57] (The Court cited *Pennsylvania Coal* as the applicable test.)

## State Court Decisions

The decisions of the state courts follow a similar checkered pattern. A Maine decision, *State v. Johnson,* shows one approach. Testing the validity of the state Wetlands Act, the court balanced the benefits resulting from wetlands protection against the loss to the individual landowner, holding:

> The benefits from [wetlands] preservation extend beyond town limits and are state-wide. The cost of its preservation should be publicly borne. To leave the landowners with commercially valueless land in upholding the restriction presently imposed, is to charge them with more than their just share of the cost of this state-wide conservation program, granting fully its commendable purpose.[58]

In the *Consolidated Rock* case, the California Supreme Court, upholding stringent regulation of gravel removal, took a different approach. That case held that the "essence of police power" is "that the deprivation of individual rights and property cannot prevent its operation, once it is shown that its exercise is . . . reasonably within the meaning of due process of law." This same approach was taken by a California court in the *Candlestick Properties* case, where an anti-fill order for Bay wetlands by a regional conservation body was sustained although the resulting losses alleged by the property owner were similar to those in the Maine case of *State v. Johnson.*

The California courts have shown more regard for public values than those in any other state when presented with allegation of a taking. In the past three or four years, courts in Wisconsin, Maine, and Maryland have also sustained state land-use controls against takings claims.

In 1972, the Wisconsin Supreme Court considered the constitutionality of a shoreland zoning ordinance that placed wetlands in a conservancy district, essentially limiting uses to those consistent with the natural character of the swampland. The court declared:

> An owner of land has no absolute and unlimited right to change the essential natural character of his land so as to use it for a purpose for which it was unsuited in its natural state and which injures the rights of

168

others. . . . [We] think it is not an unreasonable exercise of [the police power in zoning] to prevent harm to public rights by limiting the use of private property to its natural uses.[59]

In a 1973 case, the Supreme Judicial Court of Maine considered the constitutionality of a directive by the state's Environmental Improvement Commission under the Maine Site Location Law ordering a subdivider to cease development of a 92-acre tract until the commission's approval had been applied for and obtained. With respect to the takings issue, the court said: "The Legislature has declared the public interest in preserving the environment from anything more than minimal destruction to be superior to the owner's rights in one use of his land and has given the Commission adequate standards under which to carry out the legislative purpose."[60]

And the Maryland Court of Appeals sustained state wetlands legislation declaring unlawful the dredging of any tidal waters or marshlands of Charles County against constitutional attack by a gravel company. In the opinion of the trial court, adopted by the Court of Appeals, the prohibition in the law was "a limitation upon a use of property, not a taking." Thus, it was "a valid use of the police powers . . . for the state to preserve its exhaustible natural resources." "The current trend," the court observed, "is to consider the preservation of natural resources as a valid exercise of the police powers."[61]

However, the decisions of state courts on the takings issue do not show a clear pattern. Some cases throw out regulations that cause relatively minor diminution in property values, while other cases uphold regulations that appear to have a tremendous impact. The guiding beacons of *Magna Carta* and the Fifth Amendment seem to have become flickering traffic lights—now red, now yellow, now green.

## The English Experience with the Compensation Issue

Despite the same common law tradition, the English experience with land-use restrictions has been quite different from ours.*

---

*Unlike the United States, the United Kingdom does not have a written constitution against which to test the validity of legislative action. It is therefore Parliament, rather than the courts, that determines policy on compensation to owners of regulated property. Despite this procedural difference, the policy issues are the same in both countries.

While English courts stoutly maintain that property shall not be compulsorily acquired without full compensation, compensation is *not* payable for restrictions on the use of property unless Parliament so provides. Generally the English have had no difficulty, in principle, in restricting the use of land without compensation. The basic justifications are these:

1. Potential development value is speculative or "floating" and it is not possible to ascertain where the "float" will settle. To compensate for "probable" development results in overvaluation, as the "probabilities" over a wide area are more than actual development could possibly be. Thus, property restricted to current use is not considered reduced in value, since any other use is uncertain.
2. Land values are seen as largely created by public actions such as the construction of roads and utilities.

The key to the British system is the requirement of planning permission for virtually all land development (according to the Town and Country Planning Act, which codifies British planning law, "the carrying out of building, engineering, mining or other operations, in, on, over, or under land, or the making of any material change in the use of any buildings or other land"). Planning permission is usually dependent upon the closeness of the landowner's plans to the local planning authority's development plan. Although planning permission contrary to planning authority plans is difficult to obtain, it is possible under certain circumstances to obtain *compensation* provided certain statutory conditions are met. Basically, the English scheme rests on a presumption that the government is responsible for divergent land values by means of its development plan requirements, and therefore a landowner is entitled only to some "reasonably beneficial use" of his property—and not one whit more.

By far the most common of the rare situations in which compensation is payable for a land-use restriction is when an owner serves a "purchase notice" to the local council (not necessarily the planning authority) to purchase land refused permission for development. Unless the council is willing to comply (and it often is), a purchase notice must be confirmed by the Secretary of State for the Environment before it is enforceable. Instead of confirming the purchase notice, the secretary may grant permission for other development. If he does, then compensation may become payable if the permitted development value (which is what the secretary will now permit) is less than the existing use value. Note that even here there is no compensation payable unless the landowner gives up his property first.

If the secretary decides to confirm a purchase notice, he must first find (1) that the land is incapable of reasonably beneficial use in its existing state; and (2) that the land cannot be made capable of reasonably beneficial use by any other development for which permission has been granted or is being sought. The owner thus has only one ground on which to make his case for a purchase notice—the uselessness of his land in its existing state, wholly apart from any potential value for development it may have. (Purchase notices may also be served after a planning permission has been revoked or modified.)

The Ministry has interpreted this arrangement strictly, holding, for example, that land which is capable of being grazed or farmed is capable of reasonably beneficial use. If the government agrees to buy the land, it buys it at the value attributable to land for which there is no reasonably beneficial use—a catch-22 that discourages most landowners from filing purchase notices.

Thus, in England the land investor or speculator who hopes to increase his land values is given no effective recourse against the government's failure to approve his development plans, but the small farmer receives some protection against restrictions that impair the usability of his land for farming. It is this system of land-use controls that has enabled the English to preserve large amounts of open space in metropolitan greenbelts and in open country without paying compensation. Underpinning the legal powers exercised by public authorities over privately owned lands in Great Britain is a sophisticated planning process that prescribes virtually all land uses.

It seems neither practical nor desirable that we follow the English model too closely, but one cannot help but conclude that the English have achieved a more stable and socially desirable resolution of the takings issue than have the courts of most of our states. The English example at least offers the prospect that our courts may yet derive from the same basic constitutional heritage a more realistic recognition of the need for strong land-use regulations to further orderly development and protect natural, cultural, and aesthetic resources.

## Toward a More Adequate Resolution of the Takings Issue

Earlier cases struck down land-use regulations at a time when we had little knowledge of the interrelationships of land uses and their potential environmental impacts. It would be inconsistent with our constitutional tradition to adhere blindly to these past precedents now that we have better information. But how to get that information before the courts?

As long as each case interpreting the takings clause is decided by simply balancing the equities on each side, the information presented becomes crucial. Here, we believe, lies the crux of the problem. While a balancing process should, in theory, favor neither side; the landowner starts with a practical advantage. Balancing involves weighing the injury to the landowner against the gain to be achieved by the regulation. The landowner's injury is measured by the loss in land value, which is relatively easy to prove. Appraisers are available to testify to the value of the land before and after the challenged regulation, and typically there is little doubt that the regulation causes a substantial difference in value.

The government has a more difficult task. It must show the value to society of limiting development on a land area or saving a historic building. To do so, the government must relate the questioned regulation to the facts of the case and to unquantified values that will evoke the court's appreciation and sympathy. For this task, careful preparation and research are often necessary.

*Extensive case preparation is necessary to demonstrate the constitutional validity and public benefit of land-use regulations. To facilitate that preparation, the trend toward "environmental divisions" within the offices of state attorneys general and county and municipal attorneys should continue, and attorneys in these divisions should be urged to devote a substantial share of their efforts to land-use regulation.*

All too often, however, government attorneys cannot spare the time for the extensive preparation required. It is hard for the courts to strike a proper balance when a well-financed developer confronts an inadequately prepared government attorney. The recently formed Environmental Law Institute has already helped planning boards, corporation counsels, and other public bodies defend land-use controls. More sustained support and the creation of additional organizations are needed to provide such help on a continuing basis all across the country. *Existing non-profit organizations should be supported and appropriate additional organizations established that will provide government attorneys with the expert testimony, research assistance, and skilled tactical advice needed to prepare for important land-use cases.*

Foundations could support one or more institutions of this type. Financial assistance for research on the application of environmental law to land-use problems could be provided by the Research Applied to National Needs program of the National Science Foundation. Eventually, after such organizations are established, they should be financed by voluntary contributions from state and local governments in small annual amounts. These contributions would give contributing governments the right to use certain services when required. In effect, the state and local governments would be purchasing land-use case insurance.

The courts have always adapted constitutional principles to meet the needs of the times, and they no doubt will continue to do so. Judges as well as lawmakers at every level of government are becoming increasingly aware of the need for environmental protection, and this awareness will spur future adaptation. In the meantime, older court decisions continue to intimidate lawmakers in too many states and localities. Needed regulations are often not adopted for fear of adverse court decisions. Or the public need for tough environmental safeguards is left unsatisfied because of arguments that such regulation is impossible without massive payments to affected landowners—payments that are obviously unavailable in tight governmental budgets. *It is important that state and local legislative bodies adopt stringent planning and regulatory legislation whenever they believe it fair and necessary to achieve land-use objectives. This legislation, in addition to its direct benefits, can help to create a consensus that tight protective restrictions are valid and appropriate ways to achieve more orderly development and to protect natural, cultural, and aesthetic values.*

The doctrines applied by the courts need changes too.

Under the *Pennsylvania Coal* rule, the court weighs the public benefits to be achieved by a regulation against the harm threatened to the landowner. To manage this balancing process satisfactorily, the courts must have access to factual information necessary for understanding both the benefits and the harm. Too often, the courts are forced to make their decisions without adequate background.

The courts can begin to fill information deficiencies if they will acquire a healthy respect for the unknown. In the past ten years, story after story has appeared on the adverse effects of changes in land use that are recognized only after the fact. Pelicans died, and we learned that DDT was responsible. The edges of Lake Tahoe turned green, and we learned that storm water runoff from parking lots was the cause. Houses careened down hills in mudslides, and we learned that grading practices were responsible. There have been so many examples of unforeseen adverse consequences from changes in the natural ecosystem that the impact of these unknown consequences should be considered in a balancing of private and public interests.

*The courts should "presume" that any change in existing natural ecosystems is likely to have adverse consequences difficult to foresee. The proponent of the change should therefore be required to demonstrate, as well as possible, the nature and extent of any changes that will result.* Such a presumption would build into common law a requirement that a prospective developer who wishes to challenge a governmental regulation prepare a statement similar to the environmental impact statements now required of public agencies under federal programs.

Equally important is the need for the U.S. Supreme Court to reexamine its precedents that focus on the diminution of property values affected by regulations and seek to balance public benefit against land value loss in every case. We are aware of the sensitivity of this matter, and of the important issues of civil liberty associated with ownership of property. But it is worth remembering that when U.S. constitutional doctrine on the takings issue was formulated during the late nineteenth and early twentieth centuries, land was regarded as unlimited and its use not ordinarily of concern to society. Circumstances are different today.

The judiciary has accepted zoning to assure that incompatible land uses are segregated and controlled, although zoning can vastly increase or decrease the price of property. Zoning is based on the theory that the advantage to the whole of society (and in the end, therefore, to each owner of regulated property) more than compensates for any land value loss in an individual instance. Now, there is growing recognition of the need to see that urbanization proceeds in an orderly and non-destructive fashion and that our limited natural and cultural resources are conserved. These purposes should become as accepted as those carried out by zoning.

*It is time that the U.S. Supreme Court re-examine its earlier precedents that seem to require a balancing of public benefit against land value loss in every case and declare that when the protection of natural, cultural, or aesthetic resources or the assurance of orderly development are involved, a mere loss in land value will never be justification for invalidating the regulation of land use.* Such a re-examination is particularly appropriate considering the consensus that is forming on the need for a national land-use policy. Although fifty years have passed since the *Pennsylvania Coal* case, it is not too late to recognize that Justice Brandeis was right.

# Chapter V
# Creating What We Want:
# Regulating Development

In looking to the future, it is not enough to think only of protecting what we already have. Protection must be seen as part of a larger effort to create what we want in the neighborhoods, cities, and regions of the future. If urban regions are to be home for five-sixths of us by the end of the century, then the shaping of those regions must be put high among national priorities.

These future regions, which will be formed not only out of countryside but also out of today's cities, suburbs, and sprawling urban fringes, will shape peoples' lives well into the twenty-first century, and probably beyond. The regions will fall short of the mark if they achieve only functional efficiency and economic soundness. The creation of quality as well as needed quantity must be the goal.

Quality is marked by respect for human and natural values. It is harder to create quality than to preserve it, for creation requires more choices and its goals are inherently complicated. In conservation, quality values are readily translated into physical ideals and, in many cases, the ideals already exist—a community in harmony with its surroundings, a valley preserved in wilderness.

If the community or valley is instead to be transformed by development, there are no such convenient ideals. At what population level is there likely to be the greatest concern for the humanity of each inhabitant? Is it better that people live close together or far apart? That they walk to work, drive, be carried by mass transit, or perhaps by elevator within a futuristic megastructure? How much social contact should we aim for among people of different temperaments, incomes, races, and ethnic backgrounds?

No consensus exists on these issues, and none is likely to be forthcoming soon. A consensus may someday arise, most likely from a better understanding of the natural constraints on development imposed by pollution, resource limitations, and the innate needs of human beings and societies, but for the foreseeable future, the decisions that create and shape our communities and regions will continue to be made without ideal development patterns, social or physical.

Thus, creation, much more than preservation, must make peace with pluralism. The quest for quality development, which respects human values, must recognize that there is no agreement about what constitutes quality. Rather, the broadest possible range of individual choices and lifestyles must be accommodated. But even this guideline does not go far. With rapidly changing values and technology, which individual choices are long lasting and which are fleeting? As conditions change, how will individual choices change? (Would you live the same way if you worked only four days a week? If communications technology permitted you to do your job anywhere in the world?) What constraints on choice are necessary? Where must my choices be restricted to permit satisfaction of yours?

The contrast between conservation and creation is even clearer in relation to natural values. Many ideals of natural preservation can be stated as absolutes: clean air, pure water, unspoiled wilderness. Any program to achieve these goals obviously requires trade-offs. How much of the ideal can the nation afford? Who should pay? Which natural ideals or places are most important? Despite these difficulties, the ideal itself is clear. The distance between ideal and reality can often be measured, and there is the comfortable feeling that you would recognize the Promised Land if you should get there.

Development, no matter how respectful of nature, does not have the benefit of these absolutes. Its assertion of natural values comes, not in moving closer to an absolute, but in determining how far from it we must unavoidably fall. Or in determining how

178

far from it we *should* fall so that other, conflicting objectives may be achieved. Creation must, for example, focus less on unspoiled landscapes than on construction without "avoidable" grading or "needless" removal of natural vegetation. It must focus, in sum, less on prohibition than on sensitive accommodation and balance. And it needs, for success, people and institutions willing and able to seek those accommodations and strike those balances.

In most American communities, development has proceeded without many of these sensitive accommodations. Often it has seemed there was nothing to accommodate, since no one (or perhaps at most a handful of "malcontents" and "do-gooders") spoke up forcefully for quality.

Now, however, the new mood is making a difference. In a growing number of states and localities, citizens are expressing their unhappiness with what traditional development has done, is doing, or is threatening to do. Citizens in many places cannot be blamed for turning to an extreme preservationist position. The evidence in many communities seems to offer only two choices: bad development or no development. It is not surprising that more and more people are concluding that quality can best be maintained by stopping development altogether.

Many new mooders view development in the same narrow economic terms so often used to boost "progress" in the past. They see development as bringing more profits to builders and land speculators, more customers to the mayor's hardware store, and more real estate commissions to some of the members of the zoning board. And they are asking, "Who needs it?" Disregarding societal needs, they easily conclude that development is just another kind of pollution that causes congestion and destroys views.

Many builders and developers reinforce this view by defining their own responsibilities in narrow functional and economic terms. The responsibility of the state highway department, some believe, is simply to build highways where they are needed, as soon as they are needed, at the lowest possible cost. The only responsibility of the power authority is to furnish power, on demand, at the lowest possible cost. The homebuilder who builds homes, the oil company that builds gas stations, the landowner who sells land to them too often see their role as simply one of making money. They must satisfy any minimum quality standards they cannot get waived, but that is all.

*A new highway interchange in a rural area attracts surrounding develop-
ment on a scale that the rural jurisdiction may be ill-equipped to regulate.
Hence, the need for a regional or state agency to oversee development
around such growth-inducing facilities.*

"Real estate," as one dealer recently remarked, "is the last frontier. Only now people are thinking about getting up a posse." It is
often a frontier—where the risks are enormous, the stakes are
high, and the possibilities of quality easily trampled in the rush to
find gold at the edge of town. Posses are, indeed, now being
formed all across the land.

But posses can be a bit too rough and ready, missing the sub-
tleties that prove decisive when "law and order" have finally been
established. So it is perhaps understandable that some bands of
new mood adherents are interested less in delicate accommodation of development than in stopping it cold. Not in
power plant siting laws that allow all sides to be heard and contain strong protection for critical environmental lands but in
outright prohibition of power plants and refineries in coastal
zones. Not in careful siting of homes and highways to avoid earth-
moving, but in preventing urbanization and terminating highway
construction altogether. Not, in short, in sensitive refinements of
the kinds that urban planners and environmentalists have been

seeking for years, but in simply drawing a line and saying, "Stop. Enough."

The opportunity created by the new mood stems almost entirely from its growing power to draw that line and hold it. For that power means, in many places for the first time, that a counterforce has become strong enough to stand up to the juggernaut of development-as-usual.

We believe that the continuing confrontation of these conflicting forces presents an unprecedented opportunity to produce a badly needed synthesis: a synthesis of quality and quantity forces that will give us a more sensitive development process.

The synthesis is unlikely to arise where the new mood remains weak, where development-as-usual is still the rule, which is probably the case in most of the nation. It is equally unlikely to arise where the new mood virtually paralyzes development (or simply comes on too strong, as against low- and moderate-income housing or power plants). Or where both new mood and old mood are well represented but the institutional structure is incapable or unwilling to reconcile their differences creatively—where the choice remains one of bad development or none at all.

We need, therefore, to maintain a balance of power between

This site near an interchange attracted a regional shopping center.

the conflicting forces and to create institutional structures that can reconcile their differences so that we achieve quality development. If the forces of quantity are too weak, there will not be enough steam in the boiler. The result: no development. If the forces of quality are too weak, the developmental steam will leak out without ever reaching the turbine. The result: low quality development (perhaps scattered garden apartments and a few stores here and there, but no community). What is needed is a powerful head of steam and a strong protective wall and—the hardest part—devices to make sure the turbine works when the steam gets there.

In a country as varied as ours, there can be no uniform prescription for creating and maintaining that balance and establishing that institutional structure. The town where development continues as usual hardly needs the same prescription as the one where construction is virtually paralyzed. A huge city government with a sizable professional staff does not need the same institutions as a rural county or a small suburb with only a part-time clerk. But there are ways—through regulations, incentives, and the creation of special opportunities—to encourage the needed synthesis in towns and cities across the nation.

## Guiding Development at the Local Level

Since every project has impact beyond its own boundaries, governments have long acted to guide development. There are two approaches for relating development to its surroundings. One approach focuses on the proposed development, treating the surroundings as a dependent variable. ("We need a highway between A and B. Where and how shall we build it?") The second approach focuses on the surroundings and regards possible development as the variable. ("We have a pleasant neighborhood here and a woods over there. What kinds of development would be consistent with their continued enjoyment?") Both approaches must be used for a satisfactory accommodation between quality and quantity in development. Much depends, though, on how and when they are used and on how the results are combined in final development decisions.

The "development first" approach is the one used by most builders and developers, governmental as well as private. Quality controls can take this approach, too. The review of environmental impact statements, in which agencies publicly assess the effect of their proposals on the environment and present alternatives, is based on a development-first approach. So is the procedure used by thousands of localities to review proposed land subdivisions.

Zoning ordinances, on which most American localities have relied to achieve harmony between development and its surroundings, have grown out of the second, "surroundings first" approach. Early demands for zoning came from the wish to protect favored areas against incompatible development—to prevent garment factories from invading a fashionable retail district along New York's Fifth Avenue and to prevent commerce and industry from invading thousands of quiet residential neighborhoods. The original concern was defensive, focused on the place to be protected. The zoners did not start by considering society's need for garment factories, and then determine where those factories might best be located or how any undesirable impact on potential neighbors might best be minimized.

Even to accomplish their limited objectives of protecting selected places, the founders of zoning had a problem. They needed a mechanism that would be both convenient to administer and acceptable to the courts. They settled on having the local governing body establish protected zones within which specific regulations would prescribe prohibited or permitted development. But different parts of town had different characteristics, so more than one kind of zone was needed. In fact, for practical and legal reasons, it seemed wise to put the whole city into zones, with appropriate regulations for each.

Even today, zoning ordinances reflect these origins. Local ordinances contain an official zoning map that places every piece of land in the city into a zone. For each zone, the ordinance text prescribes a different set of regulations to govern development. All these rules, restricting development in great detail, are established at the time the ordinance is adopted—and, thus, without knowledge of whether, when, where, or what kind of development may later be needed or proposed.

How well does this system work?

## A Citizen's Guide to Zoning

Assume you are a town councilman responsible for fashioning land-use controls for a country town. Where would you start? Presumably, with some kind of planning. You would figure out some objectives and then try to determine the impact of the ob-

183

jectives on different places in town. If one objective was to protect important natural areas and processes, you might do a land capacity analysis, identifying swamps and floodplains that should not be developed at all and other areas which could take varying amounts of development. If one objective was to protect the integrity of established residential neighborhoods, you would identify areas not to be invaded by factories or highways or drive-in hamburger stands. If one objective was to provide an adequate transportation network, you might decide where a new state highway should go—but not without difficulty if you discovered that it had to go through either an established neighborhood or a protected swamp. Still, you could make some decisions fairly confidently, enough so that most people in town would accept them.

You would be surest of your decisions to protect something nice. ("That's a pleasant neighborhood, and it shouldn't be changed.") If development within the nice area was uniform, so much the better: you could just require new development to be like what was already there. ("All the houses over there have a 12-foot yard on each side, so I guess new houses ought to be the same.") Although you might see room for improving the simplistic rules generally used to determine what is compatible ("You mean a new house would fit in even without a 12-foot yard?"), you would find the zoning process at its best in those places where the dominant public need is protection of an area already substantially developed. This is no surprise, since protection is what the originators of zoning had in mind.

Outside the limited areas to be protected against virtually all change, you would have much more difficulty fashioning regulations. Developers and builders, not the town government, would be exercising development initiative, and you would know little about either the demand or the supply side of their development equations over time. How many people are likely to want to move into town? When? What kinds of homes will they want to live in and be able to afford? Will they be willing to live in that scruffy area by the highway, or will they insist on living somewhere in the country? Which landowner will be willing to make his land available for development at a reasonable price? When, if ever, will the legislature appropriate the state funds needed to build the highway? You could make some estimates about the answers, but you could not be certain about them.

Having planned ahead as well as you could, how would you get developers and builders to pay attention to your plans? Take the highway, for example. Perhaps you decide it ought to go through the established neighborhood, or perhaps through the swamp, or perhaps you lose your nerve and mark one route "alternate A" and the other "alternate B." You exercise your judgment, adopt the plan, and wait. You know that, if the state ever goes ahead with the highway, the route location will be re-examined. By that time, new rules may make disruption of the neighborhood impossible or may prohibit putting highways in swamps. Or the engineering study may show that the swamp is impassable.

The procedures for controlling highway location respond fairly well to these unavoidable uncertainties. The highway, if built at all, will use a combination of state and federal funds. You know that state and federal laws require hearings on the proposed route location as well as an environmental impact statement if the project will affect the environment significantly. You know that your plan will be considered at the hearings, as will the views of neighborhood residents, swamp enthusiasts, and town and state officials. You may not be wholly confident about the values that will prevail after considerable airing of views, perhaps suspecting that the highway is valued more highly than either the neighborhood or the swamp. But for highways, at least, there is a definite procedure for dealing with the uncertainties of planning, for considering all viewpoints, for exploring developmental and environmental needs, and for finally reaching a decision.

For private development of private land, the procedures are less satisfactory. Suppose, for example, that your land capacity analysis shows that the dairy farms surrounding the town could hold as many as 90,000 people without exceeding natural limits, but no one expects even 2,000 people to move to town. Nevertheless, you decide to plan for 2,000. Where will you put them? Should they be scattered evenly over the dairy-farm land, or should they be clustered on one or two farms? If the latter, which farms? Suppose the town could get a new factory or two that would employ the 2,000 people if they did come. Where among the ten physically suitable sites should a factory go, if you could get it? Any number of alternatives might be satisfactory, and you find yourself without a rational basis for prescribing which are best. You are at least as uncertain about these as you were about the highway, and probably more so.

To make private developers and builders pay attention to your plans you almost have to adopt a zoning ordinance. Unlike high-way review, zoning is not well adapted to the uncertainties of planning. You are in a quandary, for example, when you must establish regulations for the ten possible factory sites and for the dairy-farm land when you honestly do not know yet what ought to go there. To adopt the zoning ordinance, though, you must in-dicate at the time of adoption just how each bit of land in the whole town may be used. And you must make such a prescription even for those areas where you have no rational basis for one. What do you do? There are several options.

*Zoning option 1: "When in doubt, let 'em do it."* Under this op-tion, you do not restrict unless you are fairly confident about how the land should be used. Where you are confident, as in estab-lished neighborhoods to be protected against change, you es-tablish tight restrictions. But in areas where some change is desirable, but you are not sure what kind of change should occur, you resolve uncertainty in favor of unfettered use. With only a few limitations, you let the market operate. You might, for example, put all ten of those possible factory sites in industrial zones. You might put all the dairy farms in residential zones, conceivably at a density that would permit all 90,000 people. The land along all possible highway routes might be zoned commercial because you undoubtedly will want stores along there somewhere. Ordinances adopted long ago, and ordinances of localities where development pressures are slight, often reflect a preference for this option.

With experience, though, option 1 looks less and less attractive. The zoning for the 90,000 people comes to be called "overzoning." You never expected all those people to turn up; you had just been honest enough to avoid regulation when you had little idea of what regulations to establish. Unfortunately, the loose rules turn out to permit scattered development. Perhaps a subdivision is created for 120 families on quarter-acre lots out there amidst the phantom 90,000, and eight families actually build houses, so you have to run the school bus out there to pick up the children. No factories ever came, but somebody built a drive-in on one of the factory sites since the industrial zoning permitted commercial uses as well. Now there are rumors that a fellow has bought up 1,200 acres and might subdivide all of them into quarter-acre lots; who knows what the school taxes would be if people built on all of them?

What you learn from experience with option 1 is that random

scattering of development, even if it leaves the protected no-change areas alone, creates problems. You come to recognize a public interest in guiding the nature, timing, and location of development. You see that the public interest suffers because of your inability to do what the zoning process seems to demand: to prescribe a particular use for each parcel of land at the time a zoning ordinance is adopted. So you look around for another option.

*Zoning option 2: "Pretend that you know best."* Under this option, you act more confident than your planning process warrants. Although your uncertainty persists, you know that developers may propose projects inconsistent with the public interest, so you make prescriptions as best you can. Perhaps you decide to plan for two factories, and you decide that two of the possible factory sites are better than the other eight. You put those two sites into industrial zones (even though you would jump at the chance to get light industry anywhere). You decide that an additional population of 2,000 is optimum and that all 2,000 persons should be put on the two dairy farms nearest to town, with the land divided into lots of at least 20,000 square feet with 14-foot side yards.

Option 2 significantly reduces the range within which the market may distribute development: only two factory sites and two dairy farms instead of the number that existed before. Then what happens?

If the supply of sites designated for development proves to be generous in relation to demand, you may experience the same problems of scattering that you had with option 1.

But, if the site supply proves more limited than demand, you may have created something like a monopoly in developable land. You might drive up the prices of the factory sites, for example. Or, if you had decided that the town needed one shopping center and had foolishly designated only one site for it on the zoning map, you could well have driven the land price so high that no developer could touch it.

In either case, though, your very nearly arbitrary designations are likely to be rescinded or changed later, when development nears. Because you want light-industry, when somebody proposes to build a factory, you rush to change the rules so he can build at his chosen site. In itself, this retreat may well be desirable. Unfortunately, it confuses onlookers who did not know that the

187

decision was arbitrary in the first place. That leads to serious trouble. Your rational decisions become confused with the arbitrary ones. Sooner or later, changes are made even in rules that did have a sound basis (like those for protecting natural areas or established neighborhoods). Before long, both the planning and regulatory processes come to be seen as phony, simply responses to the whims of the power structure and not the result of rational analysis of public needs.

Under option 2, the crudeness of regulations for permitted development often forces you to choose between providing insufficient protection and imposing needless constraints. You find it hard to write rules that distinguish between a well-maintained animal hospital and one that you would drive out of the way to avoid hearing and smelling. Or to distinguish between a little Mom-and-Pop drug store and a giant cut-rate outlet that brings cars from all over the county. And you know that landscaping and building design could make some prohibited activities perfectly compatible with their surroundings. In effect, your pre-established rules are based on what will *probably* be compatible with what will *probably* be built. The system is not unlike an old-time traffic signal that regulates traffic flow on the basis of probable future traffic volume, without benefit of sensors that permit adaptation of the controls to what people in fact want to do.

What you learn from experience with option 2 is the difference between planning ahead and making detailed prescriptions ahead. Your plans for the future are necessarily based on estimates and probabilities. Sometimes those estimates warrant deciding in advance about the nature or location of planned new development, even though there is a risk that the estimates may turn out to be erroneous. (You might, for example, prohibit construction in the planned highway right-of-way, even though you know there is only a small probability that the highway will ever be built.) At other times, though, you recognize that advance decision-making will not achieve your objective and may prohibit construction that would be harmless or even beneficial to the community. The public objectives are so complicated, and the possible development combinations so numerous, and your vision of the future so inevitably limited, that you become hesitant to prescribe much in advance. You become aware, in short, of the risks involved in trying to decide too much too soon—and you look around for another option.

*Zoning option 3: "Wait till you see what happens."* Under this option, you turn away from detailed preregulation of new development and instead rely more on administrative review of development proposals, retaining the discretion to say yes or no until you have reviewed the proposal. Thus do you begin to transform the traditional surroundings-first approach of zoning into the development-first approach exemplified by environmental impact statements and subdivision regulations. (Perhaps the principal thrust of local land-use controls during the past quarter century has been this shift away from reliance on predetermined requirements and toward reliance on discretionary review at the time development is proposed.)

You have numerous possible discretionary mechanisms to choose among. Architectural review gives you discretionary review of the appearance of permitted buildings. Site plan review lets you review site layouts. Planned unit development provisions let you review layouts of large projects and, in exchange, let developers arrange permitted development with more flexibility than typical lot and building requirements would permit.

More far-reaching devices give discretion to determine, on a case-by-case basis, what or how much may be built. Under "special use permit" provisions, for example, designated uses are permitted if they receive specific approval. Depending on the ordinance, the "special uses" may include a handful of particularly important activities (airports or public utilities, for example) or they may include everything other than houses in a residential zone.

None of these provisions is likely to help with your uncertainties about the ten possible industrial sites or the dairy farms. There are a few discretionary devices you could use. Some towns have established so-called floating zones, authorized in the text of the ordinance but not mapped until a specific development is proposed and approved. Other towns have established standards to govern future amendments to the zoning map.

If you ask around, though, you will probably be told that none of these approaches is necessary or, given the ever-present danger that legislative innovation will invite litigation, desirable. So you probably decide, following the example of countless other communities, to employ the rule "when in doubt, prohibit." You put the more attractive industrial sites and the undeveloped dairy farms in a very low density agricultural or residential zone, thereby prohibiting virtually all construction. Anyone who wants to build or develop there will have to ask for a change in the zoning map. You then have the chance to evaluate his project and to hear what the other townspeople think at a public hearing.

In brief, this approach lets you deal with development problems when they arise. You have the opportunity to look over plans in detail and make suggestions. If proposed new residential development on the dairy farms would drive up school taxes too much, you could wonder out loud about having more one-bedroom apartments than three-bedroom ones, and you might indicate that the donation of a grade school building by the developer would be a welcome good-will offering to a town about to receive a lot of newcomers. If the applicant says no, then you can decline to amend the map, and the prohibition will remain in effect.

Having learned your lesson about not deciding too much too soon, you are now in a position to wait until more of the facts are in, to consider the alternatives carefully, and to produce a quality community. Right? Wrong. Any number of problems still arise.

First, there are the familiar problems arising out of the small scale at which development occurs. When you get a request for a small-scale change in the map, you may be as unsure about how to respond to it as you were about how to establish regulations in advance of development. The problem is most acute with small-scale changes proposed for open country or for "edge of town uses" that seek freedom from in-town restrictions. Suppose a landowner applies for commercial rezoning for one site so he can build a drive-in. No other development is nearby, and you have no idea yet whether anything else will be built near the site. As things stand, the drive-in would not hurt anything, and the landowner is a nice fellow, but if the whole area were to be developed, or if a series of drive-ins were to go in, you and most of the townsfolk would not like it. The conventional wisdom says (usually correctly) that you should avoid such "spot zoning." But you just are not sure.

Second, there are serious problems arising from the mechanics of zoning, which were established on the assumption that the rules would be determined in advance, not on a case-by-case negotiated basis. The most important of the resulting problems is one encountered before: that of misleading the public by appearing to make a decision you did not actually make. Perhaps some of the dairy farms have been zoned agricultural with the fixed intention of agricultural preservation, while others, although they are similarly zoned, are not covered by any such firm intention. Perhaps you are not sure what should happen to them, or perhaps you intend to permit development the moment a halfway decent proposal is presented. A resulting zoning change often confuses and misleads citizens—and perhaps your successors on the council or even yourself a few years later—as to the intent of the original decision. This confusion is harmful to the cause of quality development. Citizens naturally feel angry and betrayed when you approve development by changing zoning they thought was permanent.

Another problem, also related to the gulf between option 3 and the original assumptions of zoning, arises when a developer presents handsome plans of what he proposes to build to get a zoning change and then cheats and builds something that complies with the letter of the changed regulation but not with the drawings he presented. You may not be able to stop him. There are ways to prevent this cheating, such as conditional rezoning or rezoning in conjunction with a planned unit development approval, but the legality of some of these techniques may not have been confirmed in your area. Still, the problem arises because the originators of zoning did not expect you to do what you and thousands of others like you are, in fact, routinely doing under option 3.

Fourth, there are the problems—by far the most serious and fundamental—caused by a lack of trust in the decision-making process and the decision-makers themselves. Option 3 amounts to *ad hoc* decision-making under standards that are very general (if they exist at all). In the best of circumstances, this kind of decision-making is not likely to work without well prepared plans, alternative proposals, and a forum in which all points of view may be presented to qualified decision-makers. An understaffed (or nonexistent) planning department, an impecunious applicant, and some threatened neighbors, all presenting views to public officials who probably must squeeze their unpaid public service into their spare time, do not add up to a decision-making process that inspires confidence. And added to that are the common accusations of incompetence, conflict of interest, and even corruption among the decision-makers.

For these reasons, many citizens who look to land-use controls for protection against unwanted development are dead set against dependence on *ad hoc* procedures and discretionary review. They want rigid protective rules and safeguards against changing them. They point to "fast-talking" developers who mislead officials and neighbors into thinking development will be nicer than it proves to be. They point to the decades of experience with zoning variances (the grandfather of all development review mechanisms), which, despite legislation and repeated judicial decisions restricting variances to "hardship" cases, have been used in some communities as a free-ranging device to "punch holes" in the zoning. Discretionary review, these people conclude, does not produce quality.

If you conclude that none of the options can achieve quality in new development, you may decide that most development should simply be prohibited. You may then find yourself using option 3 to do in substance what you previously did only in form: prohibit more and more. What gradually drops from sight is that development, including development initiated by private developers and builders, confers essential public benefits.

How can the regulatory process be modified to produce the quality development we need and want? Would it be better to rely less on process, to go back instead to a system more like the one contemplated by the originators of zoning? We think not. Option 1, with its few restrictions, is acceptable only where the public largely trusts the market to create acceptable quality. Option 2, with its rigid mold that the market is to fill up in its own time on a scattered basis, requires trust in the ability of planners and regulators to prescribe the future in some detail. Trust in a virtually unfettered market or in human prescience seems to us to be trust misplaced.

Option 3, with its discretionary procedures that replace the mold, also requires trust—trust in a continuing process of policy-making, planning, and decision-making, trust that this process can reconcile conflicting needs and policies, public as well as private, long-term as well as short, for protection as well as for development. Although this trust, too, is in short supply today, we are confident that it can be restored. To restore it, two needs must be fulfilled. First, we need a trustworthy regulatory mechanism. Second, we need trustworthy institutions to operate it. Both may be within reach.

## The Search for a Trustworthy Regulatory Mechanism

Private projects are not the only ones for which governments have had to provide guidance. Our traditions call for governments themselves to build expressways, transit lines, airports, dams, universities, hospitals, sewage treatment plants, and much more. Although these projects present enormous potential for creating a higher level of urban quality (not only directly, in the facilities themselves, but also indirectly, in impact on surroundings), these opportunities have routinely been lost. The government office building that could have strengthened an urban center has popped up in the boondocks where land was cheaper. The sewage treatment plant that could have attracted development to a planned location has been installed instead at another site that the sewer authority found more convenient. The rich agricultural bottomlands, unavailable for urbanization as long as they were floodable, succumbed to unplanned development after a dam was built. Instead of helping to solve urban growth problems, governmental projects are often part of them.

At the heart of the problems is the frame of reference of governmental development agencies and, ultimately, of the public. For these agencies, quite as much as private developers, have judged their performance primarily in functional and economic terms. How many miles of new highway? How many cars moved and with what safety record? How much state money spent? Although the agencies have power to look beyond their own assigned functions, power to respond to human, natural, and aesthetic values, they have not usually defined their missions in those broader terms. And neither, by and large, have overseeing legislators and budget bureaus and citizen watchdog groups. Developmental values have prevailed.

Having defined their missions in roughly the same terms as private developers, the governmental development agencies have encountered continuing efforts to bring their projects into line with broader objectives. Incentives and requirements have been imposed to promote consideration of human, natural, and aesthetic values. Examples include: the relocation payments guaranteed to displaced residents by the federal Uniform Relocation Assistance Act; the requirements in the 1966 Department of Transportation Act that parkland and historic properties not be taken for transportation projects without formal findings that there is no prudent and feasible alternative to the taking; and the "3 percent money" for highway beautification, whereby a portion of highway project funds may be spent on making the right-of-way more attractive.

Even more ambitious regulatory measures have sought to look beyond individual projects and functions to whole cities and regions. Planning requirements are among the most common. Many states followed the Standard City Planning Enabling Act (model legislation released in 1928), enabling municipalities to require planning commission approval for certain public works —streets, parks, public structures, and utilities. In recent years, a series of planning requirements has been established for facilities receiving federal aid, including a requirement that governmental units possibly affected by the project be notified of the plans and given an opportunity to comment. (The "A-95 circular" issued by the federal Office of Management and Budget establishes regional and metropolitan clearinghouses for this purpose.)

The success of such measures as regional clearinghouses and the "continuing comprehensive transportation planning process" required for metropolitan areas receiving highway money has been varied. The simpler and more easily enforced measures (such as relocation payments) have come closer to achieving their objectives than measures involving complex value judgments or those whose impact cannot be easily measured. The most ambitious planning efforts, those seeking to fulfill multiple functions and multiple objectives, have often fallen farthest short of their goals.

The reasons are not hard to find. The technical problems of coordination, time constraints, staffing, and technical expertise are severe and involve development and administrative agencies at every level of government. The state highway department, the county department of public works, the airport authority, the university, the Army Corps of Engineers—each has its own responsibilities, constraints, and operating patterns. In those states and localities where governmental structure gives little power to chief executives, or where development funds are guaranteed by earmarked trust funds, some agencies are free to set their own objectives as well.

Planning agencies, charged with the task of fitting projects into a broader and longer-range context, have been conspicuously weak when confronted by big-spending, politically influential development agencies. Most regional planning agencies have suffered from an additional disability. Their role is an advisory one at best, for they lack the authority that would come from operating under an elected government. And, at all levels, planners' methods have too seldom enabled them to demonstrate persuasively that their prescriptions would be worth the extra public money they might cost.

Most development agencies continue to define their missions very largely in functional and economic terms. Measures intended to achieve broader objectives often come from outsiders, from planners or others, and are viewed by many agencies as constraints on the performance of the agency's "real" mission. Agencies have naturally tried to fight free of these constraints and, in a developmental era, they have been largely successful.

Until recently, then, public efforts to guide single-focus governmental development toward broader public objectives have often proven quite as unsuccessful as efforts to guide single-focus private development. And this despite the differences in the guidance mechanisms used. The case-by-case review of governmental projects did not seem to work any better than the preregulation applied (in theory at least) to private projects.

## The Best Mechanism So Far: Environmental Impact Analysis

Now, the balance between single-focus development and broader public objectives is beginning to change. One of the key reasons is the environmental impact statement, required by the National Environmental Policy Act of 1969 (NEPA) for each major federal action that significantly affects the environment.[1]

NEPA requires federal agencies to file with the Council on Environmental Quality (CEQ) an impact statement for all major actions, including proposed legislation, regulations and procedures, policy determinations, and proposed projects, expected to significantly affect the quality of the environment. (CEQ guidelines supplement the statutory requirements.) Impact statements must include:

—a detailed description of the proposed action;

—a discussion of direct and indirect effects on the environment that may result from the action;

—identification of unavoidable adverse environmental effects;

*A mobile home park built in an inland waterway north of Stuart, Florida, shows one response to the widespread desire for a waterfront lot.*

—an assessment of feasible alternatives to the proposed action;
—a description of cumulative and long-term effects of the action on the earth's resources;
—identification of any irreversible commitment of resources that might result from the action.

The statement is prepared by the agency involved, first as a draft statement for review by other federal bodies, local agencies, and the general public, and then, with comments from these sources incorporated, as a final statement for the CEQ. In the normal course of events, this process offers interested parties the opportunity to identify problems and propose modifications to proposals.

During its three-year life, NEPA and the provision requiring impact statements have often been in the news. Courts have interpreted the act in several important cases:

—In *Wilderness Society v. Hickel,* three conservation organizations were granted a preliminary injunction against issuance of right-of-way and special use permits for the construction of the 800-mile-long pipeline from Prudhoe Bay to Valdez, Alaska.[2] In granting the injunction, the District Court in 1970 cited failure to comply with NEPA and with the right-of-way requirements of the Mineral Leasing Act of 1920.

—A Maryland citizens' group brought suit against the Atomic Energy Commission to prevent construction of a proposed nuclear power plant on Chesapeake Bay and, more generally, to test the adequacy of the Atomic Energy Commission's (AEC) guidelines for implementation of NEPA.[3] The court found the AEC's regulations deficient in four major respects, notably in the agency's leaving assessment of the potential environmental impact of nuclear plants to state and other federal agencies. The court further ruled that the AEC must consider environmental factors beyond just radiological health and safety.

—Two conservationists brought suit against the secretary of the Army, the administrator of the Environmental Protection Agency, and the chief of the Army Corps of Engineers for failing to comply with the impact statement requirements when issuing permits to discharge into navigable waters.[4] The court's decision went against the government, concluding that each permit could require an environmental impact statement.

NEPA has been controversial from its start. Proposals are continually made to limit its scope and, occasionally, to repeal altogether the section that requires impact statements or to exempt actions from its application. Certainly no one should claim that the process is working without snags or that all the complaints about it are inaccurate. Environmental reviews are occasionally costly and time consuming. Important projects have been delayed and some whole programs temporarily paralyzed because of noncompliance with statement requirements. The agencies—and even more the citizen groups that play a critical role in making the process work—often do not have all the resources needed to prepare or evaluate statements. Needed facts and figures are often unavailable, and plans and policies to serve as a basis for project evaluation are almost invariably lacking.

But impact statements have demonstrated that both public and private developers will respond to restrictive pressures and public scrutiny by increasing developmental quality. The results can be dramatic: in Illinois, a new community was redesigned to preserve an 800-acre hardwood forest after a federal environmental agency raised a question with HUD; in Georgia, a highway was realigned to avoid major harm to a lake; in California, a flood-protection project was modified to preserve a wildlife habitat; in Kentucky, a proposed dam was moved several miles downstream to preserve a scenic area; and so on.

Some of the most serious difficulties to date, we believe, should be attributed to start-up problems. It is understandable that many agencies were not equipped to handle a process that arose suddenly. It is equally understandable that officials in many development agencies did not believe (or could not accept) that familiar ground rules for review of their projects had changed fundamentally overnight. It seems likely, though, that many problems will be overcome as agencies decide to plan in advance to meet the new requirements instead of hoping that massive foul-ups will cause relaxation or repeal of the legislation.

We are aware that the very acceptance of the process may be accompanied by a sort of bureaucratic fossilization that could destroy its early promise. Nevertheless, we believe the potential to be enormous, for two main reasons.

First, the statements provide a tool, so far a reasonably effective tool, for influencing the day-to-day workings of development bureaucracies. Project proposals must be aired in advance, publicly, in a context that invites critical evaluation. Comments from citizen groups and from other bureaucracies, whose objections might previously have gone unheard or been quietly disregarded, must be made public. Citizen-initiated lawsuits provide the all-important back-up. Already, important benefits have resulted. In a few agencies, at least, some changes in thinking appear to have come simply from contact with the new staff members or consultants hired to prepare the statements.

Second, and ultimately more important, the statement requirement implicitly establishes a higher standard of conduct for development agencies. Agency decisions must respond to the particular situation in which the agency proposes to act. New standards must thus be internalized by the agency rather than imposed in each case by outsiders. Nor can the agency discharge its responsibility simply by establishing a set of unvarying minimum standards. It must consider a broad spectrum of public objectives and respond to the alternatives available in each particular situation.

This standard is indeed demanding. No longer is it sufficient for an airport construction agency, for example, to assure that airport noise does not exceed the decibel levels prescribed by somebody's noise regulation. Nor is it enough to assure that the noise will not be dangerous to health or will not disrupt normal conversations in living rooms at a distance of 1,000 meters. In addition to satisfying minimum standards such as these, the agency must also ask how quiet the airport could reasonably be and how much each noise reduction would cost. And it must make a judgment about how much of that extra quality is worth the cost.

Despite its breadth, the spectrum of public objectives considered during most reviews of environmental impact statements is still not broad enough. In practice, review too often concentrates more on natural values than on human ones—more on fish than on people. In the case of a subsidized housing development, for example, sedimentation of nearby streams may be considered in more detail than improvement in the lives of the residents. We would hope the review process would be used to enhance public awareness of social impact rather than, intentionally or not, to divert attention from it.

A few federal agencies have established procedures for assessing social impact. The Department of Transportation, for example, requires that the impact on persons who would be displaced by a proposed project be considered. Other agencies might consider similar adjustments. Proposed CEQ guideline revisions in 1973 call for statements to include "an indication of what other interests and considerations of Federal policy are thought to offset the adverse environmental effects."

## Statement Review: Designing a Process to Withstand Incompetence, Malevolence, and Obstruction

The issues that come up in review of an environmental impact statement are so all-embracing, the objectives so broad, and the data needs so virtually limitless that the review process must be adapted to stay within the bounds of administrative feasibility. Unless these bounds are respected, the administrative burden could easily overwhelm the limited number of qualified and concerned people available to participate in the review process, especially the small bands of citizens who help stave off bureaucratization. (Cynics suggest that some development agencies may already be increasing the length and number of their statements with intent to overwhelm.) If this were to happen, the review process could degenerate into a complex ritual, costly and time consuming, but progressively less able to influence action. Even more than at present, the process could then be used to justify development decisions rather than to re-examine them, and its principal beneficiaries could be those concerned less with quality than with obstruction.

One way to streamline the review process is comprehensive planning. Planners can systematically acquire and present data now being obtained on a crash, project-by-project basis. By exploring alternatives in advance, and by offering reasons for preferred courses of action, planners can provide a sounder basis for development decisions, including more persuasive answers to criticisms raised during statement review.

Indeed, one of the most beneficial effects of the statement requirement may be a growing recognition by development agencies of their need for comprehensive planning. The most useful planning arises out of someone's need to make a decision and his realization that he is unequipped to do so. Required by NEPA to answer a flock of complicated new questions, development agencies find themselves with just that planning need. Planning then is seen less as an unwelcome constraint on agency decision-making and more as a potentially powerful aid in surmounting the formidable obstacles of impact statement review.

*Planning agencies at all levels of government should take an active part in the review of environmental impact statements and should adapt their planning processes to assist the preparation and review of statements. Comprehensive plans in environmental impact review should be used as vehicles of persuasion and evaluation, not as binding or unquestioned determinations.*

A second way to keep the administrative burden within bounds is to limit the number and kinds of actions subject to review. Available review resources need to be concentrated on the important actions, for which environmental impact assessment is so beneficial, and diverted away from the less important ones, which are so numerous that review procedures are easily reduced to meaningless paper shuffling. Federal impact statement require-

200

*This disaster occurred as a consequence of a mudslide. Impact analysis would have indicated that development here would be hazardous.*

ments are intended to apply only to "major" actions "significantly" affecting the environment. The bureaucratic tendency to play it safe has led some agencies to require environmental clearances for thousands of projects that prove too insignificant to warrant full-fledged statements. (The same tendency has led some to shy away from projects whose opponents assert environmental objections, even dubious ones.)

There is understandable reluctance to declare actions "insignificant," especially if some environmental damage may in fact result from them. And there are definite risks in establishing clear and precise criteria concerning size or impact minimums below which projects do not require statements. Little-noticed changes in criteria could be misused to exempt important projects from review. Development agencies could distort their operating practices to avoid review. ("Cut this back to 499 units. If we have 500, we'll have to do an impact statement.")

Despite the risks, we need refined means for identifying actions and issues important enough to warrant environmental impact statements—and other means for dealing with less important projects. Perhaps experience will show that projects of certain kinds or sizes, or in certain locations, are so unlikely to cause damage that blanket exemption is warranted. Perhaps some projects should be exempted if they comply with adopted, detailed plans, despite the danger that plans may have been adopted far in advance of development and may thus have failed to arouse public concern. Some needs will have to be satisfied by minimum standards, even though that approach will never achieve optimum protection. In short, there is ample room for experimentation.

*As agencies gain experience with environmental impact statement requirements, they should seek increasingly refined ways to identify the actions and issues important enough to warrant such review. Plans, minimum standards, or other criteria that assure some alternative control over the less important actions may prove most acceptable.*

Streamlining can also be accomplished by establishing procedures for licensing and project review in which any disapproval of one development proposal must be accompanied, in the same proceeding, by approval of an alternative. At present, although project reviewers may consider alternatives in an impact statement, they are usually asked only for a yes or no decision. Should this proposed power plant be permitted at this proposed location? If the answer is no, the reviewer may be under no obligation (indeed, he often has no power) to answer the next questions: Is there need for the proposed project? Should the need be satisfied by development somewhere else? If so, where? At an alternative site described in the statement? At some unmentioned site that a more thorough analysis would turn up?

Lacking a procedure to obtain answers to these questions, the proponent has no choice but to resort to a succession of individual project applications. Rejection of the first application brings forth a second, which, if also rejected, brings forth a third. Each successive proposal flushes out a different group of opponents who, because of the decision-making structure, are able to deplore the proposal in isolation, without confronting the opponents of the previous proposal or of the next one. Thus, even if each proposal is an alternative means of fulfilling the same development need, each can be separately opposed, rejected, and litigated.

The delays resulting from these successive proceedings can be devastating, especially if each is litigated through the appellate courts. More fundamentally damaging, both to the substance of decisions and to the level of public debate and understanding, is the failure of today's partial proceedings to create awareness of whole issues. Neighbors may perhaps be excused when they demand that the proposed power plant or heavy industry be put elsewhere, without specifying where. But decision-makers and the public generally must recognize that this is a cop-out that leaves key questions unanswered. The need for development must be weighed against the detriments of each alternative way to satisfy the need and, if the need is important enough, one alternative must be authorized.

Any number of practical issues will have to be resolved to make such a review mechanism effective:

—To what kinds of proposals should it apply? Proposed power plants are a prime candidate. So are projects to dispose of garbage and sewage sludge from major cities, if only because compelling arguments can usually be raised against all feasible options. But how much further should the principle be extended? Should it extend to any private projects not traditionally considered to have special claim on the public interest (oil refineries, for instance)? Should the mechanism be mandatory for certain kinds of development or merely available on request of a proponent or review body?

—How can limited geographical jurisdiction be overcome? What should happen, for example, if the "right" location is in another community or another state? We have little doubt that higher levels of government will soon have to respond to such intercommunity and interstate problems.

—How are the alternatives to be identified and evaluated? Proponents of a project should not be relied upon to make the case for alternatives originally rejected (especially the case that the proposed project is unneeded and that nothing should be done). Many review agencies share the developmental values of the proponents. Neighbors and citizen groups often lack the necessary expertise to make their points effectively. Surely a much more extensive planning process must be established. But who should do it? Should public environmental defenders be established in addition? The problem becomes especially difficult when a development proposal is approved by an administrative

When these hotels were constructed in Miami Beach, there was considerably more beach than there is today. Sound regulations sensitive to environmental needs could have kept construction well back from the shoreline. Even today, however, regulations in many areas do not prohibit beach encroachment. The luxury condominium project below was built last year.

review agency and that approval is later contested in the courts.

The most important response so far to this set of problems is contained in the power plant siting act proposed by the Nixon Administration. The bill would establish state or regional certifying agencies to evaluate the long-range plans of electric utilities and to approve power plant facilities prior to construction. The legislation would require utilities to publish annually their ten-year plans for system expansion. Specific sites and distribution routes would be identified five years before construction began, and, to allow adequate time for public comment and court review, applications for approval of new power plants and transmission lines would be submitted three to five years before construction. Certifying agencies would be responsible for assessing potential environmental impacts of these facilities in accordance with NEPA and for granting approval or disapproval within eighteen months of application.

*For power plants and other critical development, project review procedures should be modified so that disapproval of one development proposal must be accompanied, in the same proceeding, by approval of an alternative (or abandonment of the project if need cannot be satisfactorily demonstrated). A much more thorough planning process is needed for this purpose as well as review agencies with larger geographical jurisdictions. Passage of the proposed power plant siting legislation would be an important step toward fulfilling this need.*

## Statements for State, Local, and Private Actions

Development projects undertaken by the federal government are only one of many kinds of activities subject to environmental impact review. The law requires a statement for federal actions significantly affecting the environment, and the term "actions" has been broadly construed. It includes, for example, approval of a federal permit or license, a grant-in-aid, or a proposal for legislation.

The practical result is that many state and local projects are subject to impact statements. A federal agency that grants financial aid for a state-built highway, for example, must prepare a statement if the highway will have a significant environmental impact. The federal agency, in turn, is likely to ask the state to help with the statement, so the state agency finds itself assembling much of the needed information.

Environmental impact review (where there is no similar state legislation) is governed by the accident of federal participation. A state project receiving federal aid is subject to review. A nearby project of equal or greater importance without federal participation is not.

Several states have now acted, by statute or executive order, to require statements for their own actions, regardless of federal involvement. Washington, Delaware, California, Wisconsin, Hawaii, and North Carolina have various forms of environmental impact statement requirements. So does the Commonwealth of Puerto Rico. Some state requirements, though not all, extend to significant actions of local governments as well.

An environmental review process at the state level analogous to that required of federal agencies is desirable, for it is the nature and importance of proposed actions, rather than the identity of the actor, that ought to determine the scope of review. State review becomes even more important with the enactment of revenue-sharing. Whereas before federal agencies were responsible for satisfying NEPA's requirements in administering categorical grant programs, now, if no similar mechanism exists on the state level, the hard-won environmental objectives embodied in NEPA are in danger of being ignored.

*States should enact legislation, modeled on federal environmental law, requiring environmental impact statements in connection with major actions of state and local governments that significantly affect the environment.*

Private projects, like those of governments, are subject to environmental impact review if they depend on federal action. The granting of federal financial guarantees for a new community, for example, or a dredge-and-fill permit for a shorefront hotel, may bring the requirement into play. Under some state laws, moreover, a state or local permit for an environmentally significant private project can also require a statement. (The highest court of California recently upheld this position in *Friends of Mammoth v. Mono County.*)

Since local permits are required for virtually any development, these laws and interpretations could effectively require statements for all significant projects. As long as the requirement is limited to genuinely significant projects, we think this desirable. Major shopping centers, industrial complexes, and new communities, for example, have more impact on regional growth than many governmental actions. The explicit evaluation of development alternatives for these projects and a policy requiring the projects to provide achievable quality in excess of minimum standards, seem as reasonable for private as for governmentally sponsored development.

We acknowledge deeply ingrained notions that the responsibility of private development should be limited to compliance with minimum standards of health, safety, and so on. We think it clear, however, that achieving quality requires abandonment of that concept in favor of a higher standard of responsibility. The concept has long since been abandoned in practice by many local land-use regulators. Site plan approvals, planned unit development approvals, and any number of other commonplace regulatory mechanisms effectively provide a framework for project-by-project negotiations about quality.

We note also that Congress has recently gone significantly beyond the minimum standards concept in legislation dealing with air and water pollution. In addition to establishing minimum standards, the 1970 Clean Air Act requires new air pollutant sources—including private sources—to employ "reasonably available control technology." Similarly, the 1972 Water Pollution Control Act requires private water polluters to use the "best practicable control technology." In effect, these laws recognize that some sources have an opportunity to achieve higher performance than others and require those with opportunity to use it. Everyone must meet the minimum quality standards but, if a source can reasonably do better, it must.

Applying this concept to land development will be far more difficult than applying it to pollutant sources. National standards are nearly impossible for land development since conditions vary enormously and since development is at least as much an art as a science. Nevertheless, the opportunity to achieve improved quality is there and should be pursued.

Setting ground rules for impact review of private projects has special difficulties. Most serious is the problem of land ownership. The private applicant, unlike governmental agencies, normally owns or has options or other rights to the land on which he proposes to build, and he may have no way of acquiring the optimum site for the project. Is an alternative location "feasible" if it is not for sale at a reasonable price? There is also the problem of price itself: in considering proposed housing for low-income people, for example, should alternatives be considered "feasible" only if they do not increase costs to the future occupants?*

Despite the uncertainties, we think this kind of review has great promise, for it provides a procedure through which development needs and market initiatives, on the one hand, can be reconciled with protective needs on the other. Where a development would intrude on the community, the developers can be required to use all feasible means to minimize disruptive effects. *State laws should assure that impact statements are prepared and reviewed before granting permits for private projects that significantly affect the environment.*

## Local Development Review: Focusing on Actions

If environmental impact analysis continues to live up to its promise, it cannot fail to influence the methods that local governments use to guide development. In communities where extensive preregulation has been discarded but case-by-case project review has also been unsuccessful, the relative success of impact analysis as a project review mechanism should prove invaluable. How, then, can states and localities adapt the regulatory process to include impact analysis?

One essential step is to revise state enabling legislation (which empowers localities to regulate development) to fit today's regulatory methods. Under present laws, localities can take many—probably most—of the regulatory steps needed to control development. To do so, however, localities must often distort their regulatory process to fit a mold established by half-century-old state legislation. The distortion—particularly the overemphasis on detailed preregulation and underemphasis on flexible response to what is actually taking place—often obscures how development is guided (even to decision-makers), seriously misleads the public, and deprives landowners of essential procedural safeguards.

The American Law Institute is drafting a model land development code to replace obsolete state enabling acts. Recognizing that local decision-making is far more varied and complex than envisioned by most legislation now in effect, the draft provides both authorizations and safeguards that are not provided today.

---

* Similar problems have not prevented federal courts from requiring one federal agency proposing to sell oil leases to set out in its impact statement the full range of alternative means of obtaining oil, including measures not under the authority of the agency to effect.

*We look forward to completion and release (scheduled for the spring of 1974) of the American Law Institute's model land development code, which promises to furnish invaluable aid in the modernization of out-of-date state enabling acts.*

Another essential step is to fashion a realistic local decision-making mechanism. For the convenience of all concerned— builders, neighbors, administrators, the general public—a convenient, nondiscretionary mechanism must be provided so that the mass of small projects can proceed without elaborate review. Like today's nondiscretionary building permit, this mechanism will have to rely on specific rules written so that an official can readily determine whether proposed development is permitted or not. In most cases, different rules will be needed to reflect different existing conditions in different parts of town. Thus, a form of zoning will continue, although zones seem likely to reflect present, not future, land use.

The range of actions that a locality may permit without discretionary review will depend on a number of factors. How much change the locality feels capable of prescribing in advance is one. The administrative burden is another. Discretionary reviews, if too numerous, can prevent careful examination of each case and repel prospective board members by the length and dullness of the meetings Citizen acceptance of change is a third factor. In some areas (typically higher income suburbs), people expect an opportunity to comment even on relatively minor changes; in others, little say is demanded even on major projects.

Increasingly, however, we believe that nondiscretionary review will be reserved for small projects that have limited impact on their surroundings. For major and unusual development, we would hope that broad discretionary review will be the custom, not the exception.

We are aware that discretionary review means that many landowners (and their neighbors) will not know in advance whether major change is to be permitted in the use of the land. We wish it were possible to avoid this result. Developers and lenders, though, often do not decide what to build until the time of development. For the same reasons, governments seeking quality in development (not content simply to set minimum standards of health and safety) often cannot intelligently decide what to permit until all the facts are in. And landowners have long been adept at protecting their financial interests by drafting contracts that let

*"Cleared with the state, cleared with the county,
cleared with the zoning boys, the building boys, the
historical society, the ecology groups,
and now the little old lady changes her mind
about selling the farm."*

them reap benefits from whatever zoning is finally granted to the
developer.

*Except for small projects with limited impact, discretionary
review should be at the heart of local development guidance.*

As in environmental impact statements, the review process
should focus on the consequences of proposed or planned
development and on alternatives to that development. Considering consequences reduces the danger that projects will be approved haphazardly, creating unforeseen problems. Considering
alternatives helps to focus review on realistic actions rather than
on what might theoretically be desirable. In effect, assessing consequences and alternatives helps to assure that reviewers ask the
right questions. This approach has the additional advantage of
establishing a high standard of conduct for developers, of
clarifying their obligation to go beyond minimum standards when
they reasonably can. *Development review should focus on the
consequences of proposed development and on feasible alter-*

natives to it. *Conscious choice of the best of available options, instead of mere satisfaction of minimum standards, appears to be the most realistic way to achieve quality.*

## The Importance of Planning

The regulatory process will not merit public trust and respect unless decisions are based on consistent policies and plans. Without these touchstones, the process readily degenerates into what has been called "the mockery of zoning adhockery."[5] To encourage a sense of purpose and continuity in decision-making, policies and plans should be formally adopted and published.

Unfortunately, too many localities reach their decisions without benefit of effective planning. Some communities have no planning worthy of the name. Others have only a rudimentary "master plan" that consists of little more than a map of designated future land use without explanation of the opportunities and constraints that led to the designations. Formal policy statements are often so general and numerous that authority can be found to support any conclusion selected.

Effective plans and policies will need to deal less often with results of development and far more often with the objectives and constraints that shape it.

Plans and policies must deal first with protection—identifying natural and manmade features, determining how their needs should limit future development, indicating how much protection should ideally be provided as well as alternative ways to provide it. Persuasive protection plans and policies are likely to concentrate on the present—existing buildings, neighborhoods, forests, land capacity, erosion dangers, scenery.

Plans and policies must also deal with development. Quantitative needs must be identified, as well as various sites where those needs can be satisfied with various means for minimizing the impact on surrounding development and natural processes.

At times, both protection and development objectives will warrant specific regulations (grading standards, for example) or designations of future land use (to prevent disruption of natural areas and established neighborhoods, for instance). But when, as commonly occurs, decision-makers are uncertain about what to do, the uncertainty should be acknowledged. What is needed are plans and policies useful to decision-makers when they must make a decision—plans and policies that help them choose among alternative actions by showing them how their actions would affect public objectives. *A process of planning and policy-making far more persuasive than the one now found in most localities is essential, both to earn citizen respect for the regulatory process and to achieve its public objectives. Such a process will include clear protection policies and plans for certain existing neighborhoods and critical land areas as well as a frank acknowledgment of uncertainty about the nature of unforeseeable new development.*

For any number of localities, proposing that decisions be based on consistent policies and plans seems laughably unrealistic. Many local governments operate under so many constraints that their power to make and implement consistent policy is extremely limited. Local governments must usually rely on archaic property tax systems for their funds. Many have tiny geographical jurisdictions, which restrict both the range of their concern and their power to deal with regional development forces. Localities with small populations often cannot afford to hire the skilled professionals needed to deal with complex development problems. Many governments have a tradition of passivity, of acting in a more or less custodial capacity; others enjoy their adhockery.

How can more coherent policy-making be encouraged? One approach after another has been tried or proposed, including:

—Assistance, notably, federal and state grants and technical assistance. Even with the fiscal 1973 budget austerity, the Nixon Administration requested increased appropriations for the "701" comprehensive planning assistance program to strengthen state and local decision-making and management capabilities in expectation of increased responsibilities under revenue-sharing.

—Encouragement. The American Law Institute's model land development code, for example, would authorize communities with planning programs to use more sophisticated regulatory devices than those without such planning and would give those sophisticated regulations a stronger presumption of validity in the event of a legal challenge.

—Requirements. Planning is required by some state and federal laws. Specific plan elements are sometimes prescribed, and compliance with the requirements made a condition for various forms of aid. Even when localities formally comply with planning requirements, though, the result may or may not influence local decision-makers.

—Structural reform of local government. Both the Advisory Commission on Intergovernmental Relations and the National Commission on Urban Problems have recommended, for example, that, within metropolitan areas, communities having a population of less than a certain size (30,000 and 25,000, respectively) be denied zoning powers.[6] One concern was that communities be sufficiently large to have planning services.

We find it impractical to recommend any one approach or any combination of approaches to encourage more competent and consistent planning at the local level. The needs, opportunities, and likelihood of effectiveness vary too widely from place to place, even within a single region, to make a definite prescription. What is clear to us, though, is that *ad hoc* decision-making will ultimately achieve neither public respect nor public objectives.

### Strengthening Local Institutions

Local governments are often cast as villains in the urban growth drama. Damned when they act, damned when they don't, their sins of commission—principally exclusionary efforts—can be as grave as their sins of omission—largely, failure to assure that permitted development creates communities that are reasonably efficient, pleasant to live in, and respectful of nature.

Nevertheless, we have little doubt that the many decisions affecting only one local area should, insofar as practical, be made by the affected local government. No other government is likely to know or care more about the fine-grained relationships on which the quality of life in neighborhoods and communities depends. Especially in small towns, many people feel closer to local than to state or federal government, so local control keeps them in touch with changes important to their lives. Feelings of contact and control are especially important in times and places of massive change. Thus, although we recommend a number of measures to inject higher levels of government into development guidance, we think that the broad base of regulations should be established by local decisions.

In too many localities, though, neither the procedures for determining land use nor the individuals making the decisions have the public's confidence. In any number of localities, citizens suspect that the people making regulatory decisions are thinking more about themselves and their cronies than about the general welfare. These suspicions are sometimes inaccurate: builders proposing a project and neighbors opposing the same project may both privately complain that the cards are stacked against them. Far too often, though, the suspicions are well grounded. Unfortunately, the informality that is a virtue of local government can foster these suspicions. Public trust must be established if local decision-making is to be effective.

Fair, openly discussed decisions are the first essential for trustworthiness. There must be fairness when rules and policies are established, and there must be fairness when those rules and policies are later applied to proposed development.

The decision-making process must be fair not only in fact: it must also be perceived as fair by the builders, property owners, and others whom it affects. If officials are widely thought to be corrupt or if decisions are thought to be "all sewed up," both proponents and opponents of development will treat the decision-making process with growing cynicism. Opponents of development may respond by appealing to emotion rather than reason ("There are 200 people out there, and half of them look ready to hit somebody."). Or they may try to establish overly rigid restraints on growth ("At least a height limit in the city charter would keep the council from giving everything away to the developers."). Too often, the cynical citizen simply gives up trying to influence the process at all and chalks up still another area of his life in which he feels he has no control.

Any number of steps can increase the likelihood of fairness in decision-making while bolstering citizen confidence.

Open meeting requirements are a particularly important step. Decisions made at secret meetings, closed executive sessions, and even informal meetings breed public suspicions. (The absence of citizen observers can also deprive a wavering decision-maker of an excuse to put the public interest ahead of that of his friends.) Nevertheless, unannounced, closed, and informal meetings are all too common. Even where governing bodies meet in public, legislative committees or official advisory commissions may meet privately and informally beforehand to decide on a position or recommendation.

For the governmental agency, taking project plans to the public is often regarded as an obstacle to efficiency. It can be. The public may misunderstand the proposal, criticize it, or want it to do more than it can or less than it should. To avoid such responses, public officials may obfuscate, reveal noncontroversial bits of information, withhold site plans and drawings from the public as "private property" of the applicant, or maintain a silence about intentions that borders on deceit.

Citizen discontents fester in this atmosphere, leading the public to view all public action with suspicion and hostility, seeing even in innocuous decisions a malevolence that is not there. All too often, the people are frozen out of decisions affecting their lives and simply confronted with *faits accomplis*. Where a continuous dialogue between agencies and the public exists, and where agencies deal openly with public concerns, a climate of trust that tends to ward off criticism, delays, and litigation can develop.

We find it hard to overemphasize the importance of enacting open meeting laws everywhere. *Every element of the regulatory process, including deliberations and advisory recommendations as well as final decisions, should take place at advertised meetings open to the general public. Local and state laws should establish open meeting requirements applicable to all governmental agencies responsible for land-use regulations.*

Conflict of interest is another common source of mistrust. Whether the conflict is blatant—a township engineer preparing a subdivision plat privately and then approving it in his official capacity, a city councilman taking part in the decision to rezone his own property—or subtle, the problem is pervasive simply because so many officials are likely to have interests in real estate or construction. Rules to guard against conflicts are not easily formulated, especially for the many small towns where the town leaders have trouble finding enough people to serve on boards and commissions. ("An awful lot of people in this town buy a little real estate now and then, and they're about the only ones willing to sit through all those zoning meetings.")

Some states have conflict-of-interest laws—Florida, for example—but most do not. We believe such laws should be enacted by all states. The Florida law, among other things, rules out acceptance of any favor or service that might improperly influence an employee; requires disclosure of interest in any entity that is subject to regulation of or does substantial business with any political subdivision; prevents other employment that would tend to affect the independent judgment of an individual in carrying out his public duties; and prohibits employee investment in any enterprise that would create a substantial conflict of interest between-private and public interests. Yet the failure of most states to enact effective conflict-of-interest laws for elected and appointed officials at state and local levels is glaring.

*To reduce the reality or appearance of conflicts of interest, state and local laws should disqualify local and state officials from voting or otherwise participating in any regulatory decision whose outcome could confer financial benefit, or could appear to the public to confer financial benefit, to themselves, their families, or their business or professional associates. All persons having any responsibility for land-use regulation, including elected and appointed officials and employees, should also be required by law to make periodic public disclosure of their financial interests and real estate holdings within the jurisdiction over which they exercise responsibility.*

Citizen lawsuits can be an antidote to "cronyism". In addition to giving the citizen an opportunity to curb administrative abuse, they can be a convenient crutch for the administrator being pressed to grant an unlawful dispensation. ("We could grant you the permit, Charlie, but those crazies would bring suit against us all sure as anything.") The right to appeal from a regulatory decision now, though, is often limited to property owners whose land will (at least arguably) be affected by the decision. Suits to enforce compliance with ordinance requirements are also tightly circumscribed.

*Citizen suits appealing from local regulatory decisions should be permitted by any local resident or civic organization in the public interest, without regard to property ownership or other financial interest. Citizen suits to enforce ordinance requirements should also be permitted. Safeguards against premature or frivolous litigation may be necessary to guard against the abuse of citizen suits.*

Few needs are more important than responding to citizen's procedural concerns in every practical way. Are there complaints that appeals are rendered virtually impossible because no sound record is kept of proceedings? Record all that takes place at a meeting and make the record publicly available. (Meetings in some communities are broadcast over radio or television as well.) Are there complaints that the formal required notices fail to give sufficient information or are impossible to understand? Use layman's language for notices, be sure they are complete, and send additional notices to citizen groups interested

216

in land-use matters. Are there complaints that applicants "wear down" opponents by repeatedly reapplying for permissions already denied? Establish waiting periods during which denied applications may not be resubmitted. Are there complaints that meetings are held in the afternoons so that commuters cannot attend? Consider holding meetings at night. Are there complaints that applicants file the most controversial applications when citizens are likely to be away on vacation? Consider reducing the frequency of meetings at which significant applications may be brought up and scheduling them at convenient times. Is there talk because all the board members get together for coffee before the meeting? Get together after the meeting instead, after the decision has been made.

*Local officials and citizens should periodically try to identify aspects of local procedures that may give rise to citizen mistrust. Insofar as practical, measures that cause mistrust, whether or not the resulting suspicions are in fact warranted, should be changed.*

With its mechanisms revised and its institutions restored, the regulatory process can be far more effective in giving us quality development in the future than it is today. There remain, however, practical limits to what regulations can achieve. If the creators—builders, landowners (or even regulators)—find their self-interest clashing fundamentally with the public good, regulations can rarely reconcile the conflict. Nor can regulations create quality where the creators have the will to fulfill public needs but lack the opportunity to act effectively. Essential though they are, regulations are only half the story. They must be accompanied by measures that give the creators incentives and opportunities to create quality as well.

# Chapter VI
# Creating What We Want: Incentives and Opportunities

Land-use regulations that seek quality development usually evaluate, in one way or another, the end-product of the development process, the office building or the residential subdivision. If that product passes a quality test, it is approved or expedited or rewarded. If not, it is prohibited or delayed or discouraged. Zoning does this. So, with a different test and procedure, do reviews of environmental impact statements. In effect, these regulations try to coerce a "bad" builder or developer into doing what he should do instead of what he might like to do.

Incentives work differently. Instead of applying quality standards to the proposed end-product, they seek to create conditions in which each decision-maker's own motives are more likely to carry him toward quality. Incentives are of growing interest in many fields, perhaps partly in response to research that shows rewards more effective than punishment in securing desired behavior, partly out of discouragement with the growing bureaucracies needed to administer regulations.

How can quality be rewarded? By giving critics' awards? By public adulation? What? In a world where economic self-interest is a powerful force, the most effective incentives usually increase the size or likelihood of profits from quality projects, while decreasing them in the absence of quality.

But how, without individualized project review, can quality be recognized? Probability is the key. Do certain attitudes or circumstances seem to be associated with existing projects deemed high in quality? Do other attitudes and circumstances often match up

219

*Regulations can discourage this kind of strip highway development by*

with low quality? Incentive measures require or encourage the conditions associated with quality—on the theory that people will respond in the same way they have in the past and create more quality.

What, then, are some circumstances that may increase the likelihood of quality?

Private property ownership be one. Consider the experience of the Soviet Union, where land is regarded as a "free" or cheap

*prohibiting the creation of lots fronting on the road.*

resource. Forty million cubic yards of sand and gravel for cement were removed from Black Sea beaches after World War II. No longer cushioned by the sand, the shores were eroded by heavy waves. The beach area shrunk by one-half in less than fifteen years. Although laws banning the removal of pebbles from the beaches in one area were passed in 1962 and 1968, removal has continued. According to one authority, the absence of private property rights left the beaches without a "first line of defense"

221

against public contractors and "may actually have hastened the deterioration."[1]

When a person lives on property he owns, quality can be doubly rewarding. For his investment in the property, the reward can be financial. Since he lives there, his enjoyment is a second reward.

When a resident or builder or lender anticipates long-term involvement in a community, his concern with quality may increase still further. True, long-term involvement is no guarantee of concern for human and natural values. And, there are builders and investers who seek high quality even in short-lived deals. Still, the likelihood of quality seems greater when people expect to be around for a while.

Since corporations are some of the most influential participants in the development process, their incentives for quality are particularly important. A company judges its success in large part by the company's earnings per share of common stock. Thus, anything that affects earnings per share will influence the company's behavior. Accounting procedures and tax benefits, which affect the company's earnings, can therefore serve as quality incentives.

Lending practices can encourage quality, too. Consider the effect of lending institutions in an historic neighborhood where one or two banks encourage the rehabilitation of existing structures rather than support their demolition and replacement with larger new buildings.

Of course, in a market-based economic system, profitability and the public interest can and do diverge. Conditions beyond an owner's control may so reduce quality that he chooses to do what he can to recover his investment regardless of its effects on his neighbors. Or an owner may see the opportunity to profit by reducing the quality himself (and, with that profit, perhaps move to an area where the quality is still high). Thus, it makes sense for governments to prevent conditions in which owners (or builders or lenders) have the opportunity to obtain greater profit by acting contrary to the public interest.

The approach may be illustrated by considering the unfortunate practice of creating lots that front on major streets and highways. The practice can be stopped. Some localities restricted it decades ago. Yet it remains a major source of visual blight (and zoning litigation) across the country. The very existence of these lots produces pressures for commercial rezoning and strip development.

The lots may remain physically suitable for residential use but, with increasing highway noise, air pollution, and safety hazards, one or more homeowners decide sooner or later that life would be better elsewhere. When this happens, they see alternative uses, usually commercial, as offering greater profit and so they push for a zoning change. Not everyone along the street can cash in on the change, but the first few may make a killing. Thus are the pressures set up that can further reduce quality and perhaps lead to the creation of another highway junk strip. Communities need not, and usually should not, give in to these pressures, but experience has shown that the pressures are often politically irresistible. Far better, then, to prevent the pressures from arising altogether by prohibiting highway frontage lots in the first place.

*The development process should, insofar as possible, be shaped by planning and regulatory bodies, lenders, accountants, appraisers, and other participants so that developers, home-buyers, and other consumers come to perceive the maintenance and enhancement of quality as the key to profitability. Divergence between quality and profitability should be minimized.*

Even the incentives of governments can be redirected. Federal and state governments support high levels of new construction activity every year, yet federal and many state laws do not encourage the purchase (or lease) and rehabilitation of existing buildings in older neighborhoods, which could serve the government as well as (in some cases, even better than) new buildings. Governmental office buildings that might accommodate apartments and commercial uses are virtually never planned to include them. (Federal law actually prohibits the inclusion of residential units in federally owned office buildings.) The adaptation and reuse of older structures, and the creation of more vibrant office areas where life and use go on after office workers have gone home, could be achieved by cost-free changes in governmental policies.

But the public incentives most in need of change are the incentives that favor exclusion.

## Exclusionary Incentives

Local governments often see their economic interests best served by excluding new development. Consider the fable of the country club.

## A Fable of Exclusionary Incentives

Once upon a time there was a country club. Its members were a congenial group who loved their club way out in the country. The handsome old clubhouse was surrounded with trees. Beyond it was a golf course, a swimming pool, and two tennis courts.

Since it was far from the city, and even from the suburbs, the club was not exclusive. You had to pay the initiation fee and monthly dues, but they were not high. The members joked that, if your credit rating was okay, you would have no trouble getting past the membership committee.

But then things changed. The city, which many of the club members had washed their hands of long ago, crept nearer. Before long, new members started showing up around the clubhouse. The older members grumbled about longer waits to get on the golf course and having to sign up ahead to play tennis in the middle of the week. "We need more tennis courts," the president said one day when he had forgotten to sign up ahead. So a committee looked into more tennis courts and, although the estimates were high, the members went ahead anyway.

That was only the beginning. The club kept growing, and soon the golf course was overcrowded. Sometimes, on the weekends, there was even trouble finding a place to park. "It's all those new members," people started saying, although they knew that was only part of the story because the old members were buying more cars for their kids, and they used parking places too.

It was the dues, though, that caused the trouble. Every year, they went up. And every year, a few more members complained. "We can't afford any more new tennis courts." "The staff is plenty big already. They should just work harder." But the manager insisted that the club couldn't stand still. "With so many new members," he reminded them, "we can't get by on what we had before. Somebody has to be in the pro shop full time now, and keeping the grounds is a lot bigger job than it was before."

So the members began to question why the club let in so many new members anyway. The membership chairman said it was a custom and recalled the old days when the problem had been to get enough members to meet expenses. "Even now," he added, "initiation fees help keep the dues down."

"All I know," said one of the old timers, "is that we have a lot more members than we used to, and a lot higher dues, and I'd just like to be sure that we're not paying for the privilege of having all those extra people on the golf course." So the treasurer appointed a committee—and the committee's report changed everything. The report showed that each new member caused everybody's dues to go up.

Right after that, the board changed the membership policy. The initiation fee is sky high now, and the membership committee does all it can to discourage new applications. "That costs study was just the last straw," the club president explained. "I think a lot of us recognized that we had enjoyed the club more in the old days, when it wasn't crowded and everybody knew everybody. And then to find out that we were paying out of our own pockets to let the new people in. That was too much. You'll admit it's hard to see why we should pay for people to come in here and make life less enjoyable than it used to be."

Was there any regret that some people had to be excluded from the club under the new policy? "Depends on who you talk to," the president said. "A few say the new people applying for membership aren't our kind of people anyway and wouldn't fit in. I suppose they're happy about the new policy. But I think mostly it's the crowding and the costs that caused the change. I'm sorry we can't let in all those who want in. You'll admit, though, that we can't look out for everybody. Club policy, after all, is made by the members, and they wouldn't be human if they didn't think about themselves first."

*Local Government as the Representative*
*of Those Who Got There First*

Many local officials whose decisions guide the growth of urban regions find themselves and their constituents in a situation very much like that of the club members. In the midst of a mobile and expanding population, local governments represent the people already there. Prospective residents, who may be destined to double or treble the population of the community, do not live within local boundaries and therefore do not vote. The local government thus speaks for the people who got there first.

Many of these first arrivals have recognized for years that additional development has little to offer them. Some suburbs have engaged in a curious intermunicipal competition in which development (particularly low- or moderate-income housing) has been perceived as the common enemy, threatening to overrun the

225

weak or inattentive locality. Municipal efforts to combat the threat have resembled nothing so much as competitive dikebuilding by neighboring landowners, each hoping that his higher dikes will keep the floodwaters off his own land and drive them onto his neighbors' instead. Even ten or fifteen years ago, local officials would privately explain that a new zoning amendment increasing minimum lot sizes was at least partly intended to keep up with requirements in a neighboring town. ("They increased their lot sizes, and if we don't stay even, we'll just be inviting subdividers in here.")

It is impossible to isolate any single or even dominant motive for local opposition to growth because so many different motives are involved. There are undoubtedly exclusionary social motives. There is fear that those who come later will have less money or lower social status or be members of racial or ethnic minorities. There is also fear that the town may come to resemble the city that was so eagerly left behind, fear that more people will destroy the "small town" atmosphere. Given the small scale of development and the chronic malfunctioning of local development guidance, the community may well seem much more attractive before it "fills up," while the problem tracts are still vacant and while farms provide some open space.

## Economic Incentives for Exclusion

Whatever the strength of the noneconomic arguments against growth, economic motives—governmental costs and property tax rates—unquestionably are a major cause of opposition. Towns will often fight to exclude new residential development, which is seen as a net economic loss to the town, while avidly trying to attract scientific research labs and corporate offices, which are seen as economic gains.

One routine response of local governments is to shift to the developer costs that would otherwise fall on local taxpayers. Developers then bear the costs of providing and installing the streets, sidewalks, sewers—and, in some areas, open space—that serve their developments. Developers, especially the large and highly visible ones, are often informally required to bear even more costs than the regulations assign to them. A developer's decision to provide school sites, for example, or to establish a homeowners' association to maintain walkways and open spaces without public expense, may be "taken into account" by a local government in deciding whether to grant rezoning or some other needed approval for the developer's project.

Many costs, however, cannot be shifted. The cost of operating the school system as well as providing garbage collection and police and fire protection become governmental responsibilities whose cost must usually be financed largely from local taxes. Even in the case of streets and other facilities installed by developers, maintenance and operating costs are normally borne by taxpayers under local regulations requiring that installed facilities be donated to the local government. (Since local governments pay for maintenance but not for construction, they have an incentive to set construction standards very high in hopes of avoiding later maintenance expense. In effect, localities become major "customers" of the developers, and some localities engage in consumer self-protection with a vengeance.)

It is school costs, though, that are especially important in local calculations, for in many localities they are one of the biggest expenses. (In 1969, for example, school expenditures totaled 47 percent of all local governmental expenditures.)

The source of these funds is as important as the spending level. Some 65 percent of locally raised general revenues come from property taxes. And local sources—primarily the property tax—account for half of the costs of primary and secondary education.

It is the combination, then, of big education expenditures financed primarily by property taxes that makes educational costs a key issue in land development.

Aware of these and other municipal costs, localities have long turned to "cost-revenue" studies in an effort to determine whether development will pay its way.

Three recent studies have supported the argument that more families with school-age children mean higher property taxes for everyone.

A cost-revenue analysis of land-use alternatives in the Barrington, Illinois, area indicated that four-bedroom homes —even $100,000 homes on 5-acre lots—would require more in public expenditures than they would provide in property taxes, while apartments with few bedrooms would produce a net tax benefit. According to the report:

> The two residential variables found to influence school costs and revenues most were the average number of bedrooms per dwelling unit

and the average market value or monthly rental per dwelling unit. Single-family homes with three or less bedrooms and apartments with two or less bedrooms have a favorable impact upon school costs and revenues. The impact of larger dwelling units varies, depending upon size and market value or monthly rental. However, practically all dwelling units of four or more bedrooms, regardless of market value, result in a net school tax deficit.

For any given parcel of land, research-office-oriented industrial development will be likely to produce the highest net benefits in terms of local school services. Next in line is moderate rental, one- and two-bedroom apartments (developed at 30 dwelling units per acre), followed by shopping center development, production-oriented industrial development, and higher rental, two- and three-bedroom apartments (developed at 15 dwelling units per acre).[2]

The analysts concluded that retaining one 50-acre site as public open space would create a substantial deficit, particularly if the

*To enlarge housing opportunities, future growth in outlying communities is essential. Yet local residents, fearing social problems or increased school costs, often decline to accept federally assisted housing—or accept it only if residents will be elderly. Even this housing project for the elderly in Ramapo, New York, was accepted only after heated debate.*

land would otherwise be developed for one of the more "profitable" alternatives.

A study prepared for Palo Alto, California, combining cost-revenue with social and environmental criteria, recommended that the city acquire substantial open land in the foothills area as permanent open space. The analysts explored various combinations of cluster residential development, professional-administrative office development, and generous quantities of open space. The study found that:

> Of the 22 different development patterns studied, except in a few years none yielded a positive net cash flow to the City. The cost of municipal facilities and services generally exceeded revenue from property tax, sales tax, utilities (gas and electricity) sales, and other sources. Not surprisingly, cash flow to the School District was consistently negative; and because its budget is substantially larger than the City's, there proved to be a total net cost to the taxpayer in all years. Even though two-thirds of each property tax dollar is paid by non-residential development in Palo Alto, it was found that $45,000 homes would have to be priced at $62,000 and $80,000 homes at $116,500 if they were to pay their own way.[3]

Over a thirty-year period (the assumed life of bonds sold to purchase the recommended open space), the least expensive alternatives to the city and school district were estimated to cost about half as much as open space acquisition, while the most expensive would cost about one and one-half times more.

The study, as well as the city-established ground rules under which it was conducted, have been criticized. But the critics have conceded that:

> As long as local property values are the major source of income for schools, and as long as a substantial share of those values is non-residential, proportionate growth in non-residential values must accompany the development of new residential areas if the overall cost-revenue balance at a given tax rate is to be preserved.[4]

A study of development alternatives for a proposed project of 800 residential units and 30 acres of commercial development (Hollymead) in Albermarle County, Virginia (a rapidly growing area surrounding Charlottesville) found that county expenditures associated with the development would exceed county revenues by $101,745 per year over thirty years.

"The critical variable in estimating the fiscal impact of new development in an area," the study commented, is "a reliable estimate of the additional school population resulting from the development."[5] School costs for Albermarle County (excluding debt service) took 76.1 percent of the county's 1972 budget. According to the report, even if the builder contributed 37 acres of land (valued at $74,000) for a school site, capital costs would exceed revenues.

The study laid out a number of policy alternatives to offset this negative fiscal effect. They included requiring the developer to compensate the county for the deficit or obliging him to choose an alternative location within the county where existing public facilities (principally schools) may be under-utilized.

For the many communities unable to obtain proportionate growth of nonresidential development, the incentive to exclude many new residents seems undeniable so long as local property taxes are the principal source of school revenue.

With such incentives to exclude much new development, it is not surprising that many localities are doing so. They are using a variety of local powers and measures to impede new construction, sometimes aiming only at particular kinds of development and sometimes being less discriminating. Most of the techniques are well known.

Large minimum-lot-size requirements are perhaps the most common of the many techniques. The results would be hard to believe if the phenomenon were not widely documented by national commissions, state reports, and scholarly articles. A survey conducted by the National Commission on Urban Problems showed that 25 percent of metropolitan area municipalities of 5,000 or more people permitted no single-family houses on less than one-half acre.[6] A Connecticut study concluded that zoning of excessive amounts of vacant land in the state for large lots made it impossible for projected population increases to be handled.[7] (Half of all vacant land zoned residential was in minimum one- to two-acre lots.) A study of five northern New Jersey counties disclosed that more than half of all land was zoned in lots of one acre or more and 70 percent, in lots of more than one-half acre.[8]

The local practice of zoning substantial areas in large lots does not, of course, always mean that later development will actually occur on them. In some cases very low density zoning is regarded by local officials as a holding technique. But land so zoned may not easily be rezoned for development that would create property tax deficits or house low-income or nonwhite families. Thus, the proponent of development to house low-income groups or racial minorities not well represented in an area may have two strikes against him—the type of development he is proposing may be seen as presenting tax or social problems and the citizens may not even be aware that the old large-lot zoning was intended to be temporary.

Minimum building size requirements (found primarily in the Northeast) are a similar exclusionary technique. Using estimated construction costs per square foot, it is a simple matter for localities to assure expensive homes simply by setting high floor-area requirements. In five northern New Jersey counties, a minimum requirement of 1,500 square feet (or even more) is common. (At $25 a square foot, construction costs alone come to $37,500.)

Other techniques include limiting the number of bedrooms in apartments or imposing bedroom taxes. Only one-half of one percent of the land in northern New Jersey is zoned for multi-family dwellings, and of that, 83 percent is covered by restrictions on the number of bedrooms per apartment. The most common required ratio between one- and multi-bedroom units per building in the area is 4 to 1. The result: most single-family houses in northern New Jersey are large, while most apartments are small.

Public utility policies are another technique used to limit growth. A number of localities are, formally or informally, banning development unless facilities are available to serve it. San Diego, for example, adopted the following policy in 1971:

> Before giving approval to rezoning, development or redevelopment proposals, the public health and safety and the general welfare of the community and all its citizens require that provisions be made by the proponent of the rezoning, development or redevelopment in conjunction with appropriate governmental agencies to insure:
> 1. That the development, redevelopment or rezoning be consistent with a master development plan for the general area which has been reviewed by the Planning Commission and adopted by the City Council.
> 2. That the development plan includes an implementation section which sets forth in detail measures which will be taken to insure that needed public services are provided concurrent with need in the development.
> 3. That the proponent of the rezoning, development or redevelopment present evidence satisfactory to the appropriate body or agency that the required public services will in fact be provided concurrent with the need.[9]

San Diego voters have put sharp teeth in this policy. Since 1966, they have four times turned down bond issues that would, among other things, have financed the construction of schools in developing areas.

The town of Ramapo near New York City has a development timing scheme (upheld by the New York Court of Appeals) under which:

1. The proximity or availability of five kinds of facilities (sewers, drainage facilities, recreation and school sites, roads, and firehouses) serves as the basis for determining whether land may be developed.

2. The town capital improvement program (a non-binding guide) would provide facilities at such a rate that some land in the town could not be developed for nearly eighteen years.

3. Developers may develop sooner if they are willing to supply the required facilities themselves.

Some devices can have the desirable effect of assuring that new development is fully provided with services. Others, though, simply serve to keep out low-income families. Provisions that prescribe minimum building sizes, for example, artifically reduce the opportunity of much of the population to buy new housing.

There is another cost, though, that many localities do not consider—the cost of sprawl. Large-lot zoning can force development patterns that are wasteful of urban land. Several studies have indicated that low-density patterns cost more to service than do more compact patterns.

One study evaluated development alternatives for Howard County, Maryland. The Howard County Planning Commission looked at three future land-use patterns for the county, concentrating on land consumption and its implications for public service costs. Each alternative model assumed the same total county population for 1985. In the mid-1960s when this study began, the new town of Columbia was just under construction.

The three alternatives considered by the planning commission were: a continuation of prevailing development patterns (model I: sprawl); the development of Columbia with the remainder of the county developing as in model I (model II: partly clustered, partly sprawl); and all development taking place in accordance with the pattern established by Columbia (model III: all clustered).

For each of these alternatives, county planners estimated the amount of land needed to house the same number of people and then estimated the value (based on agricultural value) of the land that would remain undeveloped. The study concluded that 61,000

acres would be required for model I, 43,000 for model II, and
29,600 for model III. The cost of public facilities and services in
1985 were estimated to be $251.9 million for model I, $182.1
million for model II, and $119.2 million for model III.[10]

A second study looked at future development alternatives for
Staten Island, New York. In this case, trend development (which,

*To one local government, a wetland may not appear as part of a regional
ecological system. Thus, many coastal states are finding it necessary to
assert control over wetlands and other critical environmental areas.*

it was assumed, would take place over the next thirty-five years at densities of between 15 and 20 units per acre) was compared with three new city alternatives, defined in the study as low density (15 dwelling units per residential acre), medium density (30 dwelling units per residential acre), and high density (60 dwelling units per residential acre). While the absolute level of public investment for any of the three new city alternatives is greater than for trend development, the unit costs are lower and the returns to the city per dollar invested are higher. This study demonstrated that not only is the new community form of development more efficient on a unit cost basis but it also made good sense in terms of net revenue flows to the city of New York.[11]

A third study assessed the economic costs of a regional open space program in the San Francisco Bay area. The program, a slightly modified version of an open space proposal made by the Association of Bay Area Governments (ABAG), recommended an increase in permanent public open space in the nine-county region surrounding San Francisco from 340,000 acres in 1968 to approximately 1.8 million acres in 1990. For the study, ABAG proposed a new category, "areas to guide development," in which 600,000 acres of public open space would be placed by 1990.

The study estimated the costs of selected public services for development with extensive open space preservation and development-as-usual. Both alternatives assumed the same population over the 1970-2000 period. The conclusion: preserving the open space would present considerable cost savings because of the "tighter" development pattern that would result. Approximately 300 square miles of utility service would be "saved" by development-with-preservation. Between 1970 and 2000, the "present" value (discounted to reflect the fact that future benefits are worth less than present benefits) of savings in utility construction and maintenance and in public safety would amount to $1.5 billion, or about the cost of the Bay Area Rapid Transit System.[12]

These studies point to the economic advantages of clustering new development, both for the public and for developers (who increasingly are being required to provide roads, sewers, sidewalks, and similar services). They also demonstrate that clustering permits the conservation of greater amounts of open space.

The whole process of attempting to devise land regulatory policies that minimize expenditures or keep out the poor distracts regulators from the pursuit of quality in permitted development

234

(or even of economic efficiency in planning facilities other than schools). There is no occasion for a locality to take the essential broad view—the planner's view—that acknowledges the need or inevitability of change and asks how best to accommodate that change while doing as much as possible to protect what already exists. So long as the regulator has incentives to use his review powers to reduce the quantity of development, much needed development and quality in all development are likely to be short-changed.

How, then, can local exclusionary incentives be lessened?

State takeover of education costs, which would radically alter the impact of new housing on local real estate taxes, would reduce one important local incentive to exclude new housing. Freed of the fear of high increases in school taxes, localities might focus less on prohibiting development and more on assuring quality and compatibility in the development that did occur.

In all likelihood, though, state takeover would simply reduce, not end, the exclusionary incentives: adverse tax consequences of new housing would undoubtedly remain. So would noneconomic incentives to exclude. In fact, where the new mood represents more a defense of the pocketbook than a quest for quality, the changes might lead to significant—perhaps even excessive—weakening of environmental protective measures. Nevertheless, reducing the adverse local tax impact of new housing should increase the feasibility of responsible local action—for example, by increasing the likelihood that a suburban legislator could vote for new housing and still get re-elected.

States have generally avoided the unpleasant alternative of imposing state taxes to finance education. But growing concern about the inequality of educational opportunity that results when poor communities cannot afford to offer the education services that their richer neighbors provide may change that. The constitutions of California, New Jersey, and Arizona have recently been interpreted to bar these inequities. Other state constitutions could be similarly interpreted. (The U.S. Supreme Court recently upheld this method of financing[13]).

Reducing the tax benefit that host localities receive from new commercial and industrial development by transferring a portion of property taxes from the locality in which they are generated to all other localities in the area can reduce the tendency for every locality to try to attract its own quantity of high-tax-returning development, a practice that can work against clustering of industries. The Minneapolis-St. Paul metropolitan area has established such a measure (though it is now being challenged in court). Only 60 percent of the real estate taxes paid by new businesses go to the host locality; the other 40 percent are divided among the remaining communities in the area. With the tax benefits thus shared, localities could become more receptive to state or regional efforts to allocate commercial and industrial development in response to overall public needs.

Reducing the local tax advantages associated with businesses would reduce local incentives to treat housing (including low- and moderate-income housing) differently from commercial and industrial development. True, corporations could find themselves in a position similar to that of low-income housing builders if their property taxes were spread around outside the immediate jurisdiction. Yet, if an anti-exclusionary alliance between corporations and homebuilders should then result, the likelihood of state action to assure needed development might significantly increase.

*As part of an overall strategy to discourage excessive reliance on local cost-revenue criteria as the basis for evaluating the acceptability of new development, and to increase public acceptance of state responsibility for guiding locally excluded development, we encourage the states to enact measures that would reduce the impact of new development on local tax rates.*

### Injecting a Regional Perspective

With the costs and revenues associated with development shared, some local incentives to evaluate development in narrow, cost-revenue terms will be relieved. But local resistance to growth is based on more than concern about economic impact. One local government, like one small property owner, has only so much turf to oversee and protect, and there is little opportunity (and few incentives) to plan for its use in a scheme that includes neighbors. An ordinary locality will not see a coastal wetland as part of a regional ecological system. Or an automobile assembly plant as one element in a regional industrial, transportation, housing, and labor-supply area.

From a regional perspective, it may seem absurd for one locality to fill its portion of a great swamp or to ban multi-family dwellings when workers in its factories cannot afford single-

*Much post-World War II development failed to provide neighborhood open spaces, convenience stores, and community facilities within walking distance of homes. The result in some areas, as children and other non-drivers have discovered, is that virtually every trip must be by automobile.*

family homes. Moreover, effects of such decisions readily trans-late into discomfort and inconvenience for neighboring areas.

*Important development should be regulated by governments that represent all the people whose lives are likely to be affected by it, including those who could benefit from it as well as those who could be harmed by it. Where a regulatory decision significantly affects people in more than one locality, state, regional, or even federal action is necessary.*

The need for an areawide perspective has been clear for some time. During the 1960s, the federal government established metropolitan and areawide clearinghouses to coordinate applications by local governmental agencies for federal financial assistance.

But federal encouragements to regional planning were less effective than their proponents had hoped, for they depended on agencies with more responsibility than authority. The typical metropolitan council of governments or regional planning agency has few real powers to control major land-use decisions. In many areas, metropolitan planning has resulted in improved information exchange among governments. But rare is the area where advisory bodies have significantly affected the direction of urbanization, the conservation of environmentally critical land resources, or local acceptance of publicly assisted housing.

Many have long recognized the need to close the breach between planning, exercised by the regional agencies, and regulatory control, exercised by local governments. And they have understood the preeminence of the regulatory power—the power to say no to development if necessary to make plans work. But standing in the way of reform was a long American tradition of localism in land-use control, dating at least to the issuance of the Standard State Zoning Enabling Act in 1924, an act which most states copied and which viewed land-use controls as a matter of local rather than state control.

Major federal legislation and program documents affecting planning assistance and requirements during the 1960s nibbled at local predominance and recounted in preambles, regulations, and procedures the truism that a dynamic society had burst through local boundaries and rendered them meaningless in nearly every large urbanized area. As a result, local governments themselves were not in control of the region-forming developments—the highways, airports, and shopping centers—that were being sited in and near them and wreaking havoc with local land-use plans.

Nevertheless, it was not until 1971 that a federal administration supported transferring authority over land-use decisions of regional impact to the level of government that alone has the full powers to tax, to regulate, and to condemn land: the states.

The pending national land-use policy legislation would provide federal assistance to assure that development of "regional benefit" is not unreasonably excluded or blocked by local governments. The measure would require states to override local governments when necessary to make sure that needed development is sited.

But what form should state intervention take?

## The Role of the States

Some suggest that states should simply prohibit localities from doing the exclusionary things they want to do—that is, should try to control the content of local regulations without changing the localities' incentives. This approach makes the mistake of treating localities in the same way that regulations have so long treated developers: as untrustworthy bad guys who must be hemmed in by requirements at every turn. Such an approach may be the only one politically achievable in some states, but it is unlikely to produce quality.

In any event, statutory prohibitions (such as a ban on local requirements for lot sizes of over one-quarter acre) are useful in relatively few situations and could, if enacted, weaken legitimate environmental protection measures. Many local controls are justifiable in some circumstances but predominantly exclusionary in others (low density requirements, for example). General statutory rules are often unable to distinguish between the two sets of circumstances. In addition, since development approvals are so often granted after negotiation with local officials, localities can impose requirements that the statutes do not authorize. This is routinely the case, and developers are often unable to force local officials to back down. Statutory prohibitions, then, are desirable only when a local control is highly likely to prove exclusionary and useful only where the prohibition cannot routinely be circumvented by local negotiations.

Minimum floor-area requirements for individual dwelling units are one such case. Although health and safety presumably warrant a minimum requirement, we see little justification for minimum size requirements that vary from locality to locality, and none at all for requirements that vary zone by zone within a single locality. Since each square foot of construction adds to housing cost, the effect (and sometimes intent) of the requirements is to establish a minimum price per dwelling unit within the zone. *State legislation should deprive local governments of the power to establish minimum floor-area requirements in excess of a statewide minimum established by statute.*

Except for the rare situations that can be handled by general statutory rules, effective state action requires an administrative mechanism capable of identifying places and kinds of development that are of state concern—and capable of regulating them much as local regulations do. States may choose to intervene either to provide additional protection—as we recommend for protection of open spaces and historic properties—or to provide development opportunity where local regulations are too restrictive. Massachusetts, for example, has intervened for both purposes. Its wetlands act authorizes protective orders that can be used to prohibit development of coastal wetlands. Its zoning appeals law enables the commonwealth to approve subsidized housing development denied by local boards.

The American Law Institute's draft model land development code identifies three kinds of areas in which higher-than-local intervention is likely to be important:

1. An area significantly affected by, or having a significant effect upon, an existing or proposed major public facility or other area of major public investment.

2. An area containing or having a significant impact upon historical, natural, or environmental resources of regional or statewide importance.

3. A proposed site of a new community designated in a State Land Development Plan, together with a reasonable amount of surrounding land.[14]

In addition, the code would authorize higher level intervention when necessary to permit development of state or regional benefit, to control large-scale development, and to regulate the use of land around major growth-inducing public facilities.

Florida's Land and Water Management Act and the proposed national land-use policy legislation use similar categories. According to these measures, the state is to provide for state-level control for (1) land use in areas of critical environmental concern (wetlands, floodplains, and historic sites, for example); (2) land use in areas affected by key facilities (such as highway interchanges and airports); (3) development with an environmental impact of more than local significance; and (4) development of regional benefit (such as low- and moderate-income housing).

Any number of related measures can increase the likelihood that states will shoulder the burden of land-use responsibility. Enactment of a national land-use policy act would lend enormous persuasive force. If the act diminishes various federal grants in highway, airport, and open space aid to noncomplying states, the incentive will be even greater.

*Congress should enact a national land-use policy act authorizing federal funding for states to assert control over land use of state or regional impact and concern. Such legislation should include both incentives in the form of federal financial aid and sanctions in the form of reduced federal highway, airport, and open space funds.*

When development is considered over local objections, it is important that the decision-making process at the state or regional level be sensitive to legitimate local interests and concerns. The process must involve balancing the regional need for the development against any local problems it might raise, such as the adequacy of local public services and facilities and the extent to which the local jurisdiction may already have accepted a reasonable share of such development. Again, the problem involves accommodations and balances.

Other measures could help induce local residents to share some of their regulatory powers with higher levels of government. State assumption of a portion of local educational costs is one example. Judicial decisions restricting local exclusionary powers are another.

## The Role of the Courts

Court decisions striking down local exclusionary regulations could pave the way for state action to guide development. Developers and others have frequently gone to court to overcome such exclusionary provisions as excessive minimum lot- or floor-area requirements and discrimination against subsidized housing. The results, however, have not always been encouraging.

*Clustering of houses does not necessarily mean that people must live at very high densities. Residents of townhouses in Reston, Virginia, a new community near Washington, D.C., not only have a small private yard but also extensive community open space virtually at their doorsteps.*

Federal courts have struck down racially motivated exclusionary ordinances since at least 1927. In recent years, federal courts have held that regulations with the purpose or the effect of depriving minority persons of housing opportunities violate the equal protection clause of the Fourteenth Amendment of the Constitution. Where the purpose or effect cannot be shown to be racial, however, the equal protection clause may not supply the basis for a challenge, at least in the federal courts.

Far more difficult are challenges based on the principle that local regulations cannot lawfully put the local welfare ahead of the larger public welfare of state or region. These are difficult challenges, for several reasons.

For one thing, they are not the common zoning cases in which a landowner is complaining that a generally valid regulation mistreats his particular piece of land. Rather, the thrust of these challenges is that the regulation makes inadequate provision for a particular kind of development (such as low-income housing). Facts to support this charge can be exceedingly difficult to obtain, analyze, and present—except in extreme cases where the jurisdiction totally excludes a particular kind of development (like mobile home parks). Even in the extreme cases, the factual presentation can be difficult if the court entertains the theory (as it may quite properly do in the case of, say, atomic waste disposal sites) that all the "right" places for a particular type of development just happen to be in other localities. At the heart of the difficulty, though, for court as well as challenger, is the absence of an authoritative institution to determine what the regional or statewide public interest is.

Despite these difficulties, a few cases (particularly in Pennsylvania) have made it clear that local regulations cannot ignore regional needs. As a result, recent challenges to exclusionary zoning are based more and more on areawide or countywide plans.

If a court does conclude that a regulation is invalid, it faces the formidable problem of fashioning a remedy. Remedies to permit an individual project to go forward are relatively easy to frame, although the court does find itself dealing with planning questions such as project location. When the entire scheme of regulation is invalidated, the remedy becomes far more difficult. How much low-income housing is enough? Where shall it be located? What kind of mechanism should be established to authorize it over continuing local objections? Should the court retain jurisdiction and require the submission of affirmative action plans? Would a state-level administrative appeal procedure, such as Massachusetts has, be sufficient to validate an otherwise unconstitutional regulation? None of these questions is easily answered.

Despite these difficulties, and the genuine danger that an effective decree striking down illegitimate exclusion may sometimes be so broad that it also deprives a community of legitimate protection, the courts are performing an important service when they recognize that the public welfare justifying a regulation is not to be found simply by adding together the self-defined local welfare of each town in a state or region. We do not suggest that decrees striking down exclusionary regulations will end local exclusion: that must be done by legislation and administrative action. But judicial decisions can be an enormously important lever to obtain that needed action.

*The continuing efforts of civil rights groups and other litigants to obtain court decrees invalidating exclusionary regulations are encouraged as essential steps toward achieving the state legislation and administrative action that are ultimately necessary to safeguard fundamental rights and assure needed development.*

## The Federal Role

Suppose a watchful judiciary and an effective state regulatory process clear the tracks for the kind of development so often excluded by local government, but there is no money to initiate such development. Clear tracks then are not enough; there must be steam in the engine boiler as well. For a great deal of development, much of that steam has come from federal housing programs.

The production record of existing federal programs, particularly those introduced by the Housing Act of 1968, has been impressive. More low-income housing units have been built and rehabilitated under these programs in the few years since their inception than were built or rehabilitated in the previous thirty-one years of public effort to stimulate housing construction. In 1971 alone, over 400,000 new subsidized units were placed on the market. The yearly average of subsidized units produced since 1968 is over 300,000, five to six times higher than in the previous period of highest production. (See Figure 8.)

243

FIGURE 8
**Annual Housing Starts**

millions of units

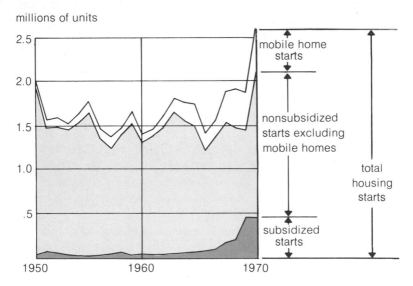

Source: Anthony Downs, *Federal Housing Subsidies: How Are They Working?* (Chicago: Real Estate Research Corporation, 1972).

The programs have done much to up-grade the quality of housing available to moderate-income families, who are the principal beneficiaries. Whether they have also helped center-city families follow jobs to suburban areas is less certain.

Federal housing subsidies are now suspended and under intensive evaluation. We consider it inappropriate to suggest how they should be reformed—how much subsidy is the right amount or what the best mechanism for achieving a given level of construction would be. Since all forms of construction have become so expensive, though, any attempt to expand the low- and moderate-cost housing stock will require substantial public funding. A strong head of steam must be kept in the boiler so that housing quality can be continually upgraded and housing quantity, expanded.

The objectives, however, should go beyond maximizing the number of dwelling units constructed at minimum cost. First, it should be possible to give needy people more housing choices than they have under current production-oriented programs.

Second, it should be possible to redesign incentives to improve the long-run quality of publicly assisted housing.

Direct consumer subsidies, whereby people are issued vouchers or cash payments to use for rent, should introduce considerable flexibility by making subsidies less visible and giving the recipients more individual choice in housing type and location. Modest evidence from HUD pilot programs suggests that consumer subsidies make good economic sense, too: recipients apparently use their extra purchasing power to shop for housing bargains, pocketing whatever portion of the rent allowance they are able to save. Direct assistance deserves careful evaluation to determine whether its social and economic advantages can be achieved on a large scale without driving up housing costs.

Where new housing is to be subsidized, improved management and maintenance can considerably increase long-term quality. Here is a case where profitability and quality have been allowed to diverge. Under the principal 1968 subsidy programs, investors made most of their profit in the early years of a project's life. This concentration of returns encouraged housing construction but reduced builders' interest in quality and long-term maintenance. Much publicly assisted housing is not expected to survive for a normal useful life—even for the life of the mortgage (which suggests that the already substantial public costs of subsidized housing may be understated).

We are impressed by proposals that would encourage developers to retain a long-term interest in the quality of their investments. A recently proposed tax bill, for example, would make it impossible for investors to depreciate a building so rapidly that its adjusted value for tax purposes falls below the amount of the building's mortgage. This proposal would eliminate some of the advantages that investors now obtain from accelerated depreciation schedules. Postponing allowable depreciation, of course, would reduce the investor's rate of return and could therefore reduce the flow of funds into housing. We believe, however, that the time has come to pay as much attention to long-term quality as to short-term quantity.

*Revisions to existing federal housing assistance programs, particularly those introduced by the Housing Act of 1968, should concentrate on a restructuring of incentives to encourage private investors to take a long-term interest in their investments. Expanding the options of assisted persons through housing allow-*

*ances should be carefully considered in the design of new housing programs.*

## Enlarging the Opportunity for Quality Development Through Scale

The construction of a few homes, the replacement of a grade school, the renovation of an apartment building—all are actions that form communities and neighborhoods and shape the lives of those who live in them. Each action affects only a few people, though perhaps significantly; the cumulative effect of many actions can change a region.

These functional pieces of a community have traditionally been set in place by any number of individual builders. Development initiative has thus been exercised, not by those responsible for putting together a whole range of functions within a geographical area, but by those responsible for only one or two functions.

The builder of each piece has usually determined his success by applying economic and functional tests. Did construction costs run over the budget? Are the homes selling; the stores renting? He has expected, realistically enough, to have his success evaluated in these same terms by those whose opinions matter to him—the board of directors or city council members, investors, bankers, and taxpayers. Human, natural, and aesthetic values have seldom been important in his thinking even about his own project ("Construction costs are high enough without hiring a landscape architect."), let alone about the neighborhood. Any assurance that individual actions will add up to enjoyable communities has been left to chance or been seen as the responsibility of someone else, usually local government. As a result, the pieces have often failed to construct quality communities.

Land development supported this kind of building by creating many lots in advance of need. A familiar two-step process arose. The land was first subdivided into lots and then built upon, lot by lot, at some future time. This process helped produce quantity construction at reasonable prices, since it gave the builder a choice among locations and lot sellers. And, of course, quantity was seen as the paramount public objective.

This "lots first, buildings later" process significantly reduced (and, where still in use, continues to reduce) the likelihood of quality development. Only at the time of subdivision can an entire tract be planned as a whole. Yet the subdivider was in the curious

246

*"I've been for quality development ever since
way back when it first became profitable."*

position of dividing the land without knowing how or when or by
whom it was to be used. He had little incentive to plan for
satisfying social relationships or imaginative physical relationships among landforms and buildings. Rather, he generally
divided the entire tract into as many saleable lots as possible. Any
opportunity to set aside open space or to adapt lot patterns to
proposed buildings or to the natural contours of the land was for-
feited. Later, when the time came for building, the lot buyer found
his opportunities tightly constrained by lot lines.

Remarkably enough, the uncertainty inherent in the lots-first
process stimulated demands for even tighter restrictions on
builders, for each lot owner found the value and enjoyment of his
lot dependent on what took place on the lots nearby. Single-
family homes were especially vulnerable to activities that brought
noise, fumes, or traffic to the neighborhood and to buildings
whose appearance was considered incompatible. The result: ever
stronger demands for deed restrictions and regulations to limit the

use of property, restrict building height, require yards, and so on.

The local land-use regulations that swept across the country in the 1920s were adapted to the lots-first-buildings-later process, with subdivision regulations established to govern the first step; zoning, to govern the second. The resulting regulations, while eliminating some of the feared uncertainty about what might happen next door, constricted still further the opportunity for imaginative building.

If we made jackets the way we have traditionally built communities, each part—sleeves, pockets, collars—would be produced over a period of years, each by a separate tailor, without any of the participants responsible for fitting the parts together.

Fortunately, the old lots-first approach has been losing ground. The changes are due not so much to the conscious efforts of government as to the growing sophistication and capacities of the real estate development industry.

Although most developers still build only functional pieces of communities, at least the pieces are bigger than they used to be. Shopping centers, industrial parks, and residential developments for hundreds of families are commonplace. Functional barriers are themselves frequently broken by commercial-residential mixtures, with industrial development sometimes included as well.

Despite this trend, the scale of most development is still far smaller than optimum. And that small scale, we believe, remains a major obstacle to quality development.

## Why Bigger Scale Is Better and New Communities Are Best

Although an increase in scale does not guarantee higher quality, it does significantly increase the developer's opportunity to achieve quality. New communities, with the fullest range of functions and the most maneuvering room, appear to offer the greatest chances, but any increase in scale is likely to bring increased opportunity.

That opportunity exists in part because large scale increases the incentives to create quality. The residents of a new community and the tenants and customers of a shopping center are likely to evaluate the whole community or center rather than just the home or store that is their immediate concern. Moreover, the developer recognizes that his profits come from the project as a whole, and, especially in the largest projects, that these earnings will come slowly, over a period of years or even decades. At the largest scale, then, the creation of some measure of enduring quality becomes a development objective and no longer just an incidental byproduct that can be left to chance or regulation. Self-interest dicates that the complex relationships within the project be planned, so planning is transformed from an outside constraint imposed on the developer to a tool he must use to achieve a satisfactory monetary return.

In some instances, "very big" can be even more profitable than just "big." A successful new community, or any very large project, can enable the developer to capture a handsome chunk of the increased land values resulting from his development. Disneyland, in California, for example, stimulated intensive development on surrounding land. The Disneyland developers could not capture the resulting land value increases because they did not own the land. When these same developers bought land for Florida's Disney World, they did not make the same mistake. They bought tens of thousands of surrounding acres as well.

Physical design is one respect in which increased scale generates increased opportunity for quality. A large project is designed as a whole from the start, without interference from pre-existing lots or owners seeking to maximize profits on each individual lot. Since the developer's profit comes from the entire project, no one fraction of it need be developed for its "highest and best use," the use that returns the most money to the owner. Instead, the developer can give his designers freedom to allocate the total quantity of planned development where they think best within the overall project boundaries. Lots, if established at all, can respond to desired development (or, later, to existing development) instead of the other way around. Such flexibility provides the chance to introduce imaginative physical relationships within and among communities and projects.

The opportunity to plan and provide a full range of urban facilities and services is another reason why the chances of achieving quality are improved with large-scale development. When the scale is very small, builders cannot economically provide many of the facilities and services needed for their projects. They and their customers find themselves dependent on local government, which often must provide the services on a catch-as-catch-can basis. Local authorities and taxpayers, equally unhappy with this situation, often try to avoid the trouble and expense of serving the new residents by requiring developers to install and pay for sidewalks, sewers, waterlines, roads, and even schools, or simply by discouraging as much development as possible.

Large-scale developers can reduce this long-standing dependency on government and, at the same time, not only mollify hostile citizens and governments but also satisfy rising consumer expectations. The large-scale residential developer, for example, may provide not only the usual streets, sidewalks, and sewers but also elaborate recreation facilities and open spaces that will help sell his houses. A shopping center developer may install (and maintain at his own expense) plazas, malls, and fountains to attract customers.

A new community can assume responsibility for planning virtually the full range of urban facilities and services. By combining both physical and financial planning and management, services can be assured when they are needed and can be sustained. The long-range perspective means that the costs of these services—even those provided at public expense, such as high schools or community health centers—can be planned for as a part of the community's development.

Yet another advantage of large scale is that it allows local governments to apply more sophisticated regulatory techniques to achieve public objectives without the constriction that is almost unavoidable when projects are small. Reviewing governments can evaluate the large project as a unit instead of applying separate sets of requirements to each component. With such a process, the need (and justification) for most of the old lot-by-lot restrictions on use and building size disappear. Hundreds of localities are already turning to this kind of overall evaluation, most often through planned unit development (PUD) provisions in local ordinances.

At the heart of PUD review is evaluation of project design. Although design review is time consuming and requires expertise that many localities lack, its potential for assuring quality seems far greater than that of any other available regulatory approach. *To promote large-scale development, communities should adopt planned unit development regulations that permit flexibility in project design, subject to overall design review. The community, as well as the developer, should have power to require that significant projects be reviewed under PUD procedures. A part of the review should be patterned after environmental impact statements.* The consideration of physically and economically feasible alternatives, as is the case with impact statements, gives the reviewing government its greatest opportunity to make realistic demands for quality.

Carefully applied design review can also substitute for some of the very low density requirements that many localities now impose. Although these requirements may have any number of rationales (such as consumer preference or the limited capacity of public facilities), the requirements often appear to be intended simply to shield the community from bad (or lack of) design.

If a community anticipates subdivision of its countryside on an essentially random basis—ten lots here this month, forty there next month—the locality is apt to decide that lots of two acres each are less likely to cause unpleasantness than lots of 8,000 square feet. The need for this crude protection disappears, however, when a project passes careful design review. A locality could find that, on a particular land parcel, a well-designed cluster project with a density of 5 or 10 families per acre provided far higher amenity levels than scattered houses on 2-acre lots. If the project is designed so that it will not overtax utilities (including, of course, those installed by the developer), there may be cause for permitting the higher density. *Even though few localities have yet been willing to grant sizable bonuses, and despite the clear risks in awarding vastly increased density (and thus vastly increased land value, which raises the risk of corruption), we believe that large density bonuses should be authorized, in appropriate cases and after careful professional design review, to new communities and other sizable projects.*

Larger scale projects, especially new communities, can also provide more housing choices to moderate- and low-income families and to racial and ethnic minorities. Harmonious blending of different priced houses is far easier when a project is planned as a whole, free of inflexible rules that each house must satisfy. In addition, a new community can accommodate a varied population from the start and perhaps avoid the resistance that is the usual response to efforts to end exclusion.

What about the possible disadvantages of large-scale development? Will it not squeeze out the little builders? Are they to go the way of the small automobile manufacturer? There is no evidence of it yet. What does appear to be happening is the separation of development functions from building functions in

*Older neighborhoods sometimes offer a sense of individuality within a community that enhances life in the city. The conservation and rehabilitation of older neighborhoods has often proved economically attractive but, unless lending institutions, zoning officials, and others are committed to a conservation policy, market pressures may force demolition of even sound old buildings and replacement with larger ones.*

some new communities and large projects. Instead of working on a few lots, the builder operates on a portion of a new community or other project, within the over-all scheme of a publicly approved development plan and subject to detailed review by the developer. In short, land is obtained differently and development is planned differently than in the past, but building goes on in much the same way.

Isn't there ample evidence from fields other than land development, though, to suggest that size is no guarantee of human concern? Hasn't the slow process of small-scale development, in which each building responds to individual choice, produced many of our most pleasant villages and most interesting urban areas? What about the knowledgeable authorities who disagree with our preference for large-scale development, citing bigness as synonomous with bureaucracy and insensitivity? And what about the many large entities, both public and private, that have produced dreadful monster projects?

The response to these legitimate concerns, we believe, lies in the enormous development needs of the nation in the remainder of this century. In some communities built over long periods, any number of constraints have helped to see that individual decisions added up to a community. Only one building material may have been conveniently available; construction technology or transportation may have been limited; natural land and water features or the need for protection may have given the community its form. Or the constraints may have been social, as when residents and builders share a sense of what is appropriate and impose social controls strong enough to protect it. ("This town has never needed a zoning by-law. We simply aren't the sort of people who build filling stations across from the common.") Much as we believe that many Americans would like to live where this kind of consensus exists, we do not see the likelihood of its arising in time to guide the huge amount of development that will take place in the next twenty-five years.

Obviously, there is no certainty of quality in large-scale projects any more than there has been in small-scale ones. Our point is simply that increased scale brings significantly greater opportunity to create quality, as well as some incentive to do so.

*Encouraging Larger Scale*

Given the disappointing results of small scale and the advantages of larger scale, we believe that public policy should encourage the latter. We think that government should use all acceptable means to channel as much development as possible into new communities. But the obstacles to success at this scale are formidable. In many locales, expected population growth will not support a new community. Even where a market does exist, net profits are not likely to begin for several years after the start of construction. Financing is therefore a problem: the bigger physical scale requires larger capital investments, including "front-end" financing, and the longer time frame requires investors and lenders willing to be patient. Land assembly becomes nearly impossible when a large number of separately owned tracts must be acquired. Difficulties over utilities, services, and zoning increase when a development is very large (and the developer, thus, highly visible). Then, there is the problem of dealing with the first residents to assure that the transformation of the community into a democratically run enterprise does not lead to citizen efforts to junk the remainder of the plan. Most formidable of all is the problem of know-how; at such a large scale, the developer assumes responsibility for an extraordinarily complex array of planning and management decisions. Few developers have experience to handle them.

Because of these obstacles, most development is going to take place at scales smaller than new communities. Even optimistic boosters of new towns hope for accommodation of only 15-20 percent of the nation's population growth over the next three decades.[15] What, then, would be an ideal size for the rest? The American Institute of Architects has recommended a basic community building block (called a "growth unit") of 500 to 3,000 dwelling units, large enough to sustain an elementary school, community center with recreational facilities, convenience shopping, and open space.[16] Some observers have concluded that even this may be too large for many developers. "You're in trouble if you build more than 500 houses at a time, trouble with the land, the permits, and the rest of it," said one builder with long experience. Although we acknowledge uncertainty about how large a scale can be achieved under varying circumstances, we would encourage large-scale development wherever feasible.

*Governments should use all acceptable means to channel development into new communities or, to the extent that these are unachievable, into "growth units" of 500 or more dwellings with related services, as recommended by the American Institute of Architects. The success of this policy will rest on the effectiveness of measures to overcome the obstacles that now keep developers from operating at larger scales.*

Financing can be a major obstacle. The federal government now guarantees bonds issued by developers to finance new communities that meet the social, environmental, and other criteria set out in Title VII of the Urban Growth and New Community Development Act of 1970. (Since the program began in 1971, fifteen new communities have been designated eligible for the HUD bond guarantees, including Jonathan, Minnesota; Flower Mound, Texas; Gananda, New York; and Harbison, South Carolina.) The problem here is federal review, which is slow and cumbersome. *A determination of eligibility for bond guarantees by HUD should clear the way for special attention by all other federal agencies. Those agencies which need to review specific elements of a new community plan or to make determinations on aid or assistance should work with HUD to develop realistic timetables for review.*

HUD assistance to new communities is valuable and should be continued. But realistic federal efforts to encourage scale should also focus on an intermediate scale that will be undertaken by developers more often than new communities. To date, the smallest community declared eligible for HUD bond insurance is Lysander, New York, where 5,000 dwelling units are planned. *The aggregate of loan guarantees now available under Title VII of the Urban Growth and New Community Development Act of 1970 should be increased and the guarantees made available for developments as small as 500 housing units together with related facilities.*

More and more communities are turning to regulations and utility installation policies in an effort to restrict the quantity of development within their borders. The suburbs of Chicago and Washington, D.C.; Savannah, Georgia; communities in Florida; Staten Island in New York City; and areas in California have all faced building shut-downs because of utility moratoriums. If this trend continues (and it seems likely to where the new mood reigns), there may be some limited benefit to measures that would grant large-scale developers relief from these restrictions (and assist developers or communities in providing needed pollution-treatment facilities). State laws could, for example, narrow the scope of local restrictions or establish administrative provisions for granting exemptions in individual cases while at the same time providing assistance where local utilities may be overburdened.

It is becoming increasingly clear that governments will need to assist developers in land assembly. But how? Should governments borrow from the land banking experience of Western Europe (where land is bought by the public and reserved or banked for future use) or from the urban renewal experience in the United States?

Despite continuing discussion at conferences and seminars, measures such as land banking have made little headway here. The reasons are clear. Dissatisfaction with the results of the development process has not, until recently, been a powerful political force. There are important ideological objections to direct governmental action in land assembly, and land banking appears so expensive as to be impractical in many situations. Most important, though, are the uncertainties about how these measures would work—about how land would be selected well in advance of need and who would maintain it. Aware that a great deal of governmental action—expressway construction, dam building, or urban renewal, to take three examples—has been less than a triumph of quality, many doubt that the uncertain benefits of more direct action warrant the costs and difficulties of experimentation.

The new mood, with its distaste for development and its distrust of governmental decision-making, does not at first glance seem likely to bring governments more actively into the development process. But it may unintentionally achieve precisely that by establishing obstacles to development that only direct governmental action can overcome. New mood conservationists are concerned principally with the quality of development; public policy must assure quantity as well. And quantity refers, not only to numbers of structures, but to the prices at which they are made available. We foresee a need for more direct governmental action primarily to serve these objectives.

We suggest that governmental action be directed through new state agencies charged to assist and encourage desired development (especially large-scale development) and even to undertake it themselves. The agencies should, we believe, have a full range of powers to deal with problems of land assembly as well as those of utilities, regulations, financing, and other needs. Any number

257

The scarcity of large undeveloped tracts of land in single ownership in and
near cities makes it desirable to consider possible alternative uses of
governmental installations for new developments or as public open space.
Fort Lincoln, a 335-acre site formerly used as a training school for boys in
Washington, D.C., is to be developed as a new community with 4,600
dwelling units for 16,000 persons. The community is to include a substantial quantity of housing for low- and moderate- income people and is
to be connected by mass transit to downtown Washington.

of states and communities promote industrial development in this way. There is also precedent (if not always with the best of results) in urban renewal statutes and programs, which assigned a positive developmental role to local governments.

The most important precedent for such an agency is offered by the New York State Urban Development Corporation (UDC). Created in 1968 by the state legislature (at Governor Nelson Rockefeller's strong urging), UDC is a public benefit corporation authorized to initiate a wide range of industrial, commercial, and residential development, including renewal or redevelopment projects. UDC's role is primarily one of catalyst, of identifying a development need or opportunity and of setting public agencies and the private sector to work on it.

UDC can put at a developer's disposal access to governmental power and programs, a sophisticated sense of financing and administrative possibilities, and legal authority to assemble land. Among the most important (and certainly the most controversial) powers granted UDC are its authority to override local ordinances and codes and to acquire property by condemnation. Of nearly equal importance is the agency's capacity (because of its statewide perspective and experience) to mobilize resources and "package" a project, telescoping the complicated, typically sequential phases of land acquisition, design, and so on into shorter time spans by harnessing public and private parties to a program.

The arsenal of tools at UDC's disposal, however, does not include money for direct subsidies. Although the agency is free to use federal and state subsidy programs, it does not itself have the resources for subsidizing projects. Thus, although UDC has ample power to float tax-exempt bonds (in 1971, $250 million in bonds were outstanding), it must retire them, so its projects cannot lose money.

In 1970 and 1971, UDC initiated close to $700 million worth of residential and nonresidential development in over sixty locations across the state. In addition to the numerous residential, commercial, and industrial projects, work began on a new community and a new-town-in-town.

What powers should the state agencies we are proposing be granted? Both the power of eminent domain and power to override local regulations, if the agencies are to have a realistic opportunity to perform their functions successfully. We do not relish the prospect of development needs overriding the wishes of property owners or local residents any more than we relish it when the construction of an airport or some other public facility makes it necessary.

If UDC experience is any guide, though, public opinion appears to preclude excessive use of either power. According to UDC president Edward J. Logue:

> It is a source of some amazement to me that in our first three and one-half years we have not had to use [condemnation], though knowledge of its availability has undoubtedly been a factor in some of our land acquisitions. UDC's unique powers to override local building codes and zoning ordinances have been our principal source of controversy. We have used the powers with the avowed or tacit support of local governments on many occasions and thus far only rarely against the opposition of local government. And then only after consultation with local officials and when compliance was not feasible or practicable.

In most cases, these powers should not have to be used. But if they are not there, the bargaining position of the agency changes fundamentally and the likelihood of success decreases markedly.

Once the principle is accepted that government ought to act affirmatively in whatever ways are needed to achieve publicly beneficial development, any number of questions arise about exactly how this responsibility should be exercised. Should the governmental entity be an agency or a public benefit corporation (as is the UDC)? Should it engage in land banking for long-term future development or should it turn over land rapidly? When should it take initiative, and when should it merely respond to initiatives taken by private developers and builders? Experience will suggest more conclusive answers to these questions.

We can, however, see a number of additional opportunities that may exist once an entity with these responsibilities is established, opportunities which may be greater or lesser depending on the choice of operating structures and methods:

—The opportunity to capture, for the public, land-value increases resulting from designation of land for intensive use.

—The opportunity to recover governmental investments in public works (such as highways, transit lines, flood-control projects) that increase the value of benefited land, since a significant amount of land can be assembled in concert with the transportation or public works agency.

—The opportunity to channel the development forces set in motion by new transportation arteries. Planners and others have long recognized the desirability of using positively the leverage

260

provided by the enormous public investment in transportation. Without governmental land ownership, however, the forces have proven exceedingly difficult to channel.

*The states should establish governmental entities, comparable to New York's Urban Development Corporation, responsible for assisting and when necessary directly undertaking large-scale projects. These entities should have the full range of powers, including the power of eminent domain, the power to override local land-use regulations, and the power to control the provision of public utilities, when necessary, to overcome the barriers that now prevent most developers from operating at the larger scales that the public interest requires.*

# Chapter VII
# Subdividing the Great Outdoors

"A place for the rich to get richer."

"Your opportunity to purchase five magnificent acres of America's dwindling real estate."

"You don't have to build immediately. You can buy now and build later."

"Your chance in a lifetime to acquire a sizable piece of choice property on exceptionally easy terms."

"Of the 5,000 miles of Ocean Front in America, less than 300 miles still remain available to the public. . . . By 1982, ocean property may not be available at all."

"There are still a few opportunities left to invest in valuable, useable, and enjoyable property. Opportunities that won't be available much longer. Maybe not past this spring."

"Don't wait to buy land. Buy land and then wait."

"Price: $4,360; cash down payment required: $45."

"A FREE DRAWING . . . and everyone visiting will be eligible for a color TV and 6 vacations."

From Martha's Vineyard to Hawaii, from Colorado to Florida, rural land is being subdivided and sold at an unprecedented rate. There is scarcely a state where subdividers are not turning farms or forests (or deserts or swamps) into lots, streams into lakes, and the hopes of the average man for investment or leisure property into sales and profits. In 1971 an estimated 625,000 recreational lots were sold by over 10,000 subdividers. In Florida alone, about 200,000 lots are registered each year in recreational and retirement subdivisions. In just one Pennsylvania county (population: under 15,000), subdividers mapped 25,000 lots and sold off 12,000 of them in just five years. Rural lot sales in Arizona have totaled 1 million acres, experts estimate.

Concern about subdivision of beachfront and countryside on Martha's Vineyard, off the coast of Massachusetts, has led to the introduction of strong protective legislation in the U.S. Senate. In Vermont and Florida, adverse publicity given to the recreational land subdividers helped pass environmentally oriented state land-use laws. In Pennsylvania, California, and Arizona, major scandals involving alleged victimization of lot purchasers have been front page news.

Some of the lots sold each year will accommodate the growing desire of American families for second homes. According to one estimate, 95,000 second homes were started in 1971—up from an average of 20,000 per year in the 1940s, 40,000 per year in the 1950s, and 75,000 per year in the 1960s. The National Association of Home Builders estimates that the annual volume of second home starts will reach 150,000 during the 1970s. With the Federal Housing Administration (FHA) now insuring mortgages on second homes (as of spring 1972), the rate of second home construction may grow even faster than predicted.

In the absence of specific problems, such as consumer victimization or environmental damage, there is nothing wrong with second homes. They can bring much enjoyment and be sound investments. Resort homes are becoming more common in many countries—in Sweden, for example, where 50 percent of the households own second homes (compared with 5 percent of U.S. households in 1970).

Most purchasers of recreational lots, though, are buying but not building. For the nation as a whole, at least six recreational lots were sold in 1971 for each second home constructed (in fact, the ratio is probably higher because many second homes are built on country property and farms that have not been subdivided). (See Figure 9.) In California, between 50,000 and 100,000 acres of rural land were subdivided annually in the late 1960s and early 1970s by recreational lot sellers. By 1971, however, houses had been built on only 3 percent of the lots sold in the previous decade. One study reportedly showed that "enough mountain lots were subdivided in 1969 to satisfy the needs of California for the next 25 years."[1]

Why is there such interest in buying undeveloped rural lots? Surveys in two California counties and in Pennsylvania suggest

FIGURE 9
**Ratio of Lots Subdivided to
Homes Constructed in Selected Subdivisions**

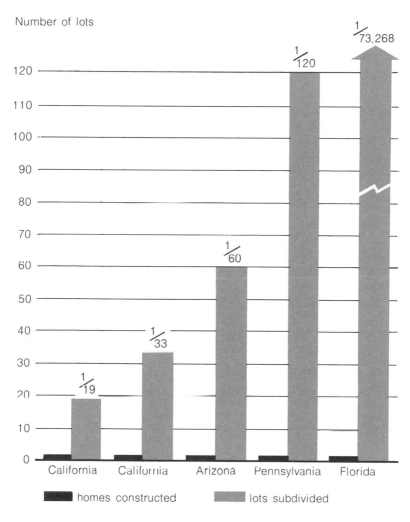

Number of lots

Note: The table reflects both lots sold and unsold because the subdividers for the most part refused to provide information on how many lots have been sold. In each subdivision, though, the sale of lots began at least 10 years ago.

Sources: Robert Cahn, *Land in Jeopardy*, reprint of a series of articles from the *Christian Science Monitor* (Boston: Christian Science Publishing Society, 1973); Morton C. Paulson, *The Great Land Hustle* (Chicago: Henry Regnery Co., 1972); Center for the Study of Responsive Law, *Power and Land in California* (New York: Grossman Publishers, 1973).

the reason: About 70 percent of the prospective customers reported that they were primarily interested in the land for investment rather than for enjoyment.

Advertising by many lot sellers encourages dreams of profit. A sales representative of a large Florida subdivision, visiting the task force offices, talked of "smart people" who were getting in "on the ground floor" by buying land that could not be developed for ten years but could be "traded up" at big profits later. Time was said to be "running out" on the opportunity to buy the kind of land the representative was offering. Although the subdivision was touted as a "new community," careful inspection of plans and federal and state disclosure reports revealed that a great many of the lots for sale were not accessible by roads and that the lands designated on plans for schools, hospitals, libraries, and shops were nothing more than white spaces on a map.

Such aggressive sales practices are common in the lot sales industry. "Most of the developers use high pressure, hard-sell tactics after attracting prospects through massive advertising and promotions featuring free dinner parties, gifts of merchandise, vacation certificates, and telephone solicitation," reported Robert Cahn of the *Christian Science Monitor*.[2]

In a series of articles, Cahn elaborated on the sales techniques of some land sellers:

> One of the most popular sales devices is the free dinner party, usually given in a small banquet room of one of the good restaurants or hotels of a city. The "guests," whose interests were whetted by direct mail or telephone, come with the expectation of hearing a sales presentation.
>
> What they are not prepared for is the intensity and skill of the sales pitch. The operation is based on getting the prospects' signatures on a sales contract before they have time to think about whether the investment is a good one or whether it meets their specific needs.
>
> Following dinner, a talk and film or slide show is presented on the virtues of land buying and of this particular development. Often the scenes are from another project of the developer—"this is what yours will look like." Television, movie, and sports stars appear in many of the promotion movies. Sometimes they are part owners of the companies. An "adviser," or "investment counselor," will start the sales pitch, with one salesman to each small table. He softens up the prospects with a primer on why land is such a good investment.
>
> ("Did you ever stop to think that the only thing you can't manufacture is earth? The world can never get any bigger. But the population will get bigger. So land will get scarcer and scarcer. And that's why the best investment in the world is a piece of earth.") He may have a choice quote

from Andrew Carnegie or Bernard Baruch at tongue-tip to prove his point.

Then he tells about this particular subdivision, what the developer is going to do and why it's a great buy.

About this time one of the "consultants" at another table may jump up and shout: "Put a hold on lot No. 122."

Often as not, this is a plant, and the "buyers" at that table are shills. But it has its effect, and pressure mounts. The salesman says he has only a few lots that can be offered this evening. He hints that the company plans to raise prices next week. Now is the time to buy. He is authorized to give a $500 discount to buyers who sign tonight.

Above all, the salesman works toward a "close"—to get the prospect to sign something. He may say it is only a reservation, or an option to buy, that he really isn't selling anything, and that there is a money-back guarantee.[3]

The aggressive sales pitch is more often than not accompanied by vague and misleading replies to specific questions. "We don't know exactly when the improvements will be completed." "We have no reason to believe that septic tanks will not be adequate. . . . It would be unconstitutional for a government not to permit them." "We don't need a reserve to guarantee the return of your money if it turns out that you aren't able to build. The reputation of our company is your guarantee." "I'm not sure exactly what it would cost to get electricity and telephone now but, of course, the cost will go down when more residences are built." "I think we're planning to keep our private security guards indefinitely." "There is no need for garbage collection service now; when there is, the company will take care of it." "I'm not sure precisely what arrangements have been made on that."

How much does the consumer-purchaser stand to gain when he buys a lot? Will he, as he perhaps imagines, be participating in a great land boom? The answer is probably no, for lots are plentiful, the buyer normally pays an already inflated price that is several times the price of raw land; and the big subdividers have the resources and sales experience to reach potential buyers far more effectively than an individual with a lot or two. The risk of future regulations—a prohibition on the construction of septic tanks due to groundwater pollution, or a building moratorium due to sewage treatment plant overload—can impede resale and add still further to the investment hazards.

Although nearly all land sellers emphasize resale profits, no company is known to produce records of how customers have fared with resales. At least one large enterprise promises that its

Recreational land subdivisions in New Mexico (above) and Florida (below).

own sales force will resell properties for its customers, but privately instructs its salesmen not to show such lots and threatens dismissal if they do. Extreme? Perhaps. But the prospectus for a debentures issue floated by one giant land sales corporation sums up the usual situation well: "The price at which [we sell] . . . land under installment contracts does not reflect the current market price for cash purchases of comparable developed or undeveloped land. . . . There is no significant resale market for installment land contracts."

What, then, of the buyer who wants to use his lot for a second home? A little checking shows that if he wants to build right away he may face unanticipated expenses.

Task force staff members inquired about properties from one recreational lot seller in Colorado. In response, the company wrote that it offered "no free dinners . . . movies . . . gift premiums . . . cut rate trips to Colorado . . . or any of the promotional incentives which characterize so much of the land sales business today. What we have to offer is good land. Land you can walk on . . . ride on . . . build on." Along with their letter came a draft contract for purchase of a designated lot. The price of the 5-acre "ranch" lot was $5,000, to be paid over an eight-year period with a 6 percent interest charge.

To determine the cost of building right away, we investigated the cost of utilities for "our" lot. According to the local telephone company, a telephone could be installed on a lot close to the old ranch house for about $130. When we described our lot, the installation man laughed. "I doubt you'll want a telephone. It'll cost you about $400 a mile from the reservoir, and the lot you're talking about is 5 miles away." According to the local power company, our lot was only a mile and a half from the power line—a better situation than with the telephone company—but the cost of installation was $5,000 a mile. The power salesman recommended the use of a gasoline powered generator, which would cost from $900 to $1,300. For water, a lot owner must drill his own well. According to a property report on the development filed with state authorities in New York, drilling would cost from $6 to $8 per foot for a well 100-250 feet deep and an average septic tank system would cost about $800.

(To a staff member's inquiry about the value of the lot, a local real estate agent spoke of finding comparable 5-acre lots for between $1,900 and $3,000. But, he suggested, a person with a little capital could purchase a larger piece of land, say 150 acres, subdivide it into lots, and sell it off himself. The agent knew of some good land for a "little less than a hundred an acre" and said he could arrange everything with the county.)

The way in which many rural lot subdivisions are created leads to two basic concerns. Consumer fraud is one. Damage both to the environment and to opportunities for quality development is the other. First, then, the matter of protecting buyers.

## Protecting Buyers

Concern about widespread deception of purchasers led Congress during the late 1960s to pass the Interstate Land Sales Full Disclosure Act (ILSFDA). This act requires subdividers of 50 or more lots of less than 5 acres each to register with the Department of Housing and Urban Development (HUD) if they wish to advertise in interstate commerce. (Industry lobbying succeeded in having HUD oversee registration rather than the Securities and Exchange Commission, as originally proposed.) Developers must also make a report available to lot buyers indicating what facilities and services (water, sewers, tennis courts, roads, garbage collection, swimming pools and lakes, etc.) have been promised and what arrangements have been made to assure that such facilities will in fact be built. (Figure 10, which shows the number of property reports on file with HUD, provides some indication of the extent of subdivision activity.)

HUD has a staff of fifty-five to administer the act, including four investigators who check out complaints. The agency has received thousands of complaints, suspended nearly 200 developers from selling in interstate commerce, and obtained indictments of six lot sellers. (Three of the six indicted were convicted; the remaining three await trial.) Since March 1972, HUD has attempted to make up for its meager staff resources by publicizing deceptive sales practices.

Several states also have laws to protect lot buyers, with those of California and New York providing the most protection.

California's most stringent regulations are aimed at out-of-state companies seeking to sell to Californians. The law requires sellers of land located outside the state to have their land appraised by the California Department of Real Estate to see whether the prices are "fair, equitable, and just." As a result, many major land sellers simply do not operate in California. Instead, prospective

270

buyers from that state are enticed, via free airplane trips, to Las Vegas or Colorado to hear a pitch that would be unlawful back home.

California law further provides buyers with an unwaivable right to cancel contracts within two weeks after signing; obligates developers to post performance bonds for the completion of promised facilities; and provides a framework within which counties can lay down environmental controls. (The California attorney general, acting on more than 500 letters of complaint, won a temporary restraining order against a major corporation and later exacted an agreement from the corporation to establish a fund of $24 million to return payments to purchasers misled by false adver-

FIGURE 10
**Indication of Interstate Land Sales**

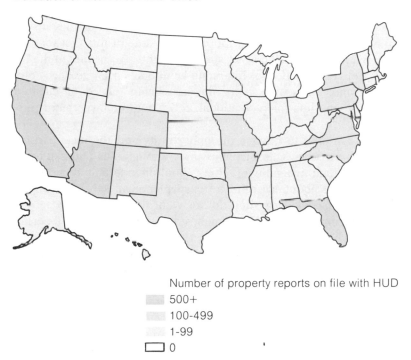

Number of property reports on file with HUD
500+
100-499
1-99
0

Based on the number of property reports on file and in the process of being filed with the Office of Interstate Land Sales, Department of Housing and Urban Development, as of March 6, 1973. It should be noted that large developments have more than one property report on file.

tising and an additional fund of $34.2 million to guarantee completion of promised facilities.)

For companies wanting to sell to New Yorkers, state law requires that prospective buyers be able to see their sites. (In many instances, now inaccessible land is sold from colored plat maps on which a hypothetical future has been sketched while salesmen suggest that, since the land can be traded back to the company, there is no need to view it.) New York State also inspects out-of-state land offerings more closely than most states and requires performance bonds guaranteeing promised improvements, a provision that has led savvy shoppers for recreational lots to ask to see the New York property report, since it will disclose in some detail any firm plans and reserves for facilities.

Federal and state laws have not stopped fraud, though. Widespread misrepresentation by land sellers continues. Many prospective customers are not shown the required reports, or they are pressured by salesmen into disregarding them, or they are so blinded by salesmen's descriptions of possible profits that they ignore warnings and sign away statutory rights. According to the director of HUD's Office of Interstate Land Sales, George Bernstein, "Thousands of people every day are being misled or cheated when buying lots for recreational, retirement or investment purposes."[4]

It is essential to remove the opportunity and the incentive for the high-pressure salesmanship that now enables companies to sell lots which, when buyers think about them later and overcome guilt feelings about accepting a free airplane trip to Nevada or a 9-piece set of cookware, they do not want or cannot afford.

At present, the ILSFDA provides a 48-hour cooling-off period during which buyers can change their minds. The right can be waived by the buyer, however, and many sellers routinely require buyers to sign waivers. The right is not even granted if the buyer goes to the site (thus, another incentive for those free airplane trips). Some sellers voluntarily permit a substantially longer cooling-off period. All should be required to do so. *The Interstate Land Sales Full Disclosure Act and comparable state acts should be amended to give buyers of lots, in projects governed by the acts, a nonwaivable cooling-off period of 30 days instead of the present 48 hours. The cooling-off period should be granted to all buyers including those who have seen the land before they buy.*

Protection now available under the ILSFDA is limited to lots containing no more than 5 acres. Buyers of larger lots are unprotected. Especially in some of the western deserts, sellers find it possible to sell much larger lots—perhaps 20 or 25 waterless acres—using the same objectionable methods that gave rise to demands for the ILSFDA in the first place. We think that buyers of these properties also deserve protection. *The ILSFDA, comparable state legislation, and other pertinent provisions protecting lot buyers should be amended so that projects containing more than 50 lots are covered, irrespective of the acreage contained in each lot.*

In many subdivisions, the buyer remains dependent on the seller to install improvements several years in the future. The buyer may also be depending on the seller's promise to resell the lot should the buyer lose interest. The buyer is thus dependent on the continued solvency of the seller, much like a buyer of stock in a corporation. The original proposals that led to the ILSFDA called for the treatment of lot sales as though they were security transactions to be governed by the prospectus requirements of the Securities and Exchange Commission. That was a good idea, which would have benefited some of the more sophisticated buyers by giving them protection they need. *Congress should amend federal securities legislation so that the sale of lots in any project containing more than 50 lots will, unless all obligations of the seller are performed before any payments by the buyer, be regarded as a securities transaction subject to the prospectus and other requirements of the Securities and Exchange Commission.*

There can be little doubt that the reliability of an improvement program—how many improvements are planned to be constructed by what dates—significantly affects the quality of the investment opportunity (as well as the quality of the resulting community). Yet, financial statements need not now provide any detail on these matters. *The Securities and Exchange Commission should require that descriptions of development programs be made available in conjunction with financial statements of land sales corporations, including pertinent information concerning the types of community facilities to be provided, the dates at which they are scheduled for completion, and who is to construct them.*

The underlying purpose of the ILSFDA (and most similar state acts) is to require disclosure of facts that might influence a buyer's

*"I think I've got it!*
*We can subdivide the back forty acres*
*in 2-acre lots, dam the stream up for a lake, and sell off*
*the ridgetop for condominiums.*
*Then we'll be able to afford a summer*
*place on the island."*

investment decisions. For sophisticated and experienced buyers, disclosure may be enough protection. For the inexperienced buyers likely to be purchasing unimproved lots, though, disclosure is not enough. Like the required small print at the bottom of cigarette ads, the unpleasant realities disclosed in the ILSFDA property report do not seem to stand up against the colorful and seductive main pitch.

If disclosure is not enough, then what is? We believe that a warranty is in order, essentially a warranty of product fitness. Fitness should include (among other elements) the availability of water and sewage disposal facilities that do not violate any law or regulation. It is likely that many local and state governments, as they catch on to the problems that lot sales projects are creating for them, will impose tougher sewage disposal requirements during the next few years. What should happen when tough

274

requirements prevent the buyer, perhaps after making payments for several years, from obtaining a building permit? We believe that the risk should be on the seller. He can much more readily install required facilities than can an individual buyer. And if the seller bears the risk, he has less incentive to shop around for jurisdictions where environmental controls are still weak.

What should be the buyer's remedy for breach of warranty? At a minimum, he should be entitled to his money back with interest and damages since he is not getting what he bargained for.

*Federal and state legislation should obligate the sellers of lots (in projects containing 50 or more lots) to guarantee to each buyer that his lot will, for a period of one year after the date on which he is scheduled to obtain title, and again for one year after the date on which the contract obligates the seller to complete all improvements, be fit for construction of a dwelling (or for any commercial or industrial use specified by the seller in the sales contract). Fitness for use should be defined, by statute or regulation, to include suitable water supply, the availability of lawful sewage disposal facilities, and safety elements (such as, that the land is not floodable, that it is free from danger of rockslides). The warranty should be unwaivable and breach of warranty should entitle the buyer to return of all his payments, with interest and damages, up to the date of breach.*

### Achieving Quality Development

Although consumer fraud is the most widely publicized misfortune resulting from today's lot sales practices, damage to the environment and to opportunities for quality development deserve at least equal attention. For what most recreational lot sellers are doing is extending, to thousands of square miles of rural open spaces, the unfortunate development method that creates "lots first, buildings later." The defects of that method—the common overemphasis on land as speculative commodity, the lack of concern with land as resource and as site for quality development—have become increasingly clear as first-home developers abandon the approach in favor of more imaginative methods. Yet the hard-learned lesson is not being applied to the countryside.

If past experience is any guide, many of the lots now being created will never be used at all: in this case, it is, "lots first, buildings never." The lot lines will remain on the record books, though, and land titles will become ever more clouded as decades pass. Tough for the land buyers? Yes. Tough also for the environment, as is shown by any number of "dead subdivisions" created forty or fifty years ago. If a few scattered lots are built upon, the subdivision may become a sparsely settled rural slum served by neglected roads and lacking essential services. Since the undeveloped lots are too small for agricultural or other nonurban use, no one bothers to manage or care for the land. The subdivision has transformed open space into idle vacant lots no one cares about.

What if the subdivided land, perhaps years later, becomes suitable for urban development? With the land divided into small pieces, with title clouded and prices driven up, there is little likelihood of reassembly for the more imaginative planning and development now possible. Once the countryside has been given over to quarter-acre or 1-acre lots (and most recreational lots sold in 1971 were one-quarter to 1 acre in size), you can forget thoughts of clustering, variable densities, common open spaces, and the like. Even if the buyers' dreams of riches have faded away, the lot lines will survive to block sensitive use of the land.

Where lots *are* built upon, a different set of environmental problems arises. Imagine an area of "unsurpassed scenic beauties" (as one promotional brochure put it), with rolling hills and falling streams, outcroppings of rock, thick stands of woodland, and perhaps a lake. A careful survey of the area would suggest what ought to be preserved and what intensity of development could be tolerated without doing violence to the environment. Often, a careful land capacity inventory will reveal that considerable development is possible in some areas; little or none, in others.

Yet lot sellers have little incentive to plan in this sensitive way. Like their predecessors in earlier decades, they typically pay little attention to the conformity of lots to the realities of topography and the hydrologic cycle. Many also try to avoid the costs of needed water supply and waste disposal facilities. The results can be disastrous.

In the Pennsylvania county in which 12,000 lots were sold in five years, soils in about half the area are unsuitable for on-site sewage disposal systems. Some water supplies are already contaminated. Nevertheless, 89 percent of the recreational lot sellers in the vicinity indicated in a survey that they provided no sewers (and 52 percent, no water). Only the low level of building activity prevents severe ecological damage from occurring.

Over two-thirds of recreational subdivisions are sited near water, often on artificially constructed lakes. While covenants on lots are often designed to protect the view of the water, the lakes and streams themselves are often neglected. Poorly planned roads, clearing of ground cover, high-density settlement—all can cause erosion and resultant sedimentation of water bodies. Once a natural drainage system is altered, rains and sudden melts may send water and soil cascading down uncovered hillsides.

In some recreational land areas, the heavy fertilizers used to keep golf courses and lawns healthy find their way into adjoining lakes. So do laundry and dishwasher detergents, oil products from cars, salts from winter snow removal operations, and the fertilizers, weed killers, and insecticides used by homeowning gardeners. The result may be a lake that is unfit for swimming in as few as five years, a putrid nuisance in ten.

The California Environmental Quality Study Council has estimated that 37 percent of stream mileage in the Sierra foothills has been damaged by siltation, stream bank alterations, and waste discharges from recreational land subdivisions. Once pristine Lake Tahoe changed color because of runoff from surrounding development. (A court there halted one developer, and the Tahoe Regional Planning Agency has drawn up plans to severely curtail future development.) In Marin County, near San Francisco, coastal lots in an area extremely vulnerable to landslides are being marketed for second homes.

What steps should be taken to reduce damage such as this? The first step has already been recommended: end the high-pressure salesmanship that concentrates the attention of lot buyers on speculative profit rather than on quality and livability. When the consumer thinks of his lot only as something to resell at a profit, he is less likely to ask the difficult questions that he would ask if he were thinking of the lot as a place for the family to spend weekends or vacations. Nowhere is the gap between profitability and livability clearer, or its consequences more damaging, than in recreational subdivisions.

The second step is to base public policy on the recognition that second homes form communities. However much we may like to dream of recreation homes as isolated refuges in the wilderness, they are rarely isolated. Most sales projects would, if fully developed, establish suburban densities. At all but the very lowest densities, these developments require most of the facilities and services—roads, sewers, trash removal, fire and police protection—needed in urban areas.

With the demand for second homes growing, then, it is essential that public policy foster the creation of recreation communities that are livable, enjoyable, and ecologically sound. Such communities can best be created by the same methods that should be used to create any other kind of community, methods based on sound planning, with development kept out of areas for which it is unsuited, with developers responsible for the full range of needed facilities and services, and with incentives for quality built into the development process.

*Recreational home developments should be required to satisfy the same environmental and land-use policy standards that ought to apply to first-home developments.* Compromise with quality standards should not be permitted simply because a project is labelled as one for second homes or for recreational use. Indeed, some excuses for compromise that may exist for first home projects, on grounds of cost for low-income families, for example, do not apply to second homes.

Experience over the decades demonstrates the problems that can arise when standards are lowered or waived on grounds that later prove spurious. ("No one is going to live in these houses in the winter, of course.") Increased leisure time and the four-day week are already leading to the "winterization" of thousands of seasonal homes. The only safe course is to take subdividers at their word: when a subdivision plat shows thousands of lots, occupancy of which would urbanize a remote area, then the development must be seen as setting forth the physical organization of a future urban community. Adequate planning and facilities for such a community should be required by law.

*Local governments should establish subdivision requirements sufficient to assure that all subdivisions, whether for first or second homes, will attain acceptable development standards and provide adequate public facilities, including water supply and sewage disposal facilities (installed or bonded), as a condition of subdivision approval. If bonded, sufficient sums should be added to the estimated cost to account for continuing inflation.*

This does not mean that all vacation home communities need have sidewalks or curbs, paved roads or street lights, any more than all communities for first homes need have them. Flexibility in planning should remain so that a natural atmosphere can be maintained. But no relaxation in standards should be tolerated simply on the grounds that "no one will be living in vacation homes." Second home developments should be planned so they are enjoyable places for people to live at least a part of their lives.

For recreation development, as for any other development, the base of protective regulations should be established by local governments. Yet, because large-scale development is new, local residents and officials of rural localities often lack experience in responding to it. They are likely to recognize that new development means income, in purchases at local stores, in construction by local contractors, in mortgages by local banks and services by local lawyers and surveyors. But they may be oblivious to the later costs that experienced localities know about—the dollar costs of providing roads and sewers and other services for scattered projects, the personal costs of congestion and changed lifestyles and disruption of cherished countryside, and the social costs of a new urban and affluent population settling among small town people and farmers.

The process of subdivision occurs at such an extraordinary rate that often the damage is done before local officials wake up to the problem. About 46,000 acres in one Pennsylvania county were subdivided in five years beginning in 1967. The rate of subdivision has now reached 10,000 acres per year. At present rates, 30 percent of the county will have been subdivided by 1980. If all the lots sold since 1968 in two Pennsylvania counties were to be built upon and occupied, the "second home" population would outnumber local residents by almost five to one. (See Figure 11.)

Small jurisdictions may also lack the resources to deal with huge new projects. Within New York's vast Adirondack Park, there are eighty-seven towns, only seventeen of which have populations greater than 2,500. Because these towns have limited financial resources and, until recently, no significant development pressures, less than 10 percent of their land has even been zoned. One firm owns 18,500 acres of land in the Adirondacks in Altamont Township (population: 6,500). The subdivider has indicated his intention to sell from 4,000 to 7,000 lots in the township, accommodating a potential seasonal population of 15,000 to 25,000 people. Throughout the sparsely populated Adirondacks, an estimated sixty developments are planned or in operation.

In one rural Florida county (population: 4,500), a major corporation is developing a "new community" for 750,000 people.

FIGURE 11
**Impact of Recreational Lot Development on Population**

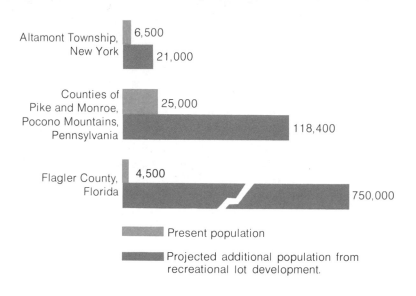

Altamont Township, New York
6,500
21,000

Counties of Pike and Monroe, Pocono Mountains, Pennsylvania
25,000
118,400

Flagler County, Florida
4,500
750,000

Present population

Projected additional population from recreational lot development.

Sources: Present population: U.S. Bureau of the Census, *County and City Data Book: 1970.* Projected Population Additions: New York State Department of Environmental Conservation. Tocks Island Regional Advisory Council. Florida Internal Improvement Fund.

The county, today, has no county engineer, no planning agency, no county health services, one elementary school, one junior high school, one high school (now under construction), fifteen school buses, no public transportation system, two volunteer fire companies, and one garbage disposal site.

The case of the Florida county illustrates still another reason why localities are often lax in defending themselves against lot sales projects. They simply cannot believe that many of the lots will be used. In the Florida case, the county sheriff pointed out that the "new community" is making no demands on his four deputies, since a private protective agency furnishes security. Asked about plans to deal with the influx of new residents, he replied, "None of us believes there will ever be that many people. If they show up, we're in trouble." The school superintendent commented, "I can't imagine that many people. If they come, I hope I've retired by then."

In Colorado, one local official seemed to treat a local lot sales project in much the same way that he might regard a speed trap that picked up a few dollars for the town from passing motorists. He saw no need to worry about the land itself, which never had been worth anything, and no need for municipal services. "After all, no one's ever going to use those lots," he commented.

A miscalculation can be devastating. If people do show up, the locality will face demands for fire, police, and garbage collection services, for street and utility maintenance, and the like. Officials of one California county were stunned by the estimated $2 million needed for repairs to faulty roads, drainage systems, and utilities installed by the developers of a recreational subdivision.

Some localities, of course, have long had adequate standards for first-home developments and simply apply the same standards to recreation developments. Other localities protect themselves later, sometimes after a good deal of damage has been done, by imposing septic tank bans or building moratoriums.

One small New Hampshire town sought to avoid environmental and growth problems by placing 50 percent of the town's area under 3- and 6-acre minimum-lot-size requirements. A developer who had purchased 510 acres, anticipating rezoning for later development at a density in excess of the existing zoning allowance, found the rezoning going the other way and challenged the new classification for larger lots as unconstitutional.

The U.S. Court of Appeals for the First Circuit, apparently impressed by how much planning had *not* been done, sustained the town's restrictive new zoning on that account:

> In effect, the town has bought time, for its citizens . . . . The zoning ordinance here in question has been in existence less than two years. Hopefully, Sanbornton has begun or soon will begin to plan with more precision for the future, taking advantage of numerous federal or state grants for which it might qualify. Additionally, the New Hampshire legislature, to the extent it expects small towns like Sanbornton to cope with environmental problems posed by private developments, might adopt legislation similar to the federal National Environmental Policy Act . . . and thereby require developers to submit detailed environmental statements; if such power does not already reside within the town's arsenal of laws.[5]

Because rural localities do face so many obstacles in guiding a rush of development, we believe it essential that the states play an active role in guiding recreation development. *Although strong local controls and standards applicable to lot subdivision are essential, states should establish their own regulations to assure that planning expertise is applied, that adequate facilities are required, and that inappropriate subdivision is prohibited, even in remote areas.*

A number of states have already acted. Pennsylvania, for example, has banned septic tank construction for new recreation subdivisions until counties develop a comprehensive plan for sewer and water systems and each township and borough within a county completes a feasibility study of the suitability of septic systems for their areas. New regulations in Connecticut make septic tanks costly (and sometimes impossible) to install.

Vermont, Maine, and Florida have statewide controls on large-scale development, controls that reach many rural subdivisions. Vermont requires a state permit for any project involving ten or more acres or ten or more units. State permits are granted only after an applicant establishes that a project will not cause "unreasonable" harm to the environment or place an "unreasonable" burden on local governmental services.

Important legislation aimed at protecting a critical environmental area threatened by lot subdivision was signed into law by Governor Nelson Rockefeller of New York in May, 1973—the Adirondack Park Land-Use Act.

Imminent subdivision plans for privately owned land in the Adirondack Park sparked statewide concern, for the local governments with power to control development had neither the plans nor the experience to handle it. The state acted to supplement scattered or nonexistent local controls with strong, comprehensive state regulations.

Forty percent of the park area is in public ownership and preserved as "forever wild" by the New York Constitution. The remaining 60 percent of privately owned land (except for land located within incorporated town limits) is now subject to a highly protective land-use plan that permits construction of only one dwelling per 42 acres on approximately 53 percent of the private area. In addition, the Adirondack Park Agency was given authority to interpret the land-use guidelines set out in the act and to review development proposals. Agency jurisdiction is over both public and private lands in the park, an area larger than Vermont.

### Reducing the Seller's Incentives to Subdivide and Run

Even the most effective regulations can usefully be supplemented by incentive measures designed to cause subdividers' own motives to carry them toward quality and livability.

*Every effort should be made to bar lot sales projects in which management and sales practices encourage sellers to disregard the suitability of projects as places to live and to enjoy. Particular attention should be given to projects in which the manner of the seller's operation enables him to make substantial profit—or to show a substantial profit on his corporate books—before he installs water supply and sewage disposal facilities and the other rudimentary essentials of community existence.*

Recreational land subdivision and sales have been sufficiently profitable to attract some of the nation's largest corporate landholders, including paper and forest products firms, railroads, and major conglomerates. Some of these corporations hold enormous amounts of land. One possesses 300,000 acres in Florida; another controls a similar amount of acreage in Arizona; a third, 180,000 acres adjoining Lake Superior. Once, a corporation that possessed large landholdings might have held them in natural condition or disposed of them to a developer. Now, the profitability of lot sales—which frequently involve markups of 500 to 2,000 percent over raw land prices—is leading some landholding firms to decline to dispose of land in large tracts to homebuilders and new community developers and to subdivide, advertise to a mass market, and sell off land themselves.

Consider how the process works. A corporation purchases substantial acreage at low prices. Or perhaps the corporation already has large landholdings it no longer needs. It lays out lots, registers a subdivision plat, bulldozes and grades roads (in some states, access to lots is not required so the road system may not have to be extensive), makes plans for promised improvements (water supply, artificial lakes, community recreational facilities, for example), and may install a few such facilities in a portion of the project labeled for "immediate development." The company registers its statement of record and property report with HUD. It may now bring on a sales force and begin its advertising campaign. So far, expenses have not been significant relative to the sales price of the land to be marketed. And the corporation is now ready to ring up sales on its lots.

The purchaser typically makes a small down payment and agrees to pay the remainder of the purchase price, plus interest, in monthly installments. During the several years over which

LAKE

LAKE

*This aerial photograph shows a 1,125-acre tract of woods, pastures, and a stream valley located in upper New York State and planned as a subdivision containing 1,500 lots of about one-third acre each. A 315-acre lake is planned for the center of the project. The lots have been platted in a simple rectangular layout irrespective of the topography, resulting in several steeply sloping lots and one road directly climbing the face of a hillside. The majority of lot buyers will have access to the lake through a marina or the common beach. While the subdivider estimates that building will take place on 2-3 percent of the lots per year, he hopes to have completed sales and withdrawn from the project (turning over administration of water and sewer systems to a property owners' association) after five years.*

*This subdivider is unusual in two respects: he has posted a bond guaranteeing the construction of water and sewer facilities, and he is not selling on the installment basis. Thus, he turns over title upon sale to a buyer and receives funds sufficient to move ahead with construction of planned facilities.*

payments are spread, the land seller is receiving a steady inflow of cash, yet has typically promised to install improvements only five to twelve years after the date of sale. In the meantime, the subdividing corporation is free to use money received from the buyers' payments for its own purposes, or simply to collect interest on the payments received.

This early positive cash flow enjoyed by the lot seller is in marked contrast to the plight of the community builder who, after undertaking a far more complex planning and management operation, must lay out large sums for improvements and perhaps wait several years before the cash flow turns positive. This cash flow inducement alone is sufficient to make lot sellers out of companies that have shown no taste for genuine community development.

Early installation of improvements can change the cash flow picture completely. Where, as a result of state or local regulations, substantial investments must be made in the construction of sewers or other facilities *before* lots may be offered for sale, the lot seller's early cash flow can turn negative, too. Some sellers have left the business rather than construct costly facilities before selling their lots.

Until very recently, accounting rules added still further to the attractiveness of lot sales for publicly held corporations by enabling them to report revenues and profits very rapidly on their corporate earnings statements. Typically, as soon as the company received 5 percent of the sales price of a lot, the company reported 100 percent of the sales price as revenue. At the same time, the company reported 100 percent of its anticipated profits on the sale.

This approach largely ignored the question of whether a small cash payment constituted a real commitment on the part of the buyer to complete his payments over the full term of the contract. Moreover, it allowed profits to be reported well before the promised development was to be completed and, in many instances, before development costs could reasonably be estimated. Substantial earnings could thus be reported with little real land-use planning and development effort, and the work of development was largely divorced from the earnings reporting process.

In April 1970, the American Institute of Certified Public Accountants (AICPA) appointed a committee to review the accounting and reporting practices of the retail land sales industry. After considerable deliberation, the committee submitted a final draft, which was approved by the Accounting Principles Board and was published, early in 1973, as AICPA accounting guide *Accounting for Retail Land Sales*. The guide is directed at the type of accounting abuses suggested above and attempts to establish more restrictive standards for the reporting of revenues and profits from retail land sales.

Among other things, it provides that no revenue or profit is to be recognized until the buyer of a lot has made cash payments that represent a significant commitment toward completing the purchase. At a minimum, the guide suggests that the buyer must have made payments equal to 10 percent of the total purchase price before a sale can be recognized. (While this requirement is certainly an improvement over earlier practices, experience may show the need for an even higher minimum payment requirement.)

In addition, the guide makes clear that, if there is a refund period (that is, if a sales contract, company policy, or law allows the buyer to cancel his contract and receive a full refund for some period after the contract is signed), no revenue or profit can be reported until the refund period ends. The impact of this provision is shown in the accompanying illustration.

# REPORTING REVENUES AND RELATED PROFITS: THREE CASES ILLUSTRATING THE EFFECT OF THE AICPA ACCOUNTING GUIDE AND OF A REGULATION ESTABLISHING AN EXTENDED REFUND PERIOD

## Facts and Assumptions of Earnings Statements A, B, and C

1. Ecological Land Corporation, an experienced land development company, sold lots in 1972 for the first time in a new project.

2. The project consisted in total of 1,800 2-acre lots with an average sales price of $5,000 per lot. The first eight hundred of the lots were sold in 1972 with a minimum payment of 10 percent on each lot. The following project costs pertain to the lots sold:

| Land and Improvement Costs and Selling Expenses | Costs Incurred to Dec. 31, 1972 | Estimated Costs to Complete | Total Estimated Costs |
|---|---|---|---|
| Land | $ 200,000 | | $ 200,000 |
| Paved access roads | 50,000 | | 50,000 |
| Utilities | 25,000 | $175,000 | 200,000 |
| Golf course and other amenities | 25,000 | 725,000 | 750,000 |
| Subtotal | 300,000 | 900,000 | 1,200,000 |
| Commissions and sales expenses | 800,000 | | 800,000 |
| TOTAL | $1,100,000 | $900,000 | $2,000,000 |

3. During the year, the corporation earned income unrelated to the project in the amount of $600,000 and had general and administrative expenses of $500,000.

## Additional Assumption Applicable to Earnings Statements A and B

The buyer's refund period expired 48 hours after the date of sale. Thereafter, a buyer who defaulted on the terms of the purchase contract would receive none of his money back. (To simplify Cases A and B, a provision for contract cancellations has been excluded from the example.)

## Additional Assumption Applicable to Earnings Statement C

The following governmental regulation establishes an extended refund period:

> Any person who engages in any sales of retail land must allow the buyers of such land to cancel their purchase contract and receive a 100% refund of all cash paid until such time as required improvements, including water supply and waste disposal facilities, are installed.

## Accounting Treatment

### Case A: Before the AICPA Guide

Before issuance of the new AICPA accounting guide for retail land sales, the corporation could have reported the total sales price of the land as revenue. It would then have deducted the total estimated costs (costs incurred to date and estimated costs to complete) related to the land sold. Thus, the corporation could have reported its total estimated profit at the time of sale.

### Case B: Following the AICPA Guide
### (Without an Extended Refund Period)

This case illustrates the accrual method of accounting as discussed in the guide. The proportion of the sales price recognized as revenue is limited to the proportion of total costs incurred (including costs of the marketing effort). On December 31, 1972, the company had incurred costs of $1,100,000, which was 55% of the total estimated costs of $2,000,000. Therefore, only 55% of the total sales price can be recognized as revenue. The remaining 45% is deferred and will be recognized in future years as costs are incurred.

### Case C: Following the AICPA Guide,
### But With an Extended Refund Period

The guide makes clear that an extended refund period precludes revenue or profit recognition until the period expires.

## Ecological Land Corporation Earnings Statement
## for the Year Ended December 31, 1972

| | Case A Before the AICPA Accounting Guide | Case B Following the AICPA Accounting Guide (Without an Extended Refund Period) | Case C Following the AICPA Accounting Guide, But With an Extended Refund Period |
|---|---|---|---|
| REVENUES | | | |
| Net lot sales | $ 4,000,000 | $ 4,000,000 | |
| Less deferred revenues | | $ 2,200,000* | |
| Interest | 400,000 | 400,000 | |
| Other income | 600,000 | 600,000 | $600,000 |
| | 5,000,000 | 3,200,000 | 600,000 |
| | | | |
| COSTS AND EXPENSES | | | |
| Land and improvement costs | 1,200,000 | 300,000 | |
| Commissions and sales expenses | 800,000 | 800,000 | |
| General and administrative | 500,000 | 500,000 | 500,000 |
| | 2,500,000 | 1,600,000 | 500,000 |
| | | | |
| INCOME BEFORE PROVISION FOR INCOME TAXES | 2,500,000 | 1,600,000 | 100,000 |
| Provision for income taxes | 1,250,000 | 800,000 | 50,000 |
| | | | |
| NET INCOME | $ 1,250,000 | $ 800,000 | $ 50,000 |
| | | | |
| EARNINGS PER SHARE | | | |
| Earnings per share of common stock (1,000,000 shares issued and outstanding for the entire year) | $1.25 | $.80 | $.05 |
| Assumed price earnings multiple | 15X | 15X | 15X |
| Assumed market price per share | $18.75 | $12.00 | $.75 |
| Total market value | $18,750,000 | $12,000,000 | $750,000 |

*Deferred revenues in Case B total $1,800,000

Even when the guide allows recognition of a sale, the seller must normally delay reporting some of his resulting revenues and profits. Suppose, for example, that a seller has received 10 percent of the sales price of a lot, that the refund period has expired, and that other requirements are satisfied so that he may recognize the sale and report revenues and profits. In keeping with earlier practice, he would usually like to report more than the 10 percent that he has received in cash from the buyer. Under the guide, however, he may not yet report more than 10 percent of his anticipated profits unless several additional requirements have been satisfied. One of these requirements is that project improvements (access roads, water supplies, sewage systems and amenities such as golf courses, clubs, and swimming pools) must have progressed beyond preliminary stages and that there be evidence that the remaining work will be completed according to plan. A second requirement is that there be evidence that the property will clearly be useful for residential or recreational purposes at the end of the normal payment period. Thus, the guide states: "There must be a reasonable expectation that the land can be developed for the purposes represented. For example, it should be expected that local ordinances and other legal restrictions, such as those arising from ecological considerations, will not seriously hamper development and that improvements such as access roads, water supply, and sewage treatment or removal are feasible within a reasonable time."[6] So long as these requirements remain unsatisfied, revenues and profits must be accounted on the "installment method," where profit recognition occurs only as cash is received.

If these and other requirements are met, the guide permits revenues and profits to be reported on the "accrual method." Even under this method, however, the seller may not simply report 100 percent of his revenues and profits as soon as he receives 10 percent of the sales price in cash. Rather, his reporting of revenues and profits must be timed to relate to the project costs he incurs for land improvements and selling expenses. In effect, the percentage of total revenues and profits reported must not at any time exceed the percentage of the total costs and expenses incurred. As a result, full revenues and profits from a sale are reported only when virtually all work has been completed. More than in the past, therefore, the earnings reporting process is tied to the development process.

By delaying the recognition of revenues and profits until nearer the time that a community is completed, the new accounting rules lessen one of the artificial inducements that encourage corporations to engage in lot sales rather than to develop genuine new communities of second homes. The rules are thus consistent with a public policy of assuring that incentives affecting land subdividers accord with the public interest—that is, the development of functioning communities served by necessary facilities. The rules may still be insufficient, however, to remove the special attraction that exists when profit precedes performance. Additional methods, going beyond accounting rules, should therefore be considered to remove that attraction and to assure that facilities are installed as promised. *One possibility is to require that a portion of lot buyers' payments be deposited in escrow until the seller has fulfilled his obligations to the buyers. We recommend that careful consideration be given to such an escrow requirement.* Escrow accounts could be held by banks and released to the sellers as facilities are completed. If promised improvements are not made, escrow money could be applied to construction costs.

### Will Changes in Laws and Tougher Accounting Rules Produce Better Communities?

Many of our recommendations for land subdivisions involve stiffer requirements for lot sellers. It is fair to ask what results these controls are likely to produce. Realistically, we expect governmental response—and thus results—to be spotty. That is why we have recommended several measures instead of only one or two.

Where governmental response is forthcoming, we anticipate that one common result will be a reduction of the long waiting periods between time of lot purchase and time of lot use. This result, though far from a complete solution to present lot sales problems, seems highly desirable from every standpoint: to subdividers who may then adjust their planning to real needs and to a market that does not depend on high-pressure sales practices; to buyers who will then run less risk of holding property that is unusable and unsaleable; to local governments, which will be able to consider subdivision registrations simultaneously with plans for provision of facilities and services; and, finally, to lenders, who will be able to make loans against real development projects where values will be less likely to evaporate as buyers walk away from contracts they got into under pressure.

But isn't there a need for fundamental change? For new values and attitudes that will consider land a resource to be wisely used rather than as an opportunity for speculation? Of course there is. We hope that attitudes and values will continue to evolve so that insensitive treatment of the land will come to be regarded, not as a sort of marginal irregularity, but as an unthinkable misuse of a valued resource.

Our recommendations, however, are designed to correct the problems now, when only a small minority are outraged over how much land is being badly subdivided and how many people are being defrauded. For the near future, it will help if consumers, state and local agencies, lenders, and accountants begin asking more pointed questions and demanding more firm assurances than many lot sellers have so far been willing to provide. Even when subdivisions are regarded solely as investment opportunities, they will be unsatisfactory in the long run if they are unattractive as places to visit or live.

Careful inquiry would be a marked improvement over the way many citizens and local and state governments are now treating recreational lot subdivisions. Gradually, perhaps fairly soon, this new attention to the importance of livability should produce a badly needed change in the treatment of the land. The need is to replace lot sellers with community builders

# Chapter VIII
# Conservation and Development:
# The Role of The Citizen

To accommodate the very large quantity of new urban development needed between now and the twenty-first century without letting it diminish the quality of our lives will require a herculean struggle to protect open spaces, historic buildings, and neighborhoods and to assure that the development that takes place is quality development. The scale of both the development and protection tasks are vast.

But the vastness of the work ahead does not mean that we should leave it to the experts. In few other fields can citizens, adequately informed about problems and alternative solutions, be so helpful to public decision-makers as in the field of urban growth. For the planner's art is just that; it is not a science. What density of development is to be planned for? How much open space is needed? How far will people walk to shops and offices? How long will they wait for a bus or subway? How important is preserving the old city hall? How offensive is the town dump? For all of these questions and more, the public must express its feelings before the planner can act responsively.

Citizens, individually and in organized groups, therefore have a special role to play in achieving quality development. Especially in times of rapidly changing values, elected officials and professionals can be victims of their experience. A tradition of bad but necessary compromises, the result in large part of citizen apathy, can persist unless citizens make it known that the old apathy is gone and the old compromises are no longer necessary or acceptable. In some cases, the need may be to confront local officials. In many others, the need is to offer a hand of support that officials have never had—and perhaps have given up hoping for.

Citizen opportunity and responsibility go beyond simply standing up for quality. Citizens must also be specific about what is needed. Several times in the report we have refrained from recommending a particular course of action because, as we have pointed out, different people in different places want—and need—different solutions. Citizens themselves must help decide what is best in each locality.

Nor is citizen opportunity and responsibility limited to working through governments. We have tried to emphasize the role of citizen groups and charitable organizations, not just as watchdogs and pressure groups but as actors, especially in protecting open spaces (the Nature Conservancy and the Trust for Public Land furnish two important examples of successful nongovernmental action).

*We believe that civic organizations can make an important contribution to the quality of life in their local areas by helping to decide what should be protected and preserved in their localities, by helping to determine how and where essential development needs are to be met, and by helping to assess systematically the adequacy of their local plans, laws, regulations, and procedures affecting urban growth. The 1976 bicentennial year would be an appropriate target date for the completion of the first phase of such an assessment. We urge that federal assistance be made available for these citizen efforts as part of the bicentennial program.*

To encourage citizen participation and help with citizen assessment, we present a partial checklist of questions that citizens might consider if they want to apply recommendations in this report to their own towns, counties, regions, or states to influence the quality and direction of urban growth.

### Areas to Protect

1. Has any governmental agency or private group designated open spaces worthy of special protection? Areas where development would be hazardous? Areas where development would disrupt important natural processes? Areas for future recreation? Buffer zones between urban areas? Highly productive farmland?

2. If so, are maps showing the designations conveniently available to property owners, real estate dealers, developers, builders?

3. Is there any evidence that the designations are influencing

*"We purchased the land in 1955 and fell right into our first battle. Some people wanted to establish a subdivision of some kind. So we formed our own water district and an association of owners to develop the valley in an orderly way. Well, we really have achieved something."*

development decisions of public officials? Of private property owners or builders?

4. Are the designations realistic and up-to-date? Are there undesignated areas that you believe worthy of special protection?

5. Are any buildings or neighborhoods listed in *The National Register of Historic Places?*

6. Are any unlisted buildings or neighborhoods historically important, at least important enough to warrant special review and consideration if a project should threaten to destroy or impair them?

### Public Open Spaces

1. How much publicly owned open space is there? Where is it?

2. How much is parkland? How are other public open spaces used?

3. How much public open space has been acquired since 1950? Since 1960? Since 1970?

4. If attendance or usage figures are available, has park usage increased? At what rate? Has the parkland supply increased as rapidly?

5. Which governments have regularly budgeted programs of

*"If one group of people or one family decided to make this not such a good place to live, I can't imagine that the rest of the families would simply accept it. We are all living here; we want the same things. Either clean up the mess you are making or leave."*

open space purchase? Have budgets increased as rapidly as land prices and parkland demand?

6. Has any governmental agency or private group designated prime recreation land (such as beaches or waterfronts)? How much has been so designated? Where?

7. Of the total prime recreation land, how much is now publicly accessible and available for recreation? How much is unavailable because of inconsistent use? Is there a practical way to make it available for recreation? Within the next ten years? Fifty years? One hundred years?

8. Of the total prime recreation land, how much is available for recreation but not accessible to the general public? What prevents public access? Private ownership of the recreation land? Or of accessways to it? Fees or regulations limiting admission or parking?

9. Is any governmental agency or private group planning to remove barriers to public access? Seeking donations? Planning purchases? Seeking changes in rules or fees? Bringing lawsuits?

10. Does state law establish safeguards to prevent needless diversion of publicly owned open space to other public use? Requirements that alternatives to diversion be formulated with full opportunity for public comment? Procedural protection to assure that open space is not needlessly condemned by public agencies? Requirements that open space taken be replaced by other open space that will meet similar public needs and have at least comparable monetary value?

11. Do local regulations establish additional safeguards?

### Asserting Neglected Rights

1. Under state law, how long does it take for the public to acquire an easement or other prescriptive right of passage across private property?

2. Are there any places where continued public passage may have established such a right? (A path across private land to the beach, perhaps? Or an old road across private land to a fishing hole?)

3. Is anyone compiling evidence of the facts that create the public right? Or seeking a court decree to formalize the right?

### Donations

1. Has any land, or any partial interest in land (such as easements or development rights) been donated to preserve open

*"We have a hillside ordinance that's an engineer's dream. It tells you where you can and can't build depending on the slope of the hill. It's very technical—and it protects any hill. It was legislated, I might add, with developers and homeowners breathing down our necks."*

space? When? What restrictions were established to prevent development of donated land? Has the donor's intent been respected?

2. Is any governmental agency or private organization actively soliciting open space donations (land or partial interests)? What techniques are they using?

3. Have governmental officials expressed a willingness to receive donations of appropriate open space—without requiring donation of funds for maintenance as well?

4. Are open spaces held by preservation organizations, such as the Nature Conservancy, exempt from real estate taxes?

5. Are subdividers and developers required to dedicate open space? Is the dedicated land sufficient to serve residents of the development or subdivision? If cash is accepted from subdividers in lieu of land, are cash amounts sufficient to buy needed land?

6. Do regulations prohibit the development or subdivision of waterfront property in the absence of adequate public accessways to the waterfront?

### Protective Regulations

1. Do local regulations establish one or more districts to protect critical agricultural and environmental areas? Are density and

other requirements in those districts sufficiently restrictive to protect those areas?

2. Does state law provide additional protection (of wetlands and agricultural areas, for example)? Is that protection sufficient?

3. To what land and water areas do these restrictions apply?

4. Are there additional areas that ought to be protected? What steps are needed to protect those areas? State or local legislative action? Administrative action?

5. Does the state have an institutional structure to review and regulate historic sites?

6. Does the state authorize local governments to protect the integrity of historic areas? Are local governments using their authority?

7. Who builds sewer and water lines? How are locations decided?

8. Is the sewer agency required by law to follow official plans when it locates new sewers? Does it in fact do so? Do the plans effectively protect open space?

## Preferential Tax Assessments

1. Does state law provide for preferential assessment of agricultural land?

2. If so, must the owner promise to preserve the land in agricultural use? For how long? What is the penalty if he breaks his promise?

3. How much could tax rates be reduced if preferential assessments were abolished?

4. Does the public benefit in open space protection warrant the expense that preferential assessments impose on other taxpayers?

## Development Regulations

1. Do regulations establish a "planned unit development" procedure that permits developers to cluster development on part of their land, leaving the rest as open space? Does the same procedure free developers from unvarying yard requirements, minimum-lot-size requirements, and other design restrictions? Does it provide for discretionary review of proposed designs or site plans?

2. In practice, is the planned unit development procedure routinely applied to important projects? Can developers be compelled to use the procedure for important projects?

3. Do regulations authorize the award of density bonuses in new communities and other large projects? Are bonuses in fact awarded?

4. Do other measures assist or encourage new communities and other large projects? What measures? How could they be strengthened?

5. When officials review proposed projects, what assistance is available to them? Are there *useful* plans and policies? Are professionals (such as planners and landscape architects) available for consultation?

6. When significant projects are reviewed, are alternative sites and designs publicly evaluated if the project is governmental? If it is private?

### Environmental Impact Analysis

1. Does state law require the preparation of environmental impact statements for significant state projects? Local projects? Private projects?

2. What measures permit or encourage citizen comment on draft impact statements?

*"We go to the beach once a year. It's such a struggle. It's an hour and a half to get there. We go sailing, but that's an hour also. We really should do something about public transportation."*

*"I'd like to get the kids I teach to realize it's their land and they can have a say in what happens to it."*

3. What rules or procedures assure that environmental impact statements need not be prepared for unimportant cases?

## Incentives for Quality and Equity

1. Do state or local regulations effectively prevent the creation of lots fronting on major streets and highways?

2. What assistance or encouragement does the state provide for local planning? For regional planning?

3. Do state or regional agencies have powers to assure that local regulatory decisions take account of state or regional needs? What powers? Are the powers used?

4. Is any governmental agency or private group seeking to have exclusionary regulations invalidated in the courts?

5. What is the impact of regulations on the opportunity to build low- and moderate-cost housing? Are regulations free of blatantly exclusionary provisions, such as those that require homes in some zones to have more floor area than those in other zones?

6. What percentage of school costs is paid by the state?

## Trustworthy Procedures and Institutions

1. Is there a requirement that meetings of governmental bodies be open to the public? Does the requirement apply to all agencies

responsible for regulating land use? Are all meetings in fact open to the public?

2. Would changes in local practices or procedures increase citizen confidence in the regulatory process? What changes?

3. Are there detailed requirements governing conflict of interest? Are they scrupulously followed? Would additional conflict-of-interest requirements increase public confidence in the regulatory process? What requirements?

4. Under state law, is there any practical way for a private citizen to compel enforcement of a land-use regulation? To appeal from a regulatory decision even if he does not own property affected by the decision?

## Rural Lot Sales

1. Are recreational lots being created or sold within your area? Or being sold to residents of the area? On what terms?

2. What protection does state law provide to buyers of recreational lots within the state? Of lots outside the state?

3. What kinds of disclosure must the subdivider make? What protection is granted in addition to disclosure? Are requirements obeyed?

4. Is there a nonwaivable cooling-off period? How long a period?

5. Do local regulations require that recreational subdivisions attain acceptable development standards and provide adequate public facilities, including water supply and sewage disposal facilities? Are the regulations obeyed?

6. Do state regulations supplement local regulations on these matters? Adequately?

# NOTES

## CHAPTER I

[1] "Paradise in Peril," special supplement of the *Miami Herald*, December, 1971.
[2] Nassau-Suffolk Regional Planning Board, *Nassau-Suffolk Comprehensive Development Plan*, February, 1970.
[3] Earl Finkler, *Nongrowth As A Planning Alternative: A Preliminary Examination of An Emerging Issue*, Planning Advisory Service Report No. 283 (Chicago: American Society of Planning Officials, 1972), p. 33.
[4] Robert S. Ayre et al., *A Proposed Analysis of Growth in the Boulder Area*, report to the city council of Boulder, Colorado, February 1972, p. 4.
[5] Environmental Land and Water Management Act of 1972, Florida Stat. Ann. §380.31; Florida Land Conservation Act of 1972, Florida Stat. Ann. §259.01; Florida State Comprehensive Planning Act of 1972, Florida Stat. Ann. §23.011; Florida Water Resources Act of 1972, Florida Stat. Ann. §373.013.
[6] *Environmental Quality*, the first annual report of the Council on Environmental Quality, August 1970, p. xii-xiii.
[7] U.S. Congress, Senate, Committee on Interior and Insular Affairs, *National Land Use Policy: Hearings on S. 632 and S. 992*, Part I, 92nd Congress, 1st Session, May 10 and June 7, 1971, p. 98.

## CHAPTER II

[1] U.S. Bureau of the Census, *Current Population Reports*, Series P-25, No. 493, "Projections of the Population of the United States, By Age and Sex: 1972 to 2020," p. 2.
[2] Commission on Population Growth and the American Future, *Population and the American Future* (Washington, D.C.: Government Printing Office, 1972), p. 38.
[3] Population Commission, *Population and the American Future*, p. 38.
[4] Department of Transportation, *The 1972 National Highway Needs Report*, Part II, p. 38.
[5] Population Commission, *Population and The American Future*, p. 36.
[6] Center for Political Research, *Federal Activities Affecting Location of Economic Development*, prepared for the Economic Development Administration of the U.S. Department of Commerce, November 1970, p. 3.
[7] Vance Packard, *A Nation of Strangers* (N.Y.: David McKay, 1972), p. 6.
[8] Charles Abrams, *Forbidden Neighbors* (N.Y.: Harper and Row, 1951), p. 260.
[9] *Golden v. The Planning Bd. of the Town of Ramapo*, 30 N.Y.2nd 359, 285 N.E.2nd 291 (1972).
[10] *Shapiro v. Thompson*, 394 U.S. 618, 629 (1968).
[11] *United States v. Guest*, 383 U.S. 745 (1966).
[12] *Appeal of Kit-Mar Builders, Inc.*, 439 Pa. 466, 268 A.2nd 765, 768 (Pa. 1970). (For a discussion of the relationship of these cases to Supreme Court decisions on the right to travel, see "The Right to Travel and Its Application to Restrictive Housing Laws," 66 *Northwestern University Law Review* 635 (1971).

## CHAPTER III

[1] B. Pushkarev, "The Atlantic Urban Seaboard: Development Issues and Strategies," *Regional Plan News*, September 1969, pp. 12-13.
[2] Vermont Land Use Law, Vermont Stat. Ann., §6001-6091 (1970 Supplement), reprinted in Fred Bosselman and David Callies, *The Quiet Revolution in Land Use Control* (Washington, D.C.: Government Printing Office, 1971), pp. 66-67.

## CHAPTER IV

[1] One of the most thorough and important analytic efforts to develop a consistent approach to the takings issue that fully acknowledges public rights to

protect the environment is Joseph L. Sax, "Takings, Private Property and Public Rights," 81 *Yale Law Journal* 149. See also Sax's *Defending the Environment* (New York: Alfred A. Knopf, 1970).

2 *Rykar Indus. Corp. v. Commissioner of Agriculture & Natural Resources,* Superior Court, Hartford County, Connecticut, No. 170229, Apr. 2, 1971.

3 *State Nat'l Bank v. Planning & Zoning Comm'n,* 239 A.2d 528, 530 (1968).

4 *Dooley v. Town Plan & Zone Comm'n of Fairfield,* 197 A.2d 770 (Conn. 1964). *Barlett v. Zoning Comm'n of Old Lyme,* 282 A.2d 907 (Conn. 1971).

5 *Turnpike Realty v. Town of Dedham,* 284 N.E.2d 891, 900 (Mass. 1972).

6 *Candlestick Properties, Inc. v. San Francisco Bay C & D Comm'n,* 89 Cal. Rptr. 89 (App. 1970).

7 *Penn Central Transportation Co. v. City of New York,* defendent's pretrial memorandum of law, p. 2.

8 *Penn Central Transportation Co. v. City of New York,* Supreme Court, County of New York, No. 14763/69, Oct. 7, 1969.

9 *Penn Central Transportation Co. v. City of New York,* plaintiff's pretrial memorandum of law, p. 8.

10 *Keystone Associates v. Moerdler,* 278 N.Y.S.2d 185 (Sup. 1966).

11 *Trustees of Sailor's Snug Harbor v. Platt* 288 N.Y.S.2d 314, 315 (App. Div. 1968).

12 *Manhattan Club v. Landmarks Preservation Comm'n,* 273 N.Y.S.2d 848 (Sup. Ct. 1966).

13 See, for example, *City of New Orleans v. Levy,* 64 So. 2d 798 (La. 1953). A recent challenge, *Maher v. City of New Orleans,* 235 So. 2d 403 (La. 1970), reaffirmed this position in dicta.

14 *Rebman v. City of Springfield,* 250 N.E.2d 283 (Ill. App. 1969); and *M & N Enterprises, Inc. v. City of Springfield,* 250 N.E.2d 289 (Ill. App. 1969).

15 *City of Santa Fe v. Gamble-Skogmo, Inc.,* 389 P.2d 13 (N.M. 1964).

16 *People ex. rel. Younger v. County of El Dorado,* 96 Cal. Rptr. 553, 555 (1970).

17 *Viso v. State,* Superior Court, Placer County, California, No. 38938, Aug. 31, 1972.

18 TRPA Land Use Ordinance §5.40

19 *Younger v. County of El Dorado,* 96 Cal. Rptr. 533 (1970).

20 *McCarthy v. City of Manhattan Beach,* 264 P.2d 932 (1953).

21 *Consolidated Rock Prods. Co. v. City of Los Angeles,* 20 Cal Rptr. 638 (1962).

22 *Turner v. County of Del Norte,* 101 Cal Rptr. 93 (App. 1972).

23 *Hill v. City of Manhattan Beach,* 98 Cal. Rptr. 785 (1971); and *Hilltop Properties, Inc. v. State,* 43 Cal. Rptr. 605 (App. 1965).

24 *Breidert v. Southern Pac. Co.,* 39 Cal. Rptr. 903 (1964).

25 *State v. Johnson,* 265 A.2d 711 (Me. 1971). See also, *American Nat'l Bank & Trust Co. v. Winfield,* 274 N.E.2d 144 (Ill. App. 1971); *Bartlett v. Zoning Comm'n of Old Lyme,* 282 A.2d 907 (Conn. 1971).

26 *Beyer v. Palo Alto,* Superior Court, Santa Clara County, California, Oct. 4, 1972.

27 *Padover v. Township of Farmington,* 132 N.W.2d 687 (Mich. 1965). See also, *Josephs v. Town of Clarkstown,* 198 N.Y.S.2d 695 (Sup. Ct. 1960).

28 *National Land & Inv. Co. v. Kohn,* 215 A.2d 597, 610 (Pa. 1965).

29 *Board of County Supervisors of Fairfax County v. Carper,* 107 S.E.2d 390 (Va. 1959). This type of case usually carries overtones of racial discrimination. See, for example, *Kennedy Park Homes v. Lackawanna,* 436 F.2d 108 (2d Cir. 1971).

30 *Clemons v. City of Los Angeles,* 222 P.2d 439 (Cal. 1950).

31 *Consolidated Rock Prods. Co. v. City of Los Angeles,* 370 P.2d 342, 351 (1962), quoting from *Beverly Oil v. City of Los Angeles,* 254 P.2d 865, 867 (Cal. 1953) (The *Beverly* case concerned the prohibition of oil production in designated areas.)

32 See *Mill v. City of Manhattan Beach,* 98 Cal. Rptr. 785 (1971); *Turner v. County of Del Norte,* 101 Cal. Rptr. 93 (App. 1972).

33 Eduardo Coke (Milite), *The Second Part of the Institutes of the Laws of England* (London: E. & R. Brooke,

1797), p. 46.

34 Robert M. Kerr, The Commentaries on the Laws of England of Sir William Black Stone, Nt., Vol. I (London: John Murray, 1876), pp. 109-110.

35 An Act Against the Erecting and Maintenance of Cottages. 31 Eliz. 1, C. 7 (Statutes-at-Large, Vol. 6, p. 409).

36 35 Eliz. 1, C. 6 (Summarized in Statutes-at-Large, Vol. 6, p. 433).

37 2 Pa. Stat. 66, Ch. 53.

38 Withers v. Buckley, 61 U.S. (20 How.) 84 (1857).

39 Davidson v. New Orleans, 96 U.S. 97, 105 (1877).

40 C. B. & Q. Railway v. Chicago, 166 U.S. 26, 236 (1896).

41 Pumpelly v. Green Bay Co., 80 U.S. 166, 177, 178 (1871).

42 Transportation Co. v. Chicago, 99 U.S. 635, 642 (1878).

43 Bridge Co. v. United States, 105 U.S. 470 (1881).

44 Bridge Co. v. United States, 105 U.S. 507 (1881).

45 See, for example, Missouri Pac. Ry. v. Nebraska, 164 U.S. 403 (1896); Great N. Ry. v. Minnesota, 238 U.S. 340 (1914); Mississippi R.R. Comm'n v. Mobile & O.R.R. 244 U.S. 388 (1916). See also, Nichols, Eminent Domain §1.42 (1), note 7.

46 Railroad Comm'n Cases, 116 U.S. 307, 331 (1886).

47 Great N. Ry. v. Minnesota, 238 U.S. 340 (1915); Missouri Pac. Ry. v. Nebraska, 164 U.S. 403 (1896); Northern Pac. Ry. v. North Dakota, 236 U.S. 585 (1915); Missouri Pac. Ry. v. Tucker, 230 U.S. 340 (1909); Missouri Pac. Ry. v. Nebraska, 217 U.S. 196 (1909).

48 Robert S. Hunt, Law and Locomotives (Madison, Wisc.; The State Historical Society, 1958).

49 Mugler v. Kansas, 123 U.S. 623 (1887).

50 Hadacheck v. Sebastian, 239 U.S. 304, 410 (1915).

51 Pennsylvania Coal Co. v. Mahon, 260 U.S. 393, 415-16 (1922).

52 Pennsylvania Coal Co. v. Mahon, 260 U.S. 417.

53 Ambler Realty Co. v. Village of Euclid, 297 Fed. 307, 311-12 (N.D. Ohio, 1924).

54 Village of Euclid v. Ambler Realty Co., 272 U.S. 365, 384, 395-97 (1926).

55 Nectow v. Cambridge, 277 U.S. 183 (1928).

56 Miller v. Schoene, 276 U.S. 272 (1928).

57 Goldblatt v. Town of Hempstead, 369 U.S. 590 (1962).

58 State v. Johnson, 265 A.2d 711, 716 (Me. 1971). See also, American Nat'l Bank & Trust Co. v. Winfield, 274 N.E.2d 144 (Ill. App. 1971); Bartlett v. Zoning Comm'n of Old Lyme, 282 A.2d 907 (Conn. 1971).

59 Just v. Marinette County, 56 Wis. 2d 7, 201 N.W.2d 761 (1972).

60 In the Matter of Spring Valley Development, Supreme Judicial Court of Maine, No. 1341, Feb. 9, 1973.

61 Potomac Sand & Gravel Co. v. Governor of Md., 293 A.2d 248, 249. The court relied on Commonwealth v. Tewksbury, 11 Met. 55 (Mass. 1846) and Goldblatt v. Hempstead, 369 U.S. 590 (1962).

## CHAPTER V

1 National Environmental Policy Act of 1969, 42 U.S.C. 4321-47.

2 Wilderness Soc'y. v. Hickel, 325 F. Supp. 422 (D.D.C. 1970), affirmed on other grounds 4 ERC 1977, Feb. 9, 1973.

3 Calvert Cliffs Coordinating Comm. Inc. v. AEC, 449 F.2d 1109 (D.C. Cir. 1971).

4 Kalur v. Resor, 335 F. Supp. 1 (D.D.C. 1971).

5 Attributed to Sir Desmond Heap, comptroller and city solicitor to the Corporation of the City of London and president of the Law Society.

6 ACIR State Legislative Program, 1970 Cumulative, "County Powers in Relation to Local Planning and Zoning Actions," (Washington, D.C.: Advisory Commission on Intergovernmental Relations, 1969), p. 31-34-00. Building the American City, report of the National Commission on Urban Problems (Washington, D.C.: Government Printing Office, 1968), p. 236.

## CHAPTER VI

1 Goldman, Marshall I., The Spoils of

Progress: Environmental Pollution in the Soviet Union (Cambridge, Mass.: MIT Press, 1972), pp. 154-63.

[2] Barton-Aschman Assoc., Inc., The Barrington, Illinois, Area: A Cost Revenue Analysis of Land Use Alternatives, prepared for the Barrington Area Development Council, February 1970, pp. vii-viii, 47.

[3] Livingston and Blayney, Openspace vs. Development, final report to the city of Palo Alto, California, Foothills Environmental Design Study, 1971, p. 4.

[4] Real Estate Research Corporation, Economic Analysis, a report to the city of Palo Alto, California, Foothills Environmental Design Study, April 1972, p. 16.

[5] Muller, Thomas and Grace Dawson, The Fiscal Impact of Residential and Commercial Development: A Case Study (Washington, D.C.: The Urban Institute, 1972).

[6] National Commission on Urban Problems, Building the American City, pp. 213-15.

[7] American Society of Planning Officials, New Directions in Connecticut Planning Legislation: A Study of Connecticut Planning, Zoning, and Related Statutes, summary report, 1967, pp. 29-34.

[8] Williams, N., Jr. and T. Norman, "Exclusionary Land Use Controls: The Case of North Eastern New Jersey," Land Use Controls Quarterly, Fall 1970, p. 1.

[9] San Diego, California, Resolution No. 199728, May 12, 1970; amended by Resolution No. 202429 (Adequacy of Public Services in Connection with Development Proposals), April 15, 1971.

[10] Howard County Planning Commission, Howard County 1985, General Plan Technical Report No. 1, April 1967, p. 30.

[11] Rouse Company, Report to the City of New York: An Analysis of Develop-ment Trends and Projections and Recommendations for a New City in South Richmond, May 1970.

[12] Development Research Associates, Economic Impact of a Regional Open Space Program for the San Francisco Bay Area, prepared for People for Open Space, 1969.

[13] Rodriguez v. San Antonio Independent School District, U.S. Supreme Court, opinion no. 71-1332, March 21, 1973.

[14] The American Law Institute, A Model Land Development Code, tentative draft no. 3, April 1971, §7-201, p. 10.

[15] Samuel Jackson, "New Communities," a reprint from HUD Challenge, August 1972.

[16] A Plan for Urban Growth: Report of the National Policy Task Force (Washington, D.C.: American Institute of Architects, 1972).

## CHAPTER VII

[1] Paulson, Morton C., The Great Land Hustle (Chicago, Ill.: Henry Regnery Co., 1972), p. 88.

[2] Cahn, Robert Land in Jeopardy, reprint of a series of articles from the Christian Science Monitor (Boston: The Christian Science Publishing Society, 1973), p. 13.

[3] Cahn, Robert, Land in Jeopardy, pp. 13-14.

[4] Paulson, Morton C., The Great Land Hustle, p. 187.

[5] Steel Hill Development Inc. v. Town of Sanbornton, U.S. Court of Appeals for the First Circuit, No. 72-1234, Nov. 24, 1972.

[6] American Institute of Certified Public Accountants, Committee on Land Development Companies, Accounting for Retail Land Sales (New York: American Institute of Certified Public Accountants, 1973), paragraph 20A.

# PHOTO AND CARTOON CREDITS

| | |
|---|---|
| Cover | Bruce G. Ando |
| page 2 | Gordon Binder |
| page 5 | Gordon Binder |
| page 8 | Gordon Binder |
| page 11 | Gordon Binder |
| page 32 | Reprint from *Freeways* by Lawrence Halprin and Associates, Reinhold Publishing Co. |
| page 38 | Janet Mendelsohn |
| page 43 | Janet Mendelsohn |
| page 45 | Janet Mendelsohn |
| page 51 | Janet Mendelsohn |
| page 59 | Janet Mendelsohn |
| page 62 | Janet Mendelsohn |
| page 65 | Janet Mendelsohn |
| page 66 | Janet Mendelsohn |
| page 69 | Janet Mendelsohn |
| page 70 | Janet Mendelsohn |
| page 74 | Bureau of Outdoor Recreation |
| page 77 | William Hamilton |
| page 90 | Paul Smolke |
| pages 92–93 | Janet Mendelsohn |
| page 95 | Bill Deits |
| page 96 | Aaron Nygart |
| page 102 | Soil Conservation Service |
| page 110 | Bureau of Outdoor Recreation |
| pages 118–119 | Bill Deits |
| page 121 | William Clift |
| page 141 | Northway Studios |
| page 142 | William Hamilton |
| page 144 | Kevin Brown |
| pages 146–147 | Kevin Brown |

| | |
|---|---|
| page 151 | Kevin Brown |
| page 154 | Wilbur Twinning |
| pages 156–157 | Andrew and Linda Williams |
| page 164 | William Hamilton |
| page 176 | Robert Lautman |
| page 180 | Soil Conservation Service |
| page 181 | Robert McCoy |
| page 196 | Bill Deits |
| page 201 | Soil Conservation Service |
| page 204 | Janet Mendelsohn |
| page 210 | William Hamilton |
| page 218 | Jerry Wachter |
| pages 220–221 | Department of Housing and Urban Development |
| page 228 | Janet Mendelsohn |
| page 233 | Kevin Brown |
| page 237 | Edward J. Lehmann |
| page 241 | Soil Conservation Service |
| page 247 | William Hamilton |
| pages 252–253 | Robert Lautman |
| page 258 | Fred Figall |
| page 262 | Kevin Brown |
| page 268 | Robert Nugent (top); Bill Deits (bottom) |
| page 274 | William Hamilton |
| pages 284–285 | Soil Conservation Service |
| page 294 | Bureau of Outdoor Recreation |
| page 297 | Janet Mendelsohn |
| page 298 | Janet Mendelsohn |
| page 300 | Janet Mendelsohn |
| page 302 | Janet Mendelsohn |
| page 303 | Janet Mendelsohn |

# INDEX

"A-95 circular" (OMB), 194
Abrams, Charles, 89
Accommodation of development, 179-82
*Accounting for Retail Land Sales* (AICPA guide), 287, 290, 291-92
Accounting Principles Board, 287
*Ad hoc* decisions, 191, 192, 213
Adirondack Forest Preserve, 117
Adirondack Park, 279, 282
Adirondack Park Agency, 282
Adirondack Park Land-Use Act, 282
Advisory Commission on Intergovernmental Relations, 213
Agricultural and environmental areas, protection of, 20, 106, 119, 127-32, 300
Agricultural classification (Hawaii), 97-98
Agricultural taxes (Hawaii), 127
Air pollution, 4, 7, 15, 33, 49
Airports, 68, 72, 79, 119
Airport funds, 27
Albany, N.Y., 91
Albermarle County, Va., 229-30
Altamont Township, N.Y., 279
Ambler Realty Company, 166-67
American Civil Liberties Union, 91
American Institute of Architects, 28, 255, 256
American Institute of Certified Public Accountants (AICPA), 287
American Law Institute, 25, 73, 122, 208-9, 212, 240
American Society of Planning Officials, 57
Appalachian Mountains, 107
*Appeal of Kit-Mar Builders, Inc.*, 100
Arizona, 235, 264, 283
Army Corps of Engineers, 194, 197
Army, Secretary of, 197
Articles of Confederation, 98
Artificial lakes, 277, 283
Askew, Reubin, 64, 70
Aspinall, Wayne, 17, 46
Association of Bay Area Governments (ABAG), 234
Atlantic region (US), 104
Atomic Energy Commission (AEC), 197
Atomic waste disposal, 242
Arvida Corporation, 67

Barrington, Illinois, 227
*Bartlett v. Zoning Commission of the Town of Old Lyme*, 149
Baruch, Bernard, 267
Bay Area Rapid Transit System (BART), 234
Beaches, 19, 20, 37, 39, 54, 104, 106, 107
Beach use, Long Island, 54
Bedroom taxes, 231
Berkeley, Cal., 50
Bernstein, George, 272
Bicentennial year, 31, 296
Bill of Rights, 145
Bills of rights, environmental, 35
Black Jack Improvement Association, 90
Black Jack, Mo. 89-91
Black Sea beaches, 221
Blackstone, Sir William, 160
Board of Commissioners, Martin City, Fla., 94
Boca Raton, Fla., 35, 39, 46, 53, 64, 67
Bonding, subdivision developers, 278
Boston, Mass., 23, 105, 162
Boulder, Col., 17, 35, 37, 46, 53, 56, 57-61
Boulder Valley Comprehensive Plan, 58
Bradley, Joseph, 163
Brandeis, Louis, 166, 167, 175
*Breidert v. Southern Pacific Co.*, 155
*Bridge Co. v. United States*, 163
Bridgeport, Conn., 148
Broward County, Fla., 94
Buffer-zone areas, 106, 136
Building moratoriums, 37, 49, 281
Bureau of Sport Fisheries, 111
Bus transit, 87
Buyers, speculative (recreation land), 30, 124-25

Cahill, William, 130
Cahn, Robert, 266
California, 12, 17, 35, 36, 46-50, 52, 53, 88, 89, 116, 117, 120, 129, 153, 155-59, 198, 206, 229, 235, 249, 256, 264, 270, 271, 281
California Environmental Quality Study Council, 277
California Supreme Court, 47
*California Tomorrow Plan*, 48

311

Candlestick Properties v. San Francisco Bay C and D Commission, 149, 155, 168
Carnegie, Andrew, 267
C. B. & Q. Railway v. Chicago, 162
Census Bureau, 75, 76-79
Chapin, Stuart, 105
Charles County, Md., 169
Charleston, S.C., 23, 105
Chesapeake Bay, 197
Chicago, Ill., 139, 256
Chicanos, 52, 54
Chief, Army Corps of Engineers, 197
Christian Science Monitor, 266
Citizen discontents with local government, 215, 217
Citizen lawsuits, 216
Citizen participation, 295-96
Citizen responsibility, 296
Citizens' Advisory Committee on Environmental Quality, 1, 2, 9
Citizens' Coordinate for Century 3 (C-3), 51
Citizens for Colorado's Future (CCF), 44
Civil rights groups, 28, 243
Clean Air Act (1970), 207
Clemons v. City of Los Angeles, 159
Cluster development, 20, 114-15, 229, 232-34, 301
Clustering, 276
Cluster principle, 138-39, 140
Coastal development, 35, 50, 52, 53
Coastal waters, federal jurisdiction, 112
Coke, Edward, 160
Colorado, 12, 17, 34, 35, 43-46, 56, 263, 269, 271, 281
Colorado Land Use Commission, 46
Colorado Land Use Policy Act, 46
Columbia, Md., 232
Commerce, Dept. of, 85
Commission on Population Growth and the American Future, 79-80
Committee for Sane Growth (Dade County, Fla.), 34
Commonwealth of Puerto Rico, 206
Concord Township, Pa., 100
Conditional rezoning, 191
Conflict of interest, 26, 215-16
Conflict of interest laws, 215-16
Congress, 30, 56, 71-72, 270, 273
Connecticut, 148-50, 282
Consolidated Rock Products Co. v. City of Los Angeles, 155, 159, 168

Constitution (U.S.), 88, 98-99, 165, 242
Consumer fraud, 270, 275
Cooling-off period, 30, 272, 304
Cost-revenue studies, 227-30
Council of State Governments, 23, 123
Council on Environmental Quality (CEQ), 71, 195-96, 199
"Country club" (fable), 224-25
Court of Appeals (Cal.), 149

Dade County, Fla., 16, 34, 36 38, 52, 63, 69, 94
Davidson v. New Orleans, 162
Dead subdivisions, 276
Deed restrictions, 128, 247
Deferred taxes, 127
De Grove, John, 52, 63-64
Delaware, 206
Density transfer, 138-39, 140, 142-43
Density zoning, Martin County, Fla., 94-95
Denver, Col., 35, 36, 43, 44, 46, 53, 57
Dept. of Environmental Conservation, N.Y. State, 41
Dept. of Real Estate, Cal., 270, 271
Dept. of the Environment, U.K., 135
Department of Transportation Act (1966), 193
Developers, 15, 67-69, 114-17, 209-10, 211, 219, 226-27, 232, 241, 245-51, 255-61, 275, 281
Developers, dedication by, 114-17
Development, 10, 14, 33, 34, 36-43, 46, 48, 49, 75-76, 88, 178-82, 219, 222-61, 275-82, 291-93
Development control, Ramapo, N.Y., 92-94
Development, economic impact, 34, 37-39
Development, inevitablity of, 76, 88
Development plan, Martin City, Fla., 94-95
Development rights, 128, 140-43
Diamond, Henry, 1
DDT (dichloro-diphenyl-trichloro-ethane), 174
Discretionary review, 189, 209-11
Disneyland, Cal., 249
Disney World, Fla., 37, 249
Di Tullio, Theodore, 97
Donations, land, 20, 113-14, 299-300
Dooley v. Town Plan and Zone Commission of Town of Fairfield, 149

Easements, 128, 299
Economic Development Administration, 85
Economic motives for exclusion, 226
Elections, 35, 38, 39, 48, 52, 98
Enabling acts (state), 208
Energy consumption, future, 82
England, 103, 133
English legal traditions, 160
English system of land ownership, 159
Environmental assessment, 4, 8
Environmental impact analysis, 25, 195, 208
Environmental impact statement review, 199-208
Environmental impact statements, 17, 25-26, 182, 185, 189, 195, 197-99, 200-202, 206, 208, 210, 219, 302-3
Environmental Improvement Commission (Maine), 169
Environmentalists, 17, 40, 47, 50-52, 54
Environmental Land and Water Management Act (Fla.), 64-65, 240
Environmental Land Management Committee (Fla.), 70
Environmental Law Institute, 172
Environmentally endangered lands, purchase of, 52, 65-67,
Environmental Protection Agency, 197
Escrow accounts, 31, 292
Estate tax laws, federal, 113
Euclid, Ohio, 166
Evaluation of project design, 250-51
Exclusionary incentives, 223-30

Fairfax County, Va., 159
Family income, 79 80
Farmlands, 40, 106, 116, 119, 120-23
Federal housing subsidies, 244
Fertility rate, 76-79
Fifth Amendment, 24, 145, 160, 162, 169
Financing (new communities), 255, 256
Fire and police protection, 227, 278, 281
Fleur du Lac, Cal., 153-54
Floating zones, 189
Floodplains, 184, 240
Florida, 12, 16, 35, 36-39, 52, 53, 61-71, 73, 129, 215, 240, 249, 256, 263, 264, 266, 279-80, 282, 286
Florida Atlantic University, 52
Florida Land Conservation Act, 64
Florida State Comprehensive

Planning Act, 64
Florida Water Resources Act, 64
Flower Mound, Texas, 256
Foothills, Palo Alto, Cal., 155-59, 229
Forest Service, 111
Fourteenth Amendment, 162, 242
France, 85
Friends of Mammoth, 47, 48
Friends of Mammoth v. Mono County, 206
Fronting lots (highway), 3, 222-23, 303
Fuel shortage, 88

Gananda, N.Y., 256
Garbage collection, 227, 267, 270, 280, 281
General Services Administration, 42
Georgia, 99, 198
Goldblatt v. Town of Hempstead, 168
Golden v. The Planning Board of the Town of Ramapo, 93
Governmental response, 39, 56
Graham, Robert, 63, 64, 68, 70
Grand Central Terminal, 150
Great Britain, 22, 85, 113, 143, 171
Greater London Plan of 1944, 133
Great Plains, 58
Great Salt Meadow (Conn.), 148-49
Greenbelts and country parks, England and Wales, 133
Green, Juanita, 68
Greenspace programs, 135-38
"Greenspaces for America," 137
Groundwater pollution, 267
Growth restrictions, 18, 89-100
"Growth units," 28, 255
Gruen, Victor, 57
Guidelines and Standards for Regional Development (Fla.), 66

Hadacheck v. Sebastian, 165, 167
Harbison, S.C., 256
Hawaii, 96-98, 120, 122, 127, 206, 263
Height limitations, 14, 35, 46, 50, 57, 60-61
Heller, Alfred, 48
Highway frontage lots, 222-23
Highway junk strip, 223
Highway locations, 54, 62, 72, 185-88
Highways, 22, 27, 82, 117, 179-80, 182-85, 188, 193, 198, 205, 222-23, 260, 303
Historic areas, 105-7, 120, 240, 301

Historic buildings, 14, 22-23, 142, 295
Historic Landmark Commission, N.Y.
City, 139, 150-52
Historic preservation, 7, 15, 22-23, 118-20, 123, 139, 150-52
Historic Preservation Ordinance, N.Y.
City, 139
Hollymead, Va., 229
Holmes, Oliver Wendell, 166-67
Household formation, 14, 79
House Interior Committee, 72
Housing, 1, 3, 42, 53, 54, 55, 61, 90, 243-46, 303
Housing Act (1968), 28, 243, 245
Housing and Urban Development,
Dept. of (HUD), 58, 90, 98, 198, 245, 256, 270, 272
Howard County, Md., 232
Howard County Planning Commission, 232
Humanism, 34
Humanistic values, 8
Hunt, Robert, 165
Hydrologic cycle, 276

Illinois, 198
Incentives (open space regulations), 126-32
Institutes of the Laws of England, 160
Interior, Dept. of, 22, 82, 138
Interior, Secretary of, 20, 113
Internal Revenue Service, 42
International Olympics Committee, 44
Interstate Commerce Commission, 163
Interstate Land Sales Full Disclosure
Act (ILSFDA), 270, 272-74
Islip, Long Island, N.Y., 41

Jackson, Henry, 10, 71, 72, 112
Job locations, 87
Jonathan Dickenson State Park, Fla., 94
Jonathan, Minn., 256
Judicial precedents ("takings"), 146-49, 152, 155

Kaiser, Henry, 153
Kalamazoo, Mich., 14, 79
Kansas, 164
Kauai County, Hawaii, 96-98
Kauai Planning Commission, 97
Kentucky, 198

Keystone Associates v. Moerdler, 152
Kilauea Plantation, 96-98

Labor unions, 52-53
Lake Okeechobee, 37, 64
Lake Superior, 283
Lake Tahoe, 174, 277
Lake Tahoe Basin, 153-55
Lamont, Bill, 59, 61
Land and Water Conservation Fund, 137
Land and water management laws, Fla., 16, 39, 64-68
Land banks, 257, 260
Land prices, 111
Land stewardship, 130-31
Land Use Act, Fla., 73
Land trusts, 131
Land use law, Vermont, 125
Land-use policies, Fla., 66-67
Large scale development, 248-61
Larson, Carlie, 40
Las Vegas, Nev., 271
Law and Locomotives, 165
Laws of 1679 and 1692, Boston, Mass., 162
League of Women Voters, 51
Lending practices, 221
Lesser San Diego, 50
Lewis Gut, 148
Lewis, Phillip, 105
Licensing and project review, 202
Limitation of growth, Boulder, Col., 57-61
Lincoln residence, Springfield, Ill., 152
Livingston and Blayney, 158
Local government, 6, 8, 9, 15, 20, 23, 24, 26-28, 213-17, 225-36, 279-82
Local planning, 211-13, 303
Location criteriafor land protection, 127
Logue, Edward J., 260
London greenbelt, U.K., 133-35
London, U.K., 161
Long Island Builders Institute, 40
Long Island Environmental Council, 40, 51, 55
Long Island, N.Y., 16, 36, 39-43, 54
Long Island Sound, 148
Los Angeles, Cal., 47, 48, 165
Lot sales, rural, 7, 29-31, 263-93, 304
Low-cost housing, 181, 303
Low-income housing, 225, 230, 236, 238, 240, 242-46, 251, 278

Lysander, N.Y., 256

Magna Carta, 160, 169
Maine, 155, 168-68, 282
Manchester, U.K., 135
Mandatory dedication, 115-17
Marin County, Cal., 35, 47, 54, 120-21, 277
Marshall, Arthur, 52
Martha's Vineyard, 263, 264
Martin County, Fla., 94-95
Maryland, 129, 232
Maryland Court of Appeals, 169
Massachusetts, 131, 243, 264
Massachusetts Coastal Wetlands Act, 131
Mass transit, 87, 178
McCarthy v. City of Manhattan Beach, 155
McHarg, Ian, 105
Merson, Alan, 46
Messer, Elliot, 67, 68
Metcalfe Farms, 97
Metropolitan areas and growth, 82-86
Metropolitan Opera House, 152
Miami, Fla., 5, 14, 16, 37
Miami Beach, Fla., 37
Miami Herald, 34, 36, 37, 68
Michigan, 158
Migration, 84-85, 89
Mineral Leasing Act (1920), 197
Minimum building size requirements, 231
Minimum floor area requirements, 27, 241
Minimum lot size requirements, 230, 241
Minimum quality standards, 179
Minneapolis-St. Paul metropolitan area, 236
Minnesota, 164
Mira Mesa, 49
Missouri, 164
Mobility, 16, 18, 76, 88-89
Mobility, individual, 88-89
Mobility, right of, 88, 98-100
Model Land Development Code, 25, 64, 73, 122, 208-9, 212, 240
Model State Guidelines for Historic Preservation, 23, 123
Monterey County, Cal., 120, 121
Moscow, U.S.S.R., 85
Moses, Robert, 40

Mountain Area Planning (MAP), 44
Mugler v. Kansas, 165, 167

Nader, Ralph, 129
Nassau County, N.Y., 39, 40-42, 54
Nassau-Suffolk Regional Planning Board, 41, 54
National Association for the Advancement of Colored People (NAACP), 16, 42, 54
National Association of Home Builders, 264
National Commission on Urban Problems, 213
National Committee Against Discrimination in Housing, 42
National Environmental Policy Act (1969) (NEPA), 71, 195-96, 199, 200, 205, 206, 281
National Land and Investment Co. v. Kohn, 159
National Lands Trust, 22, 136
National land-use policy legislation, 7, 10, 27, 72, 103, 122, 123, 238, 240
National Park Service, 111, 132
National Register of Historic Places, 23, 106, 298
National Science Foundation, 173
National Wildlife Federation, 51
Nature Conservancy, 20, 51, 113-14, 296-300
Nebraska, 164
Nectow v. Cambridge, 167
Nevada, 99, 153
New communities, 248-61, 266
New Hampshire, 281
New Jersey, 129-30, 230, 231, 235
New Mexico, 113
New mood, 6, 17-18, 33-71, 75, 180-81, 235, 256-57
New mooders, 178
New Orleans, 152
Newsday, 41
New York Central Railroad, 150
New York City, 41, 46, 91, 139, 150-52, 234, 252
N.Y. City Landmarks Preservation Commission, 150
New York Court of Appeals, 232
New York State, 12, 16-17, 35, 36, 270, 272, 279, 282
Nishimoto, Brian, 97
Nixon, Richard, 10, 72

Nondiscretionary review, 209
North Adams, Mass., 107
North Carolina, 103, 206
North Dakota, 164
Nuclear plants, 68
Nuclear power plant, Chesapeake Bay, 197

Oakland, Cal., 36
Office of Interstate Land Sales (HUD), 272
Office of Management and Budget (OMB), 194
Olympic Winter Games, 1976, 17, 35, 44-46
Open lands, diversion of, 117-18
Open meeting requirements, 214-15, 303-4
Open space(s), 8, 19-22, 103, 130-43, 158-59, 229, 276, 295-96
Open space, accessibility, 110, 112, 299
Open space classification, 106
Open space, development of, 125-30
Open space donations, 20, 112-14
Open space, expenditures for, 111, 118-20, 299
Open Space Foundation, Va., 114
Open space protection, 7, 14, 15, 18, 19-22, 104-06, 122, 123, 296 300-01
Open space purchase, 19, 35, 54, 57, 105-7, 110-12, 118-20, 298-99
Open space regulations, 21, 120-27, 300
Open spaces, England and Wales, 103
Oregon, public use of beaches, 112
Orlando, Fla., 16, 37
Orr, John B., 63
Overzoning, 186
Oyster Bay, Long Island, N.Y., 16, 42

Padover v. Township of Farmington (Mich.), 158
Palm Beach County, Fla., 94
Palo Alto, Cal., 55, 155-59, 229
Park dedication costs, 115
Parkland, 20, 115-16, 117
Parks, 14, 19, 54, 79, 104, 105, 115-16, 117
Parliament, U.K., 160-61, 170
Peak District National Park, U.K., 135
Penn Central Railroad, 150-52
Pennsylvania, 166, 242, 263, 264, 279, 282

Pennsylvania Coal Company v. Mahon, 166, 167, 173, 175
Pennsylvania shade tree law (1700), 161
Pennsylvania Supreme Court, 100
People United to Reclaim the Environment (PURE), 58, 60-61
Planned unit development (PUD), 28, 68, 207, 250, 301
Planning, 24, 27,200, 211-13, 281-2, 303
Planning assistance program ("701"), 212
Politics of Land, 129
Pollution, 1, 5, 7, 15, 178
Pooling of urbanization rights, 138-39
Population growth, U.S., 76-79
Porreca, Vince, 61
Potential development value of land, 137
Power plants, 14, 26, 180, 181, 240
Power plants, proposed, 202-3, 205
Power plant siting legislation, 205
Preferential farmland assessment, 129-30
Property tax, 15, 235-36
Proposition 20, California, 35, 50, 52
Protective regulations, incentives for, 126-27
Protective regulations, land and buildings, 21-22, 120-25, 300
Protective regulations, recreation communities, 279
Protect Our Mountain Environment (POME), 44
Pumpelly v. Green Bay Company, 162
Purchase notice, U.K., 170-171

Rail transit, 87
Ramapo, New York, 91-94, 232
Recreational development, 29-31, 263-93
Recreational lots, 263-93, 304
Recreation areas, 104-5, 107-10, 115, 299, 304
Reform of local government, 213
Regional Plan Association, N.Y., 113
Regional planning, 236-37, 303
Regional perspective, 236-38
Research Applied to National Needs, 173
Revenues and profits, reporting of (land sales), 288-90
Revenue-sharing, 117
Rezoning, 14, 63, 67, 95, 190, 281

Roads, 14, 93, 232, 278, 279, 281
Rockefeller Brothers Fund, 2
Rockefeller, Laurance S., 1
Rockefeller, Nelson, 41, 259, 282
Rockland County, N.Y., 91
Rural lot sales, 29-31, 263-93, 304
Ruvin, Harvey, 38
Rykar Industrial Corp., 148-49

St. Louis County, Mo., 89-91
St. Petersburg, Fla., 37
Sales techniques, lot sellers, 266-67
Salmon, Thomas P., 130
Sanbornton, N.H., 281
San Diego, Cal., 36, 48, 231
San Francisco Bay, 17, 149-50, 155
San Francisco Bay Area, 48-50, 234
San Francisco Bay Area Conservation
and Development Commission
(BCDC), 50
San Francisco, Cal., 36, 48
San Jose, Cal., 49
San Mateo County, Cal., 35
Santa Barbara, Cal., 35
Santa Clara County, Cal., 35
Santa Cruz County, Cal., 120, 121
Santa Fe, N.M., 23, 105, 152
Savannah, Ga., 256
Save San Francisco Bay Association, 50
Save the Otters Society, 51
Scenic easements, 104, 132
Schools, 186, 226, 227, 229, 235, 246,
250, 255, 266, 280, 303
Second homes (vacation homes), 7, 29-
30, 230-31, 264
Secretary of State for the Environment,
U.K., 170
Securities and Exchange Commission,
30-31, 270-73
Senate, U.S., 72, 264
Septic tanks, 267, 281-82
Septic tank bans, 281
Sewage disposal facilities, 30, 31, 274,
275, 276, 278, 283, 286
Sewers, 21, 59, 68, 93, 125-26, 278, 279,
301
Sheffield, U.K., 135
Shopping centers, 14, 40, 48, 60, 79, 120,
248, 250
Sierra Club, 51
Sierra foothills, 277
Site Location Law (Maine), 169
South Florida, 16, 54, 63-64, 68, 70, 71

Soviet Union, 220
Special use permit, 189
Spot zoning, 190
Standard City Planning Enabling Act
(1928), 194
Standard State Zoning Enabling Act
(1924), 238
State Land Use Commission, Hawaii, 97
Staten Island, New York, 233-34, 256
State v. Johnson, 155, 168
Starnes, Earl, 67
Stern, Claire, 40, 55
Stratford, Conn., 148
Subdivision requirements, 30, 59, 275-
93, 304
Subdivisions, recreational, 30-31, 263-
93, 304
Subsidized housing, 61
Suburban Action Institute, 42
Suffolk County, N.Y., 35, 39-41, 43, 54
Superior Court, Hartford County,
Conn., 149
Supreme Court, California, 153, 155
Supreme Judicial Court of Maine,
169
Supreme Judicial Court, Mass., 149
Sutherland, George, 167
Sweden, 264

Tahoe Regional Planning Agency
(TRPA), 153-55, 277
"Taking" of land, 145-75
"Takings clause," 23-24, 145-75
Tallahassee, Fla., 68
Tampa, Fla., 37
Tampa-St. Petersburg, Fla., 16
Taney, Roger B., 99
Task Force on Land Use and Urban
Growth, 1, 30
Tax assessments, preferential, 128-30,
301
Town and Country Planning Act, U.K.,
133, 170
Train, Russell, 72
Transportation, 1, 54, 61, 87-88, 92, 117,
260-61
Transportation Co. v. Chicago, 163
Transportation, Dept. of, 80-81, 199
Transportation, Secretary of, 117
Trustees of Sailor's Snug Harbor v.
Platt, 152
Trust for Public Land, 296
Turner v. County of Del Norte, 155

317

Uniform Relocation Assistance Act, 193
*United States v. Guest*, 99
University of Colorado (Boulder), 57, 58
University of Miami, Fla., 52
University of Wisconsin, 86
Urban Development Corporation, State of New York (UDC), 29, 259-60, 261
Urban Growth and New Community Development Act (1970), 29, 256
Urbanization rights, 21, 140-43
Urban regions, 82-88, 100, 177
Urban renewal, 257-58
U.S. Constitution, 145, 242
U.S. Court of Appeals, 1st Circuit, 281
U.S. District Court, 197
U.S. Supreme Court, 24-25, 99-100, 146, 162-67, 174-75, 235
Utilities decisions, 21, 125-26, 301

Vermont, 125, 130, 264, 282
Virginia, Commonwealth of, 167

Wales, 103, 133
Walters, Reginald, 52
Warren, Whitney, 150
Washington, D.C., 71, 256
Washington State, 206
Water pollution, 15, 33, 37

Water Pollution Control Act (1972), 207
Water supplies, 30, 31, 35, 38, 59-60, 64, 270, 274, 276, 278, 283, 304
Western Europe, 257
Westminister, U.K., 161
Wetlands, 16, 35, 40-41, 103, 106, 124, 149, 168, 236, 238, 240, 301
Wetlands Act (Maine), 168
Wetlands protection, 148-49, 168, 301
Whispering Lakes, Mo., 91
*Wilderness Society v. Hickel*, 197
Williamsburg, Va., 107
Williamson Act (Cal.), 129
Wilson, Pete, 1-2, 49
Wisconsin, 206
Wisconsin Supreme Court, 168
*Withers v. Buckley*, 162
Wright, Ruth, 60

*Younger v. County of El Dorado*, 155

Zero Population Growth, 50, 58, 60-61, 76-77
Zoning, 7, 15, 17, 21, 37, 40, 42, 49, 63, 65, 67, 68, 90-91, 92, 94-95, 100, 105, 120-23, 126, 139, 174, 183-92, 221, 226, 230-31, 242, 248, 254, 255, 281
Zoning variances, 40, 63, 139, 192